Religious Education as a Second Language

Religious Education as a Second Language

Gabriel Moran

Religious Education Press
Birmingham, Alabama

Library of Congress Cataloging-in-Publication Data
Moran, Gabriel.
  Religious education as a second language/Gabriel Moran.
  Includes bibliographies and index.
  ISBN 0-89135-072-1
  1. Religious education. 2. Christian education. I. Title.
BL42.M675 1989
291.7'—dc20   89-33871
                                                           CIP

Religious Education Press, Inc.
5316 Meadow Brook Road
Birmingham, Alabama 35242
10 9 8 7 6 5 4 3 2

Religious Education Press publishes books exclusively in religious education and in areas closely related to religious education. It is committed to enhancing and professionalizing religious education through the publication of serious, significant, and scholarly works.

PUBLISHER TO THE PROFESSION

Contents

Introduction

This book results from thirty years of reflection. In each of those years I have engaged in the activity of "teaching religion." And every year I have puzzled over the relation between my own particular activity and the whole enterprise of religious education. The experience that forms the basis for these reflections is diverse and yet a thread of continuity is captured in that phrase "teaching religion." The activity has had similar characteristics whether it was done with ninth graders or older adults, whether under religious affiliation or in secular institutions, whether in classrooms or living rooms. These reflections do not constitute a complete system by someone who has completed the course. I feel more like a beginner who is just starting to see how the pieces fit together. I need at least another thirty years to round off my thinking.

This book is offered to readers who also feel like beginners even though they may have been working in religious education for many years. I regularly teach undergraduate and graduate students who need a survey of the whole area of religious education. I do not know of a book for these students that is sufficiently comprehensive. For those people who are already at work in schools, local congregations or regional offices, this book is an invitation to reflect on

1

how their daily efforts link up with a worldwide effort in religious education. Being asked to join an international and ecumenical conversation may seem to some people like little more than a distraction. But the performance of our daily tasks is shaped by some overall theory of what we are doing.

A secondary readership for these reflections is colleagues who teach in other fields. A stimulating survey of an academic field written for specialists in another field has its difficulties. That is especially true when the topic for reflection is religion. Most of us do not presume that we know much about things which we have not studied. But scholars often do assume that they know whatever is to be known about religious education even if they have never investigated the matter. (This category of "other fields" can include Christian theology, biblical studies, church history, and the like.) This book therefore has the function of responding to a question that I am regularly asked: "How can you be a director of a program of religious education in a private university?" To the questioner there is no puzzle in what religious education is; the puzzle is in how there can be religious education when there are several religions involved.

Beyond the particular readers to whom a book is addressed, an author hopes that the text is intelligible and of interest to many other people. The assumption referred to in the above paragraph, namely, that everyone knows what religious education is, has some foundation. Most people have been exposed to some form of education in religious matters. In the United States it is a practical impossibility to avoid all contact. Thus, the difficulty of introducing people to religious education is not comparable to conveying the concepts of nuclear physics or archeology. The difficulty, rather, is one of trying to draw attention to ordinary words about more than ordinary reality. The general reader of these essays needs no special training or technical vocabulary. But there is a prerequisite: the willingness to question widespread assumptions about religion and education.

I have been writing in this area since 1961. I imagine that anyone whose writing extends over several decades likes to think that it all hangs together. One hopes that there is continuity and sameness even as there is also enrichment and progress. To the outside observer, the author may seem at times to have completely reversed positions. The writer invariably sees the movement as a shift (perhaps a "dialectical opposite") within some larger, continuing project of understanding.

The first essay that I published in 1961 was on the need for intellectual substance in high-school religion courses. I would today stand by the main idea of that essay; in fact, the message is more relevant today. And yet, I would find it impossible to read anything that I wrote in the early 1960s. The context of the writing has radically changed and therefore each text has to be rethought and reformulated.

When I started writing, my experience was one of teaching ninth to twelfth grade boys in a Catholic school. In the course of the 1960s many institutions underwent massive change, not the least affected of those institutions being the Roman Catholic church. The language that was ready at hand in 1960 no longer seemed appropriate by the end of the decade. I probably would have felt that way even if the Second Vatican Council had not occurred, but the changes in the Roman Catholic church were for me a dramatic heightening of the religious and educational changes that were going on everywhere.

By 1970 the religious education I had been exposed to both as a child and as a teacher seemed inadequate for the questions of the present. In that year I wrote a book which I entitled *Ecumenical Education*. A book club pressured the publisher to change the title because, the book club officials said, no one would understand what the book was about. I thought that those officials were lacking in vision, but they probably knew something that I did not know, at least about how to sell books. In the text of the book I still proposed to substitute "ecumenical education" for "religious education." What I discovered in the experience of trying to communicate this idea was that language does not change in this way. One cannot simply invent a new linguistic universe.

For a few years after writing that book I did not know

what to call my interest. I wrote, for example, about the "intersection of religion and education." By the middle of the 1970s I decided that "religious education" is indeed the appropriate name for what I was trying to write about. However, by that time I was acutely aware of the difficulty of language itself in the attempt to clarify what one is doing. Is it possible to develop a language of "religious education" which will describe one of the world's most pressing and universal problems, a language that will engage a sufficient number of people so that there will be real progress in addressing this problem? The answer is not yet clear.

What has been clear to me for over a decade is that the attempt to develop a language of religious education is an important enough work to make it a lifelong calling. I have no messianic pretensions; the development of language does not lie in that direction. There are at least hundreds and more likely thousands of people around the world who have a conviction similar to mine. We do not agree on all the particular details, but we can work with a degree of unanimity on the need to clarify the meaning of religious education. I have tried to give this book an international flavor without pretending that I can step outside my own historical and geographical limitations. Some day it may be possible to write a truly international book on this topic. For now I am content to suggest the opening of such a dialogue, particularly between British and United States meanings of religious education.

During the past decade I have written on various aspects of what I conceive to be the whole of religious education. When a book does not address the big picture, it may seem to some people not on the topic at all. When religion is not dealt with in the most explicit form, the author may seem to have abandoned religious education. Although nearly everything I write is intended to be part of religious education, that may not be the category which is used in publishers' lists, review journals, and people's minds. My book, *Education Toward Adulthood* (1979), may get classified as "adult education"; *Religious Education Development* (1983) may be thought of as a book on developmental theory; *No*

1

The Uncovering of Meaning

The current status of religious education became clear to me a few years ago in writing an entry for an encyclopedia of religion. I was assigned three thousand words to write the entry "religious education." It proved to be a very difficult assignment.

I began the essay by saying that one could go in either of two directions for exploring this topic: a description of the clear and explicit use of the *term* religious education; or else a description of the *idea*, what religious education could include even though the term is not used. Regarding the explicit use of the term, I said that it was found almost exclusively in the twentieth century and within countries influenced by Western religion. Even more narrowly, religious education is a term of self-description for only a few groups, such as British schoolteachers, Catholic Directors of Religious Education in the United States, and Unitarian educators. Since the term has a short and narrow history, I was able to do a manageable job in describing it.

In regard to the idea—what religious education might imply—one can conceivably include the most formative elements in all cultures at all times. I was not about to try describing that in a few thousand words. Instead, I chose some examples (e.g., the Aztecs) and pointed out the difficulty of drawing either a religious line or an educational line once one goes the route of religious education meaning everything that can possibly be called religion and education. I also compared groups (e.g., Buddhists and Jews) to show that this implied meaning of religious education can take many forms.

The editor returned my essay, saying that what I had written was fine but I should add some paragraphs on Muslims and Hindus. My chagrin was not caused by getting the essay returned but by the fact that the editor did not seem to have understood the point of what I had written. If one were to write the history of the Hindu use of the term "religious education," the most accurate thing to say is: "There is none." In contrast, if one wishes to know what could conceivably be implied by religious education, the most accurate thing to be said in the entry would be: "See Hinduism." Instead, I was instructed to write two paragraphs on Hindu religious education, a gesture which does justice neither to Hinduism nor to religious education. What I was hoping was that the editor(s) might begin to wonder why three thousand words in fourteen volumes were assigned to religious education. If the editors really wanted to know what religious education could mean and some day may mean, why didn't they assign several of the fourteen volumes of the encyclopedia to the topic?

This experience suggests to me where religious education is these days; it falls between an actual meaning that is very narrow and a potential meaning that is too wide for anyone to comprehend. As soon as one moves out of the parochial limits of one's own religion, any full-blown theory of religious education seems absurdly inadequate to the task of addressing everyone's religion and education. I stake no claim to speak authoritatively on how Hindus should practice religious education (indeed, I have little to say about how Jews and Christians should practice it). My modest hope is to approach this area in such a way that if Hindus or any other religious group wish to join the conversation, they could find their way into it. I am reflecting on what people do and how they might better describe their efforts so that a language of religious education might have more reality than it currently has. A fully developed language of religious education will undoubtedly take several generations.

This book is an answer to the question: "What is the meaning of religious education?" This first chapter is about the meaning of asking that question. That is, before examining the meaning of religious education, I first explore some questions about meaning in general.

ARGUING ABOUT MEANING

In this chapter, I describe in a general way the form that my arguments take. The subsequent chapters will illustrate this approach. My arguments are almost always about the meanings of words. Such an approach may seem to some people abstract and impractical. However, attentiveness to language has its own concreteness and practicality. The most important changes in the world spring from restating questions, distinguishing terms, and uncovering deeper levels of meaning.

It is almost a truism that twentieth-century thinkers are concerned with language. In any debate, everyone is likely to agree that there is a need to clarify terms. What is hidden under this apparent agreement is that the concern with language goes in two opposite directions. One is a concern to define terms as a prelude to argument; the second is a concern to resist defining terms so as to allow more meaning into the argument. The first direction completely dominates our culture. If one wishes to go the second route—as I do in this book—one has to keep pointing out that the main question is *meaning* not definition, and that language is the beginning, middle, and end of the argument.

The first direction is so common that it hardly needs describing. It is the basis of much of our scientific and technical culture. Its most preferable language is numbers which have no ambiguity about them. Where numbers cannot convey the reality, then unambiguous words are used, preferably words that are not used in everyday speech. If possible, the meaning of words should be legislated by a group of experts. The ideal, as Alvin Gouldner says, is "one word, one meaning for everyone and forever."[1]

This approach has had spectacular success in scientific investigations of our physical universe and in the developing of technology. However, when it is applied to all aspects of human life this approach can be illusory. When Thomas Hobbes set out to found a "new science of politics" in the eighteenth century, he claimed that it would have more certainty than the physical sciences because the terms would be defined at the beginning.[2] Hobbes's criticism of Aristotle centered on the fact that Aristotle did not define his terms; he started from ordinary speech. Aristotle's definitions, if they emerged at all, were at the end rather than the beginning of the argument.

The concern to define the words at the beginning is found throughout much of social science, theology, educational writing, and political discourse. The effect is sometimes salutary in clarifying the limits of a discussion or in cutting through a lot of pious puffery. That strength turns into a weakness in areas where the dimensions of a question have not begun to be explored. The closer one gets to the qualities of human life, the greater is the likelihood that our existing definitions are already too narrow. We need to break open the words not define them.

In recent years the language of "models" has become widespread. This particular image has been used to advantage in some questions, but often it provides a false clarity where the answers cannot be reduced to three, four, or six models because the question is not yet clear. In the future, there may be a use for "models of religious education." Such a discussion today would be premature because there is far more that must first be said about the actual and possible meaning of the term "religious education." There is as yet no agreed upon thing that is ready to be modeled.

A language that employs the image of model is a particular use of language that can obscure other uses; it is weighted in the direction of the scientific and technical. No doubt there are aspects of education and religious education that can be described by two or more models (for example, the ways in which a classroom instructor interacts with students). But the full meaning of education and religious education requires inquiry that is historical, political, and aesthetic.

My arguments are about words and how the words go together. Meaning cannot be explored apart from words although it is not very accurate to say that the words "have" a meaning. Most dictionaries do in fact make this presumption and therefore operate in closed circles; one simply finds that this word means approximately the same as that word. The most helpful dictionary in English is the Oxford English Dictionary because there one can get a history of the words and often the political issues implied in that history.

The meaning of the word is found in its use. The most important words are usually the most ambiguous in their usage. Instead of this being a reason to banish these small, old words (life, love, passion, desire, freedom, good, and so forth), the ambiguity is precisely what is worth arguing about. The argument can be frustrating and convoluted because we cannot step outside language to clarify language. We are, as Hannah Pitkin says, like sailors who must rebuild our boats on the high sea without ever putting into dry dock.[3]

But is it worth arguing at all? If no single answer is right, who am I or anyone else to say what words should mean? In our culture there are two extremes for an answer to this question. There is a band of experts who lay claim to being the guardians of what is proper and improper in the use of the English language. The rules are well-established and the experts have endless examples of how football announcers, politicians, and business executives mangle syntax and misuse words. Violators of correct speech must be prosecuted. In tracking down the perpetrators of incorrect speech, these experts are often oblivious to the political issues of power that language embodies.

In reaction to the snobbish enforcement of correct rules, there is a common attitude of "anything goes." Language is alive and changing all the time. It is assumed that anyone who thinks that he or she can control language is silly. If a rule gets broken enough times it eventually ceases to be a rule and none of us is the poorer for the change.

The position I begin from is between these extremes. Language is always changing and it often changes in unpredictable ways. No individual or group has the power nor should have the power to control those changes. Nonetheless, the political and educational life of human beings throughout the centuries can be traced in the movement of language: Who has the most control and who are excluded? What are the main metaphors that guide thinking? How do the main distinctions enhance or diminish life?

A question I constantly return to in these pages is: Who or what are we excluding by this particular use of language? If the metaphor is mechanical, are we blinded to organic relations? If the metaphor is organic, are we missing something specifically human? Do commonly used political names hide the existence of whole groups of people? Do black people, old people, disabled people disappear into categories that do not quite fit them? These are not rhetorical questions intended to produce guilt. They are questions whose answers must be patiently explored case by case, context by context.

As a general rule, I begin with the assumption that definitions of words reflect the success of one group in being able to speak for humanity. Robert Frost wrote: "Whoever controls the words controls the world." The words provide power and in turn the powerful of the world do the defining or limiting of words. A main task, therefore, is to try opening the discussion to representative voices both from the past and the present. The past is available to us in etymology and the history of words. The past may be buried deeply in words but it seldom, if ever, disappears.

The excluded voices of the present offer an even richer variety of meaning but a more complex problem than the past. Who or what is representative of the present? Sometimes one is helped by noticing different meanings of a word in different countries or even in different regions of the same country. Sometimes it is highly revealing that a word is used with different meanings in different academic disciplines.

If one takes the major power splits in the human race (age, gender, race, wealth, health), one can be fairly sure that the very young and the very old, women, nonwhite people, poor people, sick people cannot get their voices adequately heard. Such categories do not begin to exhaust the question, but they do suggest likely places to start looking in each case.

Although the process I have just described is one of increasing the voices and letting in more meaning, the whole purpose and result cannot be described simply as *expansion* or *growth* of meaning. Indeed, the language of expansion or growth is one of the main modern images that needs challenging. Acknowledging that a word has several meanings can be a way of avoiding an examination of how it functions as a whole. The argument has to be about both coherence and consistency. Variations in the meaning of a term need to fit within some consistent (not necessarily logical) pattern of usage.

Meaning in language cannot be invented. A private language is a self-contradiction. What does happen with great thinkers is that they bring forth something that seems utterly original; yet at the same time what they say has roots in previous thinkers. A famous biologist of the twentieth century has said: I get all my original ideas from reading. If Plato, Kant, or Heidegger argue for a certain interpretation, we tend to listen because they incorporate the wisdom of many previous thinkers even though they are at times idiosyncratic.

In principle, anyone can argue that any word can mean anything. However, if no one from the past gives support to the position, if no one else in the present agrees, then the cause is hopeless. Wittgenstein notes that we do correct children in their use of language because one can be mistaken about the meaning of words. We ought to correct children's mistakes not to give them the right answers but to get them into the flow of human conversation.

As meaning is not invented neither is it destroyed; at least one can say that this is usually if not always the case. No matter how many times repressive governments and vicious dictators redefine freedom, democracy, justice, and so forth, the meaning latent in those terms awaits its time. There is no guarantee that it will surface on its own, but the creative stirring of an individual or a group can retrieve the meaning. Very often it is not on the basis of scholarly argument but out of the moral response to grave injustice that language is given rebirth. It may simply be one man or woman who at risk of life stands up and says: no. Our agreements, said Wittgenstein, rest not on a kind of seeing but on our acting.

As human beings we agree or disagree in language. The person who says "it doesn't matter what you call it" or "isn't that merely semantics" does not grasp the nature of dialogue and argument. Dialogue seems to have arisen in Greece when listeners interrupted the speaker with the question "What do you mean by that?" or just "Would you repeat that?"[4] Simply to repeat oneself is the beginning of dialogue. The speaker has to reflect on what he or she has said; the second saying has a different meaning. I take it as a compliment when someone says to me "What do you mean?" (unless it is said with obvious hostility). In responding to a student in class, I consider it my main responsibility to help the student understand what the question does or does not mean, how the question might be better formulated, and how the beginnings of an answer are already found in a well-stated question.

Language is a much larger reality than any individual; it is even larger than the whole human race at any moment. We are not totally powerless before it, but our *intentions* count for very little separated from the power of language in its historical reality. People who get accused of racial, ethnic, sexual, or religious slurs usually reply: "But I didn't intend to insult you." That is not much of a defense. Intending to insult someone is bad enough; if one does not know that the words are insulting, then the problem is buried deep in the language itself. There are, of course, individuals who take umbrage at all kinds of statements. But if a major segment of the human race finds a statement offensive, there is something wrong with what was said no matter what the intention of the speaker.

Writers who begin a book with a first footnote that reads

"The term "x" is the subject of much disagreement; for the purpose of this book I define "x" to mean . . ." have usually closed the door on one of the basic questions the book should be asking. Writers who have a footnote saying that "the term "y" is used incorrectly in popular speech but because it is too difficult to change the usage and everyone understands it, I go along with it in this book" have usually abandoned the vocation of writer.

Samuel Coleridge in the nineteenth century wrote: "Few would be the errors of men if they knew what their words meant, and fewer still if they knew what the words themselves meant." It is a brilliant insight marred by one irony. Coleridge could not have imagined that some people in the twentieth century would take him to task for his use of the word "men." His defense, no doubt, would be that by the word "men" he obviously intended to include both men and women. And indeed at an earlier period of the English language one could construct a defensible case that "man" did mean men and women. Over a period of centuries, that meaning changed. As a result, the man (or woman) who today would begin a book by saying "I know all about the objection to sexist language, but there is no smooth way in English to correct the problem; therefore, in this book by 'man' I mean men and women," does not yet understand what the question is.

This issue of gender sensitive language is one of three examples I wish to use for illustrating the above principles. These three examples may not seem central to religious education, but in the way I propose to go—burrowing into what is ostensibly secular language—each of the three illustrates a facet of the overall inquiry. The first is a term that needs distinguishing, the second is a pattern of speech, the third is the dominance of a particular image.

1) *Half the world disappearing in a word: America*. For more than two decades the use of the words "America" and "American" has been a chief interest of mine. I have tried to convince people of the importance of a consistent distinction in using these words. Everyone knows the distinction and everyone knows that the distinction is a correct one. Yet, the distinction is regularly violated in practi-

cally every book, every newspaper, and every journal published in the United States. Not only is the distinction
violated but the violation is celebrated in the backdrop and
substance of most political, religious, and advertising discourse in this country. I refer to the difference between
America and the United States of America. The confusion
of these two terms was deliberate from the beginning of
the country.

The reason why it is difficult to get at this issue is its
religious character. "America" began as a religious term in
1507, and it has continued to have religious connotations.
America was Europe's name for the promised land out in
the Western sea. America was another name for the kingdom of God on earth. The nation that identified itself with
America laid claim to being the fulfillment of that religious
dream. In doing so, this one nation took for its own the
whole of the American land: North, Central, and South.
The results have been devastating for Canada, Mexico,
and the nations of Central and South America. The transition period the United States is now entering is so difficult
because the United States and its neighbors have no language in which to begin a conversation.

It may seem that this issue has been written about at
great length, but there has been no attention to a consistent use of the distinction I am advocating. Discussions, for
example, of "American civil religion" have buried the
problem more deeply before the discussion begins. Pick up
the *New York Times* any day of the week. The front page is
likely to have a story from Central America in which a
reporter talks about U.S. policy. Many reporters in Central
America have been forced to realize that there is something peculiar about referring to American policy in conflict with a (Central) American country. Turn to the editorial page of the same paper and you will find not a hint of
this problem in all the pronouncements about what America should do and what Americans think. The editorial
writers at the *Times* apparently do not read the front page
of their own newspaper.

The question always asked is: "Yes, but what word would
you substitute for 'Americans'? Everyone knows who the

Americans are." The answer is that if there were an obvious term for the people between the Canadian and Mexi-
can borders, then the problem very likely would not exist.
The proper response to the problem is to stop and hear
oneself; after that, one has to try some creative moves with
available language. If someone replies that such change
takes too long and is too complicated, then he or she is not
willing to find out how deeply this problem runs. In this
case, the absence of a crucial word is a symptom of a five-
century-old question that will take at least a few generations to resolve.

I cannot begin to pursue here the reverberations of this
distinction in all areas of life. Much of the necessary material is already available, but it does not get through the
filter that U.S. Americans have in their language. U.S.
people will need help from other people. Europeans could
certainly help by not saying "America" when they are in
fact referring to the United States.

It is not only other American peoples who have a vested
interest in this topic. U.S. foreign policy everywhere in the
world is profoundly influenced by the absorption of
American religion (that is, the religious meaning of America) into U.S. politics. At times this confusion leads to policies of remarkable compassion and altruism. At other
times, it can generate extraordinary violence accomplished
with seeming innocence in the name of the sacred cause of
liberty. Richard Hofstadter puts it well by saying: "It has
been our fate as a nation not to have an ideology but to be
one."[5]

Eventually, this ideology must be broken through. I
doubt that generals or politicians will lead the way. But the
task is a central one for religious people and educators,
especially those who are not quite in the mainstream. For
example, the name "Native American" could be a step in
rethinking the meaning of "America." Most native people
are rightly suspicious of the term. Whereas "Indian" was
simply the mistake of a lost European, "Native American"
is manipulative unless "American" is no longer used to
mean United States citizen. Suppose people did take seriously the meaning of "Native American"; then all the For-

eign Americans might have to rethink their politics and religion.

2) *Half the people of the world disappearing: Women.* The issue of "gender sensitive language" (what to call this question is itself a big question) is a hot topic in the U.S. In the course of less than two decades, the issue passed from being the concern of a few feminists to being proper protocol for politicians, textbook publishers, and television reporters. A writer who appears to be unconscious of the problem today is most likely taking a negative stand. One would have to have been hidden in a mountain cabin for the last decade not to be aware of the question.

In contrast to my previous example, this one may seem to be taking care of itself or even to be practically solved. But has the conversion been that swift and that complete? The fact that a lot of "he and she" is sprinkled through speech today is a hopeful sign, but it is only a start. The change has to be run through one's linguistic system for a few decades before all the implications become clear. The movement ought not to be given over to political lobbyists. It is important to think about the religious and educational complexities of this major change in language.

The name that emerged in the 1970s for this movement was "gender inclusive language," a phrase unfortunately often shortened to "inclusive language." As most names for movements do, it said something obvious while possibly obscuring the more difficult levels of the problem. All language includes and excludes at the same time. To name a particular person, thing, or event is not to name other persons, things, and events. The more vital and effective language is, the more it deals in concrete detail, fine distinctions, and poetic precision. In contrast, bureaucratic language is highly inclusive because it seldom takes note of any individual; it can be grandly inclusive in its abstraction.

Most of our language in political, academic, and scientific circles is already inclusive by being abstract. We must be careful not to push it toward higher abstraction. Excising the word "man" does not always name the world better; the worst of our language already has forgotten about flesh and blood men. If the word "man" actually refers to a male human being, then the word "man" ought to be cheered by feminist critics of language.

At other times, "man" or "he" is used when the reference is actually to human beings. Today it is not enough to say that "by 'man' I intend to include man and woman." One can usually find alternatives for "man," such as person or human. Often the best we can do with "he" is to add "she." To avoid cluttering our speech pattern, a shift into the plural is sometimes helpful. I suspect that in the future evolution of the English language, "they" and "their" will become singular as well as plural.

The main point is that if a group is excluded by our typical patterns of speech, then they tend to be slighted in our concerns. If $x=a$ and $x=a+b$, then b tends to get overlooked. Sometimes the way to overcome exclusion is by simple addition (he and she, his and hers, man and woman), but that can be cumbersome and sometimes miss the point. For example, instead of always adding "actress" to "actor," it is more effective to recover the meaning of "actor" as a term that is not sex specific. When enough women call themselves "actor," then people will not think only of men when they hear the word "actor."

Consider one of the main philosophical problems of Western culture, embodied in the language of "man and nature." I deal with this question in chapter eight as central to what morality is. I would only note here that the language would not be improved by including women and therefore referring to "man, woman, and nature." This quick fix would further obscure the question of power reflected in that language. We need a larger reformation of language that brings out the relations of men and men, women and women, men and women, human and nonhuman animals, human community and biotic system.

Case by case one has to decide what is the most felicitous and accurate way to describe the world of relational realities. Every choice will have some disadvantages and will seem to slight one group or another. The aim of feminist criticism has to be a simpler, more poetic, more revealing language even if some temporary convolutions may be necessary.

As in the previous example of "America," the issue of sexual or gender exclusion is in part a religious one. That is why the contemporary handling of the issue is problematic and why the issue is central to religious education. The relation of men and women has always had a symbolic connection to the relation between human beings and what is ultimate. Religions have always sensed this connection and to some extent embodied it. Religion is not necessarily where one starts in bringing about these changes of language, but religious changes are an integral part of the story. Without some grounding in the wisdom of the past, contemporary political and economic changes may easily become ruled by cultural biases. Granted that every supposed piece of wisdom from the past should be scrutinized by people today. But that is different from trying to replace complex patterns that have a long human history with a single principle from twentieth-century politics.

Not long ago only a few radical critics were attacking Judaism, Christianity, and Islam on feminist grounds. But the milder criticism of institutional patterns in these religions has been turning toward the foundations of their existence. The central figure in the Hebrew Bible, the Christian New Testament, and the Qur'an seems to be a male figure; and the pronoun "he" sticks in the throats of many women (and some men) today. A religious education that starts out discussing "God in his heavens" needs to stop and to take a step backward. We have to consider the entry points to peoples' religious questions while not using language that—usually subconsciously—obstructs a pursuance of the questions. No question is more important to this book than gender sensitive language, but for its own effectiveness it needs a context of other questions similarly explored.

3. *Half of human activity disappearing: The image of making.* I said above that meaning is not something lodged in single words. What needs attending to are the governing images that shape our language. I examine here the seemingly harmless image of "making" which has spread into all areas. After absorbing much of human life, it threatens to take over the very idea of meaning. At stake here is not

just the meaning of a single term but the meaning of meaning.

I was recently asked to speak on a panel at a religious conference on the topic: "How do people make meaning in their lives?" I began by expressing surprise at a religious group choosing this title. Of course, the idea of "making meaning" is a favorite one in twentieth-century philosophy, psychology, and sociology. Indeed, the phrase is so confidently assumed in many quarters that one would be considered hopelessly naive to challenge the assumption that "man is the maker of meaning." And yet it is a presumptuous, not to say, arrogant phrase; it is not based on any kind of proof or discovery but is an assumption reflected in a choice of language. The claim can seem to be self-evident today only because the way has been prepared by turning everything over to "man the maker."

If the artist were the controller of the meaning of "to make," that would not be bad; but the making or construction that the twentieth century loves to talk about has the context of a consumer economy. Western culture over a period of several centuries had substituted the language of industrial economy for the story of a creator in heaven. The philosophical spread of the image of making is traceable to Immanuel Kant, who at the turn of the nineteenth century began a shift toward emphasis on human agency. There was a valuable truth in his perception that human beings are not wax waiting for an imprint or a slate board awaiting the chalk (favorite and misleading images of a period preceding Kant). For Kant and most of science and philosophy afterward, the human mind is active rather than passive.

Friedrich Nietzsche is the pivotal thinker of the late-nineteenth century, the one who forced open the frightening conclusion to a long process of Western thought. If there is no God, no human nature, no meaning that is given to humans, then "man," man the maker must invent everything. The everything includes himself, or more exactly, a better version of himself than has hitherto existed. The use of gender exclusive language here is no accident; it is always "man" who is the maker. I think if one speaks of men and women in their relation to meaning, other active verbs emerge, such as revelation, discovery, or birth.

One of the most telling lines in nineteenth-century philosophy was written on a postcard by Nietzsche from the insane asylum shortly before his death: "I would much rather be a Basel professor than God, but I will not push my egotism so far as to desist from the creation of the universe." Medically, it was not the attempt to create the world that drove Nietzsche crazy (syphilis had a lot to do with it). But I would wager that the attempt to "make meaning" in their lives is today driving many people into despair.

One of the immediate precursors of "making meaning" is the phrase "making decisions." This phrase has become so much a part of our language that people are often unaware they use it and how their lives may be distorted by the effort to make decisions, instead of simply deciding or letting decisions emerge. Psychologists, ethicists, business experts, newspaper columnists, and television advice givers claim to be helping us by their constant hectoring that we should make decisions. Life having been put into our hands by those who de-divinized the heavens and the forests, we are like industrial engineers supposed "to make something of ourselves." And if you cannot make decisions, what are you? Obviously, nothing at all. In contrast, the religious concern is not making something of yourself; its concern is living in relation to other human and nonhuman beings on this earth. Just because one is not trying to construct oneself does not mean that one is living a passive or subservient life.

My criticism of the spread of the image of "to make" into areas where it does not belong is not an attempt to expurgate the word from the language. "Making" is a quite good and serviceable word in its place. It is the pattern of its usage that concerns me. Organic, mutual, and communal relations should not be described in the reductionistic language of maker, owner, and user. I wish the use of the image of making were not so prevalent, but I recognize that not every questionable use of the term is demeaning.

For example, when someone says "I am trying to make

sense of this story," that probably suggests that the story's meaning is not to be made but to be discovered. Or, a phrase like "making a living" is terribly reductionistic, but we also know pretty well that we are merely talking about holding a job. Obviously, the phrase "making love" is a strange euphemism that we use in the absence of an acceptable, mutually involving verb. These and other uses of the image of making deserve our attention. Whether any one of them is worth constant and loud protest is debatable; we all have only limited passion with which to fight linguistic battles. Nevertheless, for myself I draw the line with "making" when it comes to taking over the idea of meaning. Resistance to "making meaning" is necessary if religious education is to be possible.

LEARNING A SECOND LANGUAGE

One final issue to be addressed in this chapter is the image of second language that is in the title of this book. I compare the development of religious education to an individual's learning a second language. Like all analogies, this one eventually limps, but the comparison has several features I wish to develop. Religious education has the characteristics of a language people learn after they have learned a native language. My thesis is that although religious education is somewhat alien to most speakers today, its development and spread are important to tolerance, understanding, and peace in the world.

Language is one of the great mysteries of human life. A child's learning to speak is a miracle that no one comprehends. The child does not so much *acquire* language as become immersed in it. By whatever the mysterious means involved, the child grasps both human situations and patterns of speech, and then the child is able to relate the two. Everyone learns to speak; even those who are cut off from the usual flow of sounds and sights can be helped to enter into human conversation.

We are "acquired" by speech before we are aware of the process occurring. Human awareness follows upon the capacity to engage in language. The particular language in which we are immersed is so close to us that we are not aware that it is *a* language. If we were never to meet a person who speaks another language, we would be unaware that we spoke *a* language. Nearly everyone does meet people who speak a different language. At least, modern means of communication make us aware that they exist.

A few fortunate children are born into families where two or more languages are spoken. The only thing more miraculous than a child learning a language is a child learning several languages. Before the age of reflective self-consciousness, children are able to move between languages with little difficulty. As many people know, learning to speak another language later in life is extremely difficult.

Whatever the fluency attained, there are two good reasons for studying a second language. First, one gets to understand other people better if one attempts to learn their language. Translations can be of some help, but depth of understanding and emotional identification are limited if one cannot get inside the particular language of another person.

The other reason for studying a second language is a paradox well-known to any student of language, namely, we come to understand our own language better when we study a second one. Teachers of English grammar have a nearly hopeless task in convincing students of the importance of gerunds, nonrestrictive clauses, and subjunctives until the student has to move between English and another language. Struggling with the regularities and irregularities of someone else's language forces us to be conscious of the structure of our own language. And the mystery of humanity itself confronts us when we meet a well-developed form of human communication that bears little resemblance to what we have assumed is the normal way to speak.

One's first language has elements that can be called "religious," that is, expressions which imply a relation to what is ultimate in life. The culture's underlying assumptions about body, freedom, evil, redemption, prayer, and so forth, are reflected in each particular religious language. A child in a Muslim family and a child in a Christian family will assimilate different religious ideas from the language that is at hand. Parents or religious leaders may reinforce this process, but even where a child is shielded from direct religious formation, some influence will get through. The child has little say in this early education; one is acquired by a religion before one has a chance to decide about being a member.

Religious education emerges with the first stirrings of comparison between religious languages. Almost everyone has some experience of religious diversity as he or she is growing up. But it is usually only as an adult that most people seriously engage an entirely different religion. As a late second language today, religious education gives the appearance of being artificially contrived. It need not be that way and perhaps in the future will not be. People of any age are able to hold in fruitful tension a passionate involvement in one religious group and a sympathetic understanding of other religious groups.

Religious education should not be a kind of esperanto, an invented language removed from everyone's ordinary life. It ought to be more like a Spaniard learning to speak Italian or a German learning English. The major difference with religious education is that thus far in history this second language has not entirely emerged. So the closer analogy may be to someone learning Italian when it was not entirely separate from Latin. There have been historical moments in the emergence of a language when the speaker had no choice but to provide vitality, originality, and style to the particular language in its birthing. Anyone trying to speak religious education today has to help give birth to the language, not just settle into its syntax and vocabulary. The comforting side to this situation is that there are no native speakers to laugh at one's accent.

A different way to think of religious education as a second language is with the analogy of dialect and *lingua franca*. This latter phrase refers to a language formed from several dialects for the purpose of mediating communication between communities. Religious education can be seen as the attempt to bring into one conversation many religious languages. At the least, the human race has to find a way to stop one group from killing other people whose beliefs and practices differ. There is a great urgency to develop this framework for understanding now that an incident in one part of the world can affect everybody. If Jews, Christians, and Muslims lived respectively on Mars, Venus, and Mercury, there would be little problem. But can all three live in Jerusalem or in Brooklyn?

The contrast between local dialect and common language should not be equated with a split between the private and the public. Religious language is external, social, and visible; it cannot be confined to the private. The real contrast here is between the language that is of a community and a language that has the chance to be intercommunal. We do need on the one side a language of intimacy, what Krister Stendahl calls a "caressing language."[6] Such language is characterized by lively, concrete imagery, wild exaggeration, and meaning that is found in the silences as well as in the words. In contrast, the language spoken by many communities in many places can have greater clarity of a logical kind; the language of the mathematical sciences is a supreme example. The meaning of the words is less dependent on the immediate context; it is speech that can be translated and transferred. Something is gained, something is lost.

The question of a second language is nothing new for the human race. But most of the time the question has been which one will win. Individuals throughout history have learned two or more languages and did not necessarily see them as competitors. But when communities, tribes, or nations are in conflict, the survival of a people's language becomes a sign of the resistance of rebels, and the suppression of a language becomes a tool in authoritarian oppression.

There is an interesting passage in the Hebrew Bible (2 Kings 18) which illustrates the struggle around two lan-

guages. I borrow here from the insightful commentary of
Walter Brueggemann.[7] The Assyrian army is at the gates
of Jerusalem in a mismatch of power between Assyria and
Judah. An Assyrian negotiator stands at the city walls and
shouts terms of surrender. He taunts the soldiers of Judah,
saying that they are going to die a miserable death if they
do not surrender. The leaders of Judah respond to the
Assyrians: "Speak to us in Aramaic. Do not speak to us in
Hebrew within the hearing of the people." Aramaic was
the language of international diplomacy. The leaders of
Judah fear that the soldiers, if they understand, will be
intimidated. The Assyrian negotiator, for the same reason,
continues to speak in Hebrew.

Brueggemann contrasts this "conversation at the wall"
with a different use of language which he calls "conversation behind the wall." This latter concerns the ordinary life
of the people and includes the most intimate and sacred
dealings in the community. And for Judah, of course, this
conversation is in Hebrew. King Hezekiah consults the
prophet Isaiah about what to do. The prophet warns that
more military power is not the road to success. The pray-
ers (said in Hebrew) and the faith of the people eventually
lead to deliverance from the hands of the Assyrians.

As it was in 701 B.C. when this event is thought to have
occurred, so today we have struggles between people in
which the use or nonuse of a language plays a key role.
And unfortunately the issue is still often played out as
language at the wall against language behind the wall. The
survival of Judah depended on not letting the people (that
is, soldiers in imminent danger) know what was going on.
On their side, the Assyrians had learned enough Hebrew
to hold it in contempt. The problem today is probably as
bad and the stakes for the world are higher.

The interesting twist in the biblical passage is that the
Assyrians knew Hebrew. At least they knew enough to
taunt, insult, and threaten the soldiers at the wall. How did
they know it? Perhaps by spies? Why did they learn it? For
this occasion or was there some element of sympathy? If
one carries the issue into today's context, do Soviet com-

mentators who speak flawless English on U.S. television simply have good technical training or do they share some of the United States's ideals? There is no guarantee that knowing another's language will lead to friendship, but a knowledge of each other's language by many people on each side would be the sign of a thaw in the frozen positions of two hostile groups.

Consider how hostility may arise. Two communities of people who do not share a common language cannot be close friends. If for some reason they come to have regular interactions, hostility is likely to arise because of misinterpretation of gestures, tone, and movement. If the situation is not to degenerate into warfare, community "A" must learn the language of community "B" or community "B" must learn the language of community "A" or both communities must learn a mediating language "X." A truly mediating language would not do violence either to "A" or to "B." I am proposing that one way to imagine religious education is as a second language for people in communities "A" and "B." This language would be grounded in experiences broad enough to offer a bridge between "A" and "B," but it would not substitute for the languages of either "A" or "B."

To some extent this "religious education" already exists, or at least parts of the language exist in the form of modern languages that give such positive meaning to neutrality, objectivity, civility, tolerance, and similar qualities. The whole project of Western Enlightenment has been an attempt to save certain "values" that are rooted in religious history (for example, the dignity of the individual) while at the same time to get rid of religious elements that seem to cause conflict (for example, election or chosenness). Kant and Hegel, Marx and Freud, Weber and Durkheim, saw themselves as discovering a basis in science for some beliefs once held on religious faith.

The conflicting religions were to be replaced by a secular language that everyone would agree to speak. An explicit religious language would be tolerated only if it stayed in its place. One's first language could be Jewish or Christian or Muslim, but one's second language, to be used in public discourse, had to be secular; otherwise a civilized world would be impossible. It was naively expected that in time there would be reasonable replacements for those passionate first languages that embody religious dreams and activities.[8]

The development of modern forms of secular discourse could thus be called the emergence of "religious education," except that the religiosity is so thin as to be barely visible. The human race lost some valuable time while its scholarly leaders pursued a policy of suppressing the dialects of religion in the name of a universal reason. The time could have been better spent in establishing settings that channel religious forces in fruitful ways, that is, in developing an adequate language of religious education.

A religious education cannot abandon traditional religious language on the basis that it conflicts with what the modern world says is true. But equally important, religious education cannot be a settling for one's religious dialect without asking how it interacts with the modern world. The emergence of a language of religious education requires people who speak a secular language but who realize that secular language is a fragile compromise of conflicting ideals. We have to hold on to the real gains of modern tolerance even while unearthing religious dimensions of that speech.

Most of the chapters of this book center around a term from our ordinary secular language (for example, education, morality, professional). At the surface level, these terms may seem to have little or nothing to do with religion. My claim is that if we open up the term in the context of our contemporary crises, then the relevance of religious traditions will be evident. The premise of the inquiry is that religious and secular are not opposites or parallels. Secular language is a second language that often jumped too far from its own foundations. The world needs a new mediation to confront ancient wisdom with modern knowledge and at the same time to uncover the religious traditions in secular language. This work of developing an adequate language of religious education is occurring in all parts of the world, but it is still only a gentle murmur in the midst of the clash of ideas and the conflict of weapons.

NOTES

1. See, C. Bowers, *Elements of a Post Liberal Theory of Education* (New York: Teachers College, 1987), p. 83.

2. Thomas Hobbes, *De Corpore* in *The English Works of Thomas Hobbes*, vol. I, ed. William Molesworth (London: John Bohn, 1839-45).

3. Hannah Pitkin, *Wittgenstein and Justice* (Berkeley: University of California, 1972), p. 297.

4. Eric Havelock, *Preface to Plato* (Cambridge, Mass.: Harvard University Press, 1963), p. 208.

5. Richard Hofstadter, *Anti-Intellectualism in America* (New York: Vintage, 1963), p. 235.

6. Krister Stendahl in *Christ's Lordship and Religious Pluralism*, ed. Gerard Anderson and Thomas Stransky (New York: Orbis, 1981), p. 14.

7. Walter Brueggemann, *II Kings 18-19: The Legitimacy of a Sectarian Hermeneutic* (Indianapolis: Christian Theological Seminary, 1984), pp. 1-5.

8. George Steiner, *In Bluebeard's Castle* (New Haven, Conn.: Yale University Press, 1971).

2

Education's Religious Problem

An answer to "what is the meaning of religious education" requires, among other things, answering the question: "What is the meaning of education?" This latter question is the one that I explore in this chapter. I cannot think
of a more comprehensive or more important question to
ask about education. However, I quickly add that there are
innumerable questions about education which I am not
asking, questions about how to practice education with
various groups in various places at different stages of life.
This chapter's sufficiently ambitious aim is to provide an
adequate statement about the meaning of the term "education."

That religious education is a part of education may seem
almost too obvious for saying. And yet, in the United
States and elsewhere, there is a widespread assumption
that religious education belongs to churches and synagogues and that it is, therefore, a subdivision of theology
or a part of the religious institution's need for self-preser-
vation.

The same conclusion is reached starting from opposite
ends. On the one side, those who disparage religious education think that it should not be dignified by inclusion
within education; religious education, they would assume,

31

cannot measure up to the standards of the modern ideal of education. On the other side are people who work under religious auspices. While they usually do not wish to be dissociated from education, they have a sense of "going beyond education" in their religious work. They are therefore resistant to confinement within an academic subdivision.

I am not without sympathy for the protest of this second group who wish to go beyond education. But their protest needs to be funneled in a fruitful direction. If our present meaning of education is too confining, too rigid, too biased, then the protest ought to be about the meaning of education. One ought to argue on the basis of history, logic, and the crisis of our culture that education can have a richer meaning than is allowed today in many discussions. A religious protest ought to be from within education itself.

In the United States we have a crisis in the relation between education and religion. One would never guess that from the several dozen national reports on education that have been published since 1983. The religious problem is buried deeply in the meaning of education. People who are surveying classrooms or testing seventeen-year-olds can be oblivious to the larger patterns of meaning that thread together the idea of education.

Until the nineteenth century in the United States there was some recognition that education required both moral and religious meaning. The impetus for establishing schools was most often religious, and schools were generally under religious auspices. When the public schools were begun in the 1840s, the aim was to overcome sectarian religious divisions with the teaching of a common religion. The common religion was to be taught during the week in the common schools, while the Sunday school was charged with conveying denominational particularity. John Dewey, the best known educational reformer of the twentieth century, did not completely break with that tradition. Dewey had little trust in the Sunday school religion of the churches, but he had almost unbounded trust in the public school to convey the "common faith." The work of the school, said Dewey, is "infinitely religious."[1]

While acknowledging the intrinsic connection between religion and education, Dewey and other reformers placed almost all of their educational hopes in a state-supported system of universal schooling. Dewey's belief that "education is the fundamental method of social progress and reform" coupled with his belief that family, church, and apprenticeship were no longer sources of education, placed all the hope for progress and reform on the shoulders of public school children.[2]

As the school became the hoped for agent of salvation in the late-nineteenth and early-twentieth centuries, its chief opponent became the traditional centers of religion. A leading social reformer in 1901 saw "an almost worldwide drift from religion toward education as the method of indirect social restraint."[3] Education now had to do what religion had traditionally done; the school was to be more religious than were the religions.

Once this opposition is linguistically in place—religion versus education—then people who identify themselves as educators have to prove their claim by distancing themselves from all taint of religion. And on the religious side, there is endless sniping at education. The theological attack has ranged from the rantings of a Billy Sunday to the sophistication of a Reinhold Niebuhr. In all these cases, the religious group has to use a "noneducational" language in which to state its attack and carry on its business.[4]

On the secular side, the school is always threatened with becoming an idol. Without a larger context, the school is subject both to the unrealistic hopes and to the periodic thrashings of people who expect miracles. In some of the poorer sections of the world, eight or twelve years of schooling can still inspire hope of salvation. In some of the rich, industrial nations there is almost constant fretting at the failure of the schools. Why have they not saved us?

EDUCATION AND MEANING

The late 1960s were a time of intense criticism of education. Numerous experiments were started, most of which did not last long. Although some beneficial changes did result from that period, what unfortunately did not change was the fundamental language in which we ask educational questions. Some new phrases were coined (e.g., open classrooms, schools without walls, life experience credits) but they embodied more than they challenged the fundamental assumptions of modern education.

Self-proclaimed radicals of educational reform usually become very vague when they get past the attack on the existing system. They know that education should mean something other than tired schoolteachers talking endlessly to bored schoolchildren while administrators make announcements on the public address system. But if one tries to break the total control of education by school, if education is not a commodity sold in school, what is the alternative?

As I indicated in chapter one, there are two main places to look for the recovery, reform, and restatement of a term's meaning: the history of the word and the excluded voices of the present. The two sources often overlap as they do here; various excluded groups (e.g., women and blacks) have their own history of education. Thus, the history of education has to be attended to but with a wary eye on the sources of that history. For a few years there was much talk about a "revisionist history of education." That phrase unfortunately suggested a one-time uncovering of some conspiracy and the subsequent revelation of the true history of education. The revisioning of or relistening to history is a patient, never-ending process.

The relation of men and women is especially important here. One can easily miss the point by assuming that the problem has been the exclusion of women from education and that the solution is to give women equal access to education. Since we now seem to be moving in that direction, we may seem to be approaching a solution. But I think we must dig deeper.

Women were excluded from institutions that controlled the *meaning* of education. Two things resulted. Because women could not get their education in the place which the cultural spokesmen called education, women developed other aspects and forms of education. And because women's experience was not included in the meaning of the term "education," that meaning has been radically deficient. Education became a different kind of thing and the later entrance of women into *that* thing does not automatically correct the problem.[5]

Feminist criticism of education, I think it safe to say, has barely begun. It will take several generations of women as professors, administrators, and educators in positions which have yet to be named before the question becomes clear. At present, women are doing the necessary digging at male theories of education that have dominated recent centuries. In addition, much of the necessary data to fill out the meaning of education come not from books on the history of education but from places like social history, history of the family, or the history of work. And one should not exclude religious history.

Another excluded group are those who are voiceless because of age. Here there is the strangest twist of language which prevents us from identifying who the excluded are. Education in the last century became identified with the schooling of the young. Within a few decades there began to be a protest against this narrowing. The movement was called "adult education," a term almost but not quite accurate.

In adult education literature, there seem to be only two groups: children and adults. This is not the most precise or most helpful way to relate age and education. Infants and very young children are invisible in adult education literature; so are the very old. In reality, if there is a competition by age for the meaning of education, the main division has the young and the old on one side of the divide and people in their middle years on the other side. This middle has the most control of the meaning of education.

In asking who controls the meaning of a term, the main issue is not to whom the word is applied but who controls the applying. Thus, education is a term that is mainly the affair of young and middle-aged adults exercising power in the lives of older children and young people who are soon to join the ranks of these adults. The literature of adult education has generally been oblivious to any subtleties or complexities in stating the issue of age. Writers complain that children have been getting more than their fair share of education (an amazing assumption) and that adults have been shortchanged. Thus, the cry has been for more money and bigger programs for adults.

The first need is not a theory of adult education but a meaning of education which, among other things, includes all ages of adults. As it is, theories of adult education have made almost no impression on educational writing other than adult education. Why, for example, does the community college population, whose average age is near thirty, get spoken of as part of education, not adult education?

A few years ago I was preparing to teach a course on "curriculum." I went to that section of our large university library and went through all the monographs and textbooks that looked readable. In all these books, curriculum was assumed to mean what goes on in primary and secondary schools. I could not find a book, a chapter, or even a paragraph to suggest that the curriculum of education could include what adults learn. There is, of course, an adult education section of the library where authors discuss such things. Writers in adult education all too easily accepted the deal: There is "education" and its literature; there is "adult education" and its specialized concerns. That division of labor prevents the term "education" from ever being seriously tampered with.

HISTORICAL PATTERNS OF EDUCATION

In thinking about what constitutes education, historical studies help to provide an opening for the imagination. We need to move away from the single system that has dominated our thinking for over a century. The "radical" reform of education that would simply liberate young people from school is inadequate. However, the radical reformers are right in pointing out the illusion that education is a product available in school. Education always has been and always will be more complicated than that. Giving the whole task of education to schoolteachers and their young charges has not proved effective. We add schooldays to the year, schoolhours to the day, and even schoolyears to the young person's life, but such changes do not uncover our assumptions about the meaning of education.

History is helpful in showing that the person who questions today's meaning of education is not being merely "speculative," not denying what everyone has always known is the meaning of education. Not so many centuries ago, education meant something wider, something deeper, and at times something longer than what education in the twentieth century has generally been assumed to mean. That earlier meaning did not entirely disappear, especially among people away from the centers of economic and political power. The task is not simply to restore the meaning of education from the sixteenth or seventeenth centuries. Even if education in some past century were adequate to that day, it would not be appropriate to ours. But part of the meaning of education is waiting to be recovered so that we can think more imaginatively about education in the present.

At an earlier period in the English language, education referred to the nurturing and rearing of the young. Interestingly, the term could also apply to the nonhuman world so that a horse or even a plant could be educated.[6] The verb "to educate" clearly refers to a highly directive process. Education was neither a self-invention by the individual nor a sharing among equal partners. One generation had valuable things to pass on to the next generation within a limited amount of time.

The difficulty with this meaning of education, especially in our day, is how to have effective education without its being authoritarian. The liberal wing of educational discourse tends to slide over this issue by concentrating on attitudes as opposed to behavior, or by saying that education should be available to everyone but imposed on no one. In practice, this wing of education seems to be based on trying to change people's thoughts while hoping that there will be a connection between thinking and behavior.

On the conservative or behavioristic wing of educational discussion, the issue is directly confronted. Education is thought to be the practical business of changing the world. At the beginning of Ralph Tyler's influential book, *Basic Principles of Curriculum and Instruction,* he writes: "Education is a process of changing behavior patterns of people."[7] This way of speaking about education scandalizes liberal critics. One of them asks in reference to Tyler's definition: How does this differ from hypnosis, shock treatment, or brainwashing?[8]

Many writers with a behavioristic orientation seem oblivious to profound questions of human freedom. However, some of their assumptions about education are on firmer ground than their liberal opponents. Education has been and continues to be concerned with changing the world, that is, changing physical organisms in their relation to the whole environment. I think this conviction is present in most people's thinking about education; they think it should make a practical difference.

As often happens in such disputes, the liberal opposition to behaviorism is the other side of the behavorist categories rather than a genuine alternative. While behaviorists take the outside ("behavior"), liberals take the inside with thoughts, values, feelings, attitudes, and so forth. What joins the two parties is their assumed image of education: an instructor facing a group of children. The problem of education becomes the limits of an individual schoolteacher's control of schoolchildren.

Suppose instead that education is the interplay of several institutions. Suppose further that what education results in is a change of human *activity,* that is, persons in relation to other people and to the nonhuman world. Then the first question of education is not the dilemma of a classroom instructor facing schoolchildren, but how to describe the institutional interplay that constitutes education. Classroom instruction has its dilemmas but any fruitful discussion of their resolution requires a wider context of education.

How does one describe the institutional pattern of education? A helpful book on the history of education that tried to provide the details of this meaning was *Education in the Forming of American Society* by Bernard Bailyn.[9] Published at the beginning of the 1960s, Bailyn's essay influenced the thinking of many people, including myself. Bailyn started from the fact that histories of education in the United States were very sketchy about the actual practice of education between the 1640s and the 1840s. Did the school do all the educating? In answering this question, Bailyn brought to it a meaning of education as "the entire process by which a culture transmits itself across the generations." The answer he found to his question was that schools did have a part in education but probably a much smaller part than most people have generally assumed.

Bailyn describes in his book a configuration of educational institutions: the family, the school, the church, apprenticeship. Each of these four helped to shape the culture, and they reshaped that culture as they transmitted it to the young. The four poles of education worked in unison and with some overlapping. Schools were not set up to take something away from the family but as extensions of the family. The school and the family were to cooperate in educating the young. (In this partnership schools are necessarily ambiguous in their effect on the family, a point which I return to below.) The church was also closely related to the family, and it was a chief impetus for schooling in literacy; one could not be a good church member unless one could read the Bible. Apprenticeship was, besides "job training," a new family experience. Each young man learned a trade in the context of a new family; and even the young woman who was not learning a trade underwent something similar.

Bailyn's four-part description of education provided a definite pattern of language that has historical credibility. It also generally had a lot going for it in our present-day world. Certainly, the family is still as central as ever in the nurturing and rearing of the very young, despite the shift in the nineteenth century which moved economic production away from the family. The school has spread in all directions; it is the centerpiece of education for nearly all young people and of increased importance for older people. Apprenticeship, whether housed within the school building or elsewhere, is as important as ever; education now and always is about the preparation for and the engagement in work.

The most problematic of Bailyn's four elements is the church. For better or worse, the church does not exercise the kind of power it once had. In the seventeenth century people were required to listen to the sermon even if they were not church members. This provision of "adult education" by the seventeenth-century church does not provide the most helpful guide as to how the church might be in education. The twentieth-century diversity of religion has to be acknowledged in the exploration of the religious question. But the Christian church might in fact be freer to contribute to education as a whole when it is not assigned to keeping children and adults on the one right path.

For a few years in the late 1960s, I adopted language proposed in an essay by Donald Oliver and Fred Newmann.[10] They referred to a threefold pattern of community seminar, schooling, and laboratory. Bailyn's description of family, school, and apprenticeship is evident in their language. Community discussions could include the family, and laboratory might refer not only to preparing for a job but of continuing to learn on the work site. Eventually, I decided that this language did not represent appreciable progress in clarity and concreteness. What struck me was that there was need for further distinctions within the main elements of education. Only in that way could we get a better description of the interactions that *are* education.

The Oliver and Newmann category of community seminar was the element I found most stimulating. More particularly, the relation between family and community became for me the nub of the problem. I sensed that one of the keys to the meaning of education revolved around the meaning of community and its relation to the family. Much to my surprise, I found what I was looking for when I was not looking. That is, I was engaged in what I thought to be an entirely different interest—the history of the family in the Reformation period—when one of the pieces of the educational puzzle fell into place.

The Reformation was in large part a fight over where

one finds the religious community. Medieval Catholicism had located it in the monastery; in reaction, the Reformers wanted every family to be "a little church." What struck me was that both sides had a piece of the truth but neither had the whole truth. What Christianity then needed and still needs is the maintaining of a healthy tension between family and community. To separate the two, as Catholicism tends to do, or to conflate the two, as Protestantism tends to do, is destructive. The idea of community should ordinarily include the family but should not be equated with it. The term "community" ought to connote something larger than family (although not too much larger) and something more diverse than any family can be (although something cohesive enough to be a personal and personalizing group).

This delicate and ever-changing relation between the family that each of us is born into and the community that we are called to become requires education. I do not mean—at least I do not primarily mean—that this is a topic for a social studies class. I mean that education is the shaping, the reshaping, the intelligent living out of this relation between family and community. Education is always a "learning," but it can be what one learns by living with a spouse, caring for one's children, and participating in a neighborhood organization. That is not the whole meaning of education, but any claim to state the meaning of education that neglects this primordial relation has missed the point.

I hasten to add that I am not speaking about "informal" as opposed to "formal" education. How to use the word "form" is precisely the issue. And one of the clearest places to begin thinking about form in education is with the form of the family: How has it existed for several thousand years, what have been variations in its form, what are the limits in proposals to change the form today?

A distinction between family and community implies the reality of other communal forms besides the family. For its own good, the family needs other groupings which have personalizing characteristics but need not be modeled on the family. A neighborhood, a religious congregation, or a baseball team can be community experiences distinct from the parent and child experience of the family. I think it should be possible to describe the most important of these nonfamilial, communal forms.

I have tried elsewhere to name patterns of life in which tens of millions of people find inclusion, care, and a sense of personhood.[11] It is not a matter of advocating that these forms come into existence but of recognizing them and naming them better. For example, since the mid-1970s I have regularly named homosexual relations as one such communal form. It is clear to me that homosexual people who live in caring and loving relations constitute a nonfamilial but personalizing form of life. But we are still at the beginning of trying to understand what the similarities and differences may be in relation to heterosexual marriage, and even to recognizing differences between gay and lesbian relations.

My discovery of the relation of family and community while studying the Reformation era had a bonus attached to it. The relation of job and work (or task and vocation) formed an almost exact parallel in the sixteenth century. Medieval Catholicism had placed religious work in the monastery; the Reformers wished to have every task be part of God's work. Like family and community, we are still in need of an educational approach to the relation of job and work.

I can sum up my educational pattern by saying that it consists of four forms, each of which has a tension within it. A sequence of four institutional involvements corresponds

FAMILY	SCHOOLING
JOB	RETIREMENT

to the chronological stages of life. We proceed from involvement in the family, to a great emphasis on school, to tasks in the world of work, to retirement from preoccupation with some of these tasks.

Each of these involvements is related to a universal value of which it is a partial embodiment: family in relation to community, schooling in relation to literate knowledge, job in relation to work, and retirement in relation to contemplative wisdom.

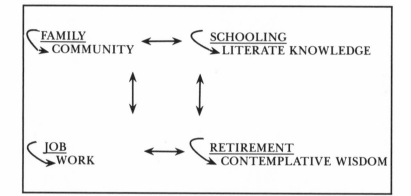

Education consists in developing the most fruitful relations both within each of these four forms and among the four forms. Although one of these forms is likely to predominate at any one stage of life, the other three ought never to disappear. For example, the school can convey knowledge only in a context where the school is a kind of community, where school is experienced as real work, and where a sense of retirement or retreat is also present.

DEVELOPMENT AND EDUCATION

The final key to the pieces of education falling into place was an idea that I had often used but had never really reflected upon. That was the idea of "development." From the time I had read Bailyn's essay in the early 1960s I was keenly aware of not speaking of education as a product that schools provide. But adding the family, apprenticeship, and perhaps other institutions does not necessarily correct the problem. Such addition might only diversify the agents of production without changing the nature of education. We might end up with more attention to the producers while still not getting a better understanding of what education is, why there is so much fighting about it, and how we can dramatically improve it.

The problem, it seemed to me, was not that education was thought to be a product of the school but that it was thought to be a product at all. The idea that it was a product, a thing, an object, a commodity, a concluding state of affairs, seemed to me to be self-defeating. But what is the alternative? The word most frequently paired and contrasted with product is "process."

In Bailyn's meaning of education quoted above, he says that education is "the entire process." Is that the correct way to start a description of education? Many people think so, but many other people think that the product is more important. The argument is one of those hardy perennials in which the pendulum makes its swing every few years. For a while, process seems to be in the ascendancy. What counts then is that students learn how to think and how to go about educating themselves; social interaction is part of the process. But periodically we discover what the students know and what they do not know. In the early 1980s the fear arose that great numbers of high-school or college graduates know very little about history, geography, and literature, not to mention math and science.

Whenever I sit through one of these academic disputes over process and product, I feel a mixed allegiance. One can always say (and someone always does): The answer is that both are important. But saying both/and is usually a way of evading the argument or failing to understand why there is an argument. In this case, if I have to choose I go with "process" simply because being in favor of a good product seems to miss the point of education. And yet all the talk about process leaves me uneasy.

The idea of "development" helped me to locate the reason for my uneasiness. If the concern with process is with a process that leads to a product, then talking about process is merely an indirect or a preparatory way to talk about product. That is, once one accepts the language of process versus product the argument is intramural and the differences are fairly minor. If one listens carefully, what is usually presupposed in the product/process discussion is that education takes place in school and that the product of the school is seventeen- or twenty-one-year-old educated students. The argument is mainly about efficiency, effectiveness, and quality control. The process in question is one of making, the conclusion to the act of making is a product. Education fits all too well into our dominant metaphor of making.

People who use this language probably do not wish to turn students into manufactured products. But it is very difficult to avoid this way of thinking. Twentieth-century philosophy has tried to find a new meaning of process, one that differs from most of our ordinary images. The modern Westerner is deeply rooted in Aristotelian thinking in which change is the transition between two static conditions. The final state is the object first imagined in the agent of change; there is a process of change needed to get from the first object to the second object.

In this context education can be the process that an individual or society undergoes in order to get "x" result in the lives of young people. Or alternatively, education is the "x" (the product) in service of which all the efforts are made. In the first case, education is called process; in the second, education is called product. In both we have the same assumptions, the same hopes, and the same struggling educators.

Can there be an alternative? One would have to have a process that is different from the making of products. Education in this case is a process that has no end point, no end state, no object to be attained. There are two ways in which one can imagine such a process.

The first image is that the process leads toward unlimited growth; the second is that the process leads to a deepening of the harmony, balance, and integrity of the process itself. In both cases, what emerges is a "religious" question, that is, the nature of infinitude and the relation of human life to some unimaginable unity.

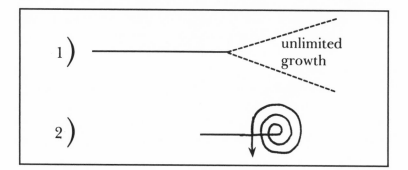

This is the reason why education has a religious problem and why a kind of religious crisis underlies all the efforts at reform. Education's problems are manageable when one is concerned with training a young person to have a "skill" or listing the great books that everyone is supposed to have read. But as soon as education itself comes into question, we have profoundly disturbing questions about the origin and purpose of life. Why be educated? What does it mean to be educated? Who is to judge? Where if anywhere do all these questions lead?

Here is where I found the idea of development to be so intriguing. I finally realized that it is with this term that the modern world was struggling to find a new religion. Development is closely related to both progress and evolution, but I think it has become the more comprehensive term with biological, individual, social, economic, and cosmic meaning. It is also the more flexible term in wrestling with the peculiar process of education.

Development is the modern world's alternative to providence, predestination, and heaven. At least, it is the alternative to what are assumed to be the constraints of Christian piety. Development is the idea that life has a direction although it has no end point or final state. Human life can get better right here on earth. Modern people who dismiss the idea of heaven as childish still have to believe that their lives are going somewhere, that is, to a better condition.

Theories of development combine empirical fact with fervent belief. Human life is guaranteed to get better if we can just clear away the obstacles to continuous improvement.

The idea began in the ecomomic arena at the beginning of modern times. That there could be progress in wealth, that we could develop more goods indefinitely, was what helped to define modernity. No one had a preordained plan for the world; poor countries need not stay in poverty; machines could substitute for human labor. As Marx put it, we must take back from the heavens what has been stolen from earth. The modern world is intent on emancipation or liberation from laws which Christianity had claimed were written in the economic universe. The modern idea of development was anti-Christian though not anti-religious in its origins. It needed the idea of infinity, the hope for unlimited growth as the driving force of a process that has endless products but no final product.

The nineteenth and twentieth centuries carried the idea of development into personal life. Psychologists sometimes speak today as if they invented the idea, but psychology was actually rather late on the scene. The emancipation of the individual from hereditary, physical, or social restraints spread slowly. Developmental psychology was thought to be part of child psychology. A developmental psychology that still presupposed a fixed point of adulthood was not yet completely developmental. Starting about 1950, however, adults were included with children and the dominant word became "growth." Nothing should interfere with the growth of the individual; neither tradition, nor parents, nor spouse, nor one's children should take precedence over the individual's personal growth.

The idea of growth as unqualified good came into educational theory through John Dewey's writing. He tirelessly repeated the position that "not perfection as a final goal, but the ever enduring process of perfecting, maturing, refining is the aim in living."[12] What we think of as educational goods "are directions of change in the quality of experience. Growth itself is the only moral end." With growth the only end, Dewey saw the enemy as any fixed standard, any object before which human beings must bow.

Dewey and other growth advocates acted with genuine religious impulse against the idols of the marketplace. But as often happens with idol smashers, the enthusiasts of this religion created a worse monster in the idea of unlimited growth. One can make some allowance for Dewey's celebration of growth fifty or seventy-five years ago. But it is astounding to find writers in education today who, oblivious to what the ecological question is about, still assume that "growth in growth" is a good beyond question. Growth in its proper place and in right proportions is a healthy sign. However, as the governing metaphor of personal life and civilized culture, growth quickly becomes pathological.

Education cannot have a fixed point of termination. Dewey was right on this issue, perhaps even more right than he realized. While denying that education has an end, he still spoke of education as being an affair of children, thus implying that adulthood is in fact the end of education. I think that Dewey was disastrously wrong in offering growth as an alternative to a termination point as end. And, unfortunately, Dewey's idea, riding the crest of industrial civilization, has spread everywhere.

What is the alternative both to education having a termination point and to education being a process of unlimited growth? One has to imagine a movement that has very definite ends (purposes) but no end (termination). The ends that are sought should be of a kind that can be reintegrated into the process itself. Money, for example, is not that kind of end. But activities such as play, art, sex, politics, or worship have a privileged position in education. We passionately seek an end within these activities, and each end that is reached simply enriches the activity. There is no object outside the activity whose attainment would terminate the activity. In this kind of movement, sometimes growth is desirable, sometimes contraction is desirable, and sometimes the question of growth does not apply.

Education has to be described in such a way that, within the finitude of human (and by implication, nonhuman) life, the full range of possibilities is allowed. It took me many years to come up with the following description, but I think it is comprehensive and consistent. It is also framed in ten simple words, eight of which are one syllable. I suggest that a starting point for discussing education is: "The reshaping of life's forms with end and without end." The play on the double meaning of "end" is intentional: end in the sense of purpose, aim and design; end in the sense of conclusion, termination, and final result. It is in the tension and play between the two meanings of end that fruitful discussions of education can occur. Most attempts to "define" education try to remove all the paradox before we start. That simply covers over the question of why education is endlessly argued about.

The meaning of education is itself an educational question to be endlessly debated. The debate ought not to be formless or without direction. Education does connote human design and the attempt to improve the world. However, one individual's conviction about how the world could be reshaped for the better ("This eight-year-old needs to know fractions" or "This teenager should be prevented from experimenting with sex") needs to be placed in the context of the flow of generations as well as in some community of today's wisdom.

One way to summarize this picture is to say that education is about "tradition," that it is about the transmission of what is most valuable from one generation to the next. Such a contention flies in the face of most twentieth-century writing on education which denigrates tradition. I think that sooner or later tradition has to be restored and that its close associate, transmission, has to be saved from the numerous thrashings it has taken. There is an aspect of education that concerns the criticism of tradition; however, one cannot criticize it until one recognizes that it is within us and all around us. Education does not hand on tradition; education *is* tradition, the process of handing on, and within the process the asking of critical questions about the past.

Tradition is a well-known term, used in many situations today. It is often mistaken for a denial of change, whereas the process of handing on is the most powerful form of change. Mere ideas, removed from the physical contact of handing something to another hand (trans-mission), have little power. To understand the full meaning of tradition it is helpful to consider its more than casual relation to religion.

In nearly all the major religions, tradition is a peculiar and paradoxical idea. A particular religion after the age of its founder tends to become fixed in written texts and commentaries. It happened with Moses, Gautama, Jesus, Muhammad, and even with nineteenth-century founders of religion. Tradition arises as a subtle counterforce to fixity. Tradition is the oral stream which does not contradict the text but instead provides the origin and larger context of the writing. Tradition awakens us to the oral nature of truth. The teaching is passed from master to disciple in secrecy; it is often thought to be, and in some ways is, subversive and dangerous. The danger is controlled by subjecting tradition to writing but the tradition is liable to spring up anew. After Jewish (oral) tradition became a written source, Jewish mystical tradition arose as a secret, oral teaching. Eventually, that also became written and controllable. In the modern world, Jewish tradition breaks out anew in both secular and religious expressions. For example, one of those expressions is psychoanalysis; its continuity with Jewish mysticism is something that Freud was quite aware of.[13]

Education as tradition means that it starts as physical handing on. The family conveys its rituals of life and death; parents are a kind of secret society with knowledge not available in books. The family's tradition becomes verbal in the telling of stories, some that pertain directly to the family, others that are about a larger community. The individual parent's intention in telling a story may be dwarfed by the intentionality embodied in the story itself. The story can carry the intentions of generations of parents. The tradition is the teller of the story—whether Irish, Jewish, Afro-American, or smaller groups of people—while the parent is a kind of sounding board.

EDUCATION AND SCHOOL

Within modern education the school plays a critical role in both senses of the word "critical." School is critical in the sense of being so important that it tends to become equated with the whole of education. That tendency is not a healthy one given the other meaning of critical. That is, within education the school's role is mainly to be critical: to probe, to cut through with the mind, to criticize. The negative connotation of the word "critical" is not undeserved. To criticize is to raise questions about whether what is assumed to be true really is the case.

Criticism, to exist at all, needs a tradition in which it is embedded; within that tradition school is a peculiar element that turns back on elements within the tradition. By the time that tradition is entirely made into the object of critical concern, it is no longer tradition. When the process is turned back on itself, it ceases to be a process; the tradition then gets viewed as the things that are passed on, as in the phrase "handing on tradition." Schooling, as a particular form of education, rightfully casts a skeptical eye on everything—every statement—that is assumed to be true.

This description of education and tradition brings out the fact that schools are almost self-contradictions. They exist in modern times because some community pays the bills to maintain them. The community wishes to have schools that pass on its tradition to the next generation. Insofar as the school is a community that socializes young people, it does indeed maintain tradition. But insofar as a school provides classrooms for appropriating tradition through literary tools, schooling makes the tradition vulnerable to doubt. People discover that there are multiple readings of every text and they also discover that there are other books to be read than the officially approved body of writing in the tradition.

One of the most dramatic examples of this conflict was the teaching of slaves in the North American colonies during the seventeenth and eighteenth centuries. The slave-masters thought it would be good for the slave's training

and the perpetuation of the community tradition that the
slaves should learn to read the Bible, especially such parts
as the Letter to Philemon. However, in the early nineteenth century some slaves were reading other books than
the Bible and reading parts of the Bible that the slaveowners did not really understand, especially the Book of
Exodus. The result was rebellion against the slaveowners
led by literate slaves. It then became a crime in the 1830s
to teach a slave to read. Schooling had been educationally
successful for the slave, but as a consequence the slaveowners put a stop to this form of education.[14]

Every religious group has something of this problem
even though its adherents are not slaves. The written text
which seems to safeguard orthodoxy within the tradition is
open to varying interpretation and commentary. When
great numbers of the "faithful" learn to read and to think
for themselves, the tradition comes under scrutiny and
sometimes under attack. The leaders must then ask themselves: Should the religious school be allowed to keep turning out potential heretics?

Not just the religious school has the problem. Every little
town and school district that financially and otherwise sup-
ports a school is eventually dismayed that the children do
not think like their parents. And some of the ideas that the
schoolteachers dabble in seem to be dangerous. Some tension between community and school is not bad, but schools
cannot be in severe conflict with the community's standards. Ultimate failure would occur only if the community
were to close the school for failing to produce orthodoxy
or if the community were to put the schoolteacher in the
impossible position of having to accept and to teach uncritically the views of the community.

This ambiguous position of school in education illustrates a more general principle, that what I have called
"forms of life" have a definite and conserving pattern but
that the interplay of forms is a constant transforming of
life. The family conserves and passes on the acquired wisdom and knowledge of centuries. And yet, families in relation to each other, families in relation to nonfamilial but
personalizing groups, transform the world toward a com-

munity still coming to be. Schools in relation to one another, schools in relation to other sources of literate knowledge, subvert the established knowledge that a school is set up to disseminate.

The need for reform of family or school is constant, but one cannot reform what does not have form. If the school becomes a "shopping mall," as has happened in some places today, the student's world is never really challenged and transformed. The student simply looks for what fits into his or her existing viewpoint. When school becomes equivalent to education and takes on the task of doing everything, it is sure to neglect the specific things that the form of schooling can do and should do, especially the teaching of reading and writing.

People who work in schools should have very definite ends in view. These are not the ends of education so much as the ends of schooling. Schoolteachers do not have a blueprint for the educated person; that has to be discovered in and through a lifetime of education. But schoolteachers ought to be clear about what a well-schooled person should know after eight, twelve, or sixteen years of school.

These ends, the designed-for results of school, are not subject to democratic vote by schoolteachers or students. This fact does not mean that school ought to be conducted in an authoritarian manner. Most procedures in a school can be democratic in the sense of respecting the person of the student and allowing for choices in the curriculum. The ends of schooling invite imaginative experiments on how to get there. For example, there is no guaranteed way to get students excited about reading or writing. There are many ways to get students disciplined in both.

I referred earlier in this chapter to a modest little treatise written by Ralph Tyler in 1949.[15] It became one of the most influential books on curriculum. In this book, Tyler proposed four steps in designing a curriculum: 1) choice of "educational purposes the school should serve," 2) experiences needed to attain those objectives, 3) organization of the experiences, and 4) evaluation of the process. From one point of view, Tyler was describing what every school and every schoolteacher do, whether or not they do it consciously and systematically. Every school has some kind of curriculum guide that specifies "objectives" and something about how to get there. Every teacher who walks into class with notes and a lesson plan wishes to arrive somewhere one or two hours later. Evaluation is the element that may be postponed until a later time, although any experienced teacher is constantly taking stock through eye movements, feet shuffling, questions asked and answered.

The most crucial of Tyler's four steps is the first; the other three follow from the first and are at the service of the educational purposes of the school. How does one find the answer to this first key question? Tyler gives three sources: 1) studies of learners, 2) studies of contemporary life, and 3) subject matter specialists. These sources, however, hide a simple fact: If one is talking about the purpose of education, no one can adequately formulate the answer. If in contrast one is talking about the purpose of schooling, then the answer is generally evident without conducting surveys. I grant that as one proceeds to spell out the curriculum in detail Tyler's three sources do come into play. To write a math curriculum for a junior high school, one needs expert knowledge of math and some knowledge of the abilities of the particular students.

An extraordinary amount of curriculum writing since 1950 has consisted of "Tyler bashing," that is, denunciations of "the Tyler rationale" as a reductionistic and mechanistic approach to curriculum. Ralph Tyler has generally stood his ground in responding to critics. He has acknowledged that his four steps need not always be in the same order. Evaluation might be the first step when considering curricula. Or a literature course might begin with the literature itself and only later ask about objectives. With the admission of such flexibility, Tyler's position is all but invulnerable. To the extent that he and his critics assume schools, school departments, classrooms, courses, and lesson plans his description is accurate.[16]

What gets Tyler's critics irritated is that they are certain that education consists of more than setting goals, trying to convey a definite body of material, and then finding out if one has succeeded. But the critics usually share with Tyler the tendency to talk of school as if it were the one place of education and classroom instruction as the one form of teaching.

Tyler's position is invulnerable unless one distinguishes the curriculum of schooling from the curriculum of education. Curriculum planning in the school is largely what Tyler describes, but the curriculum of education is a different kind of question. While education can go many different ways and its goals cannot be stated, the school has to have fixed standards. The ends of schooling are largely determined by the nature of schooling and have to be maintained by people prepared to be the staff of a school. While there ought to be a place for the student voice, the school that is run by the students is close to being no school at all.

Curriculum reforms in U.S. schools often go in the direction of expanding the curriculum to include all kinds of "practical" things. The premise is sound that education ought to be practical. The problem is the assumption that the whole curriculum of education belongs in the school. If there are problems in the culture—traffic deaths, drugs, AIDS, racial discrimination—the school is presumed to be the place that takes care of such problems. Why not one more course? But the school is often confused as to its essential nature, and its trying to cope with all kinds of contemporary problems further obscures the limited but invaluable contribution that school can make to education. Most of the "practical problems" belong elsewhere in education.

Tyler effectively responds to his critics by saying that if no one will hire seventeen-year-olds, then a better curriculum will not help. He is right, provided that we are talking about the school curriculum. What we need, Tyler goes on to say, is new cooperation of job-study for young people and an examination of "other educational environment." I heartily agree, although that kind of statement must be worked into a consistent and comprehensive way of speaking about education. Otherwise, people nod their heads on the question of "other educational environments," but go right on speaking of education as what happens in school.[17]

Tyler's reference to job-study is especially telling. The school subverts its own mission by becoming just a job-training center. As the history of so-called vocational schools shows, when the school does nothing but prepare people for jobs, it does not even do that well. The jobs that the school prepares for are likely to be outdated by the time the student gets a job.

This is not to say that the school should have no relation to jobs and, more so, work. Instead of there being a radical split between academic and vocational schools, all schools ought to have a sense of both the academic and the vocational. School should itself be an experience of real work for young people before they have a job. Furthermore, the school should be related to the job world so that when students do have jobs the job will be educational, that is, it should be experienced as genuine work and not just a means for making money.

Most young people in high school and college do in fact hold jobs. While maintaining its academic responsibility, the school could be aware of the job world and try to create some fruitful relations with it. Youngsters need the experience both of holding a paying job and doing service work for which they are not paid.

In this context there has been an interesting, possibly revolutionary, proposal in the Carnegie study, *High School:* "We recommend that every high-school student complete a service requirement—a new 'Carnegie unit'—involving volunteer work in the community or at school."[18] Here the high school is envisioned not only as housing classroom instruction (including preparation for a job) but also as the place for another *form* of education. Many religiously affiliated schools already have such programs. Anyone involved in their organization will testify that this is not "informal" education; it requires at least as much form and organization as does the classroom.

I think the idea of young people experiencing this form of education—learning by service—deserves exploration in every public and private school. My only reservation is that the Carnegie study does not adequately discuss the

high-school student's freedom in this context. This form of
education engages the student in another kind of learning;
it necessitates new protections for student freedom. There
ought to be a range of possibilities for how a student moves
into this area and what kind of service work he or she does.
Simply assigning a fifteen-year-old to work in a nursing
home is not necessarily educational; it could be counter-
productive. But where young people exercise some choice
and where they work with helpful supervision, the experience can be transforming.

CONCLUSION

Discussions of educational reform in this century have
been skewed by the assumption that the question is whether adults should tell children what to think and how to act.
The conservative side believes that it knows what youngsters should know and how they should behave. The liberal side believes that the youngsters should discover the
truth for themselves and that behavior is not what education is about. And so we have the standard arguments of
content versus method, product versus process, authoritar-
ianism versus laissez-faire.

I have suggested in this chapter that it is possible to have
a conservative-looking school curriculum for the sake of a
liberal and liberating education. School cannot be all
things to all men and women. When children or adults
agree to take part in school, they agree to enter into a
disciplining of the mind under the guardianship of those
who are knowledgeable. The authority of a schoolteacher
or any teacher should not be confused with the power that
adults have over children.

This confusion is less likely when "student" is not equivalent to young person. Sometimes there is good reason for
all the students in a room being eight years old or teenagers. On the whole, however, we ought to speak of the
school as a place for people of any age. In this context, the
recent rise in the age of many college students has been a
healthy development.

An adequate meaning of education, therefore, requires

the inclusion of adults of every age as well as infants and children. I doubt that we will be able to maintain the tension between education as always having ends (purposes) but never having an end (termination) without a religious dimension to education. We turn the school or knowledge or skills or career into an idol; education then ceases to be the intelligent and continuing reshaping of human life. Or we canonize mere "openness," the right to choice and individual idiosyncracy; here, too, education ceases to be a reshaping of our common life.

Religion is, above all, a resistance to idols. It de-idolizes everything, including whatever becomes the end of education. Skills are desirable but they lead to something further; knowledge is good but it is not G-d. Religions insist that we must strive for particular goods even though none of these goods will perfectly satisfy us. That means living in a tension between the end of any form of education and the end of education which is not under our control.

At its best, religion holds together the individual and the collective, what has already been attained and what is still to come, bodily life and a unity beyond bodily imagination. The religious issue is not a peripheral addition to education. At the center of the interplay of educational forms, religious questions emerge. Our way of responding to those questions shapes the whole process of education.

NOTES

1. John Dewey, "Religion and Our Schools," in *Characters and Events,* vol. II., ed. Joseph Ratner (New York: Henry Holt, 1929), p. 514.

2. John Dewey, *Dewey on Education,* ed. Martin Dworkin (New York: Teachers College, 1959), p. 30.

3. Edward Ross, *Social Control* (New York, Macmillan, 1901), p. 176.

4. See, Reinhold Niebuhr, *Moral Man and Immoral Society* (New York: Scribner's, 1960), p. xiii; for Billy Sunday's views on education, see, Richard Hofstadter, *Anti-Intellectualism in America* (New York: Vintage, 1963), p. 22.

5. Jane Martin, *Reclaiming a Conversation: The Ideal of the Educated Woman* (New Haven, Conn.: Yale University Press, 1985), p. 179.

6. *The Compact Edition of the Oxford English Dictionary,* vol. I (London: Oxford University Press, 1971), p. 833.

7. Ralph Tyler, *Basic Principles of Curriculum and Instruction* (Chicago: University of Chicago Press, 1950).

8. Herbert Kliebard, "The Tyler Rationale," in *Curriculum: An Introduction to the Field,* ed. David Purpel and James Gress (Berkeley: McCutchan, 1978), p. 259.

9. Bernard Bailyn, *Education in the Forming of American Society* (New York: Vintage, 1960).

10. Fred Newmann and Donald Oliver, "Education and Community," in *Religion and Public Education,* ed. Theodore Sizer (Boston: Houghton Mifflin, 1967), pp. 184-227.

11. Gabriel Moran, *Education toward Adulthood* (New York: Paulist, 1979), pp. 96-100.

12. John Dewey, *Reconstruction in Philosophy* (Boston: Beacon, 1957), p. 177.

13. David Bakan, *Sigmund Freud and the Jewish Mystical Tradition* (New York: Schocken, 1965).

14. See, Thomas Webber, *Deep Like the River: Education in the Slave Quarter* (New York: Norton, 1978).

15. Tyler, *Basic Principles of Curriculum.*

16. Ralph Tyler, "Specific Approaches to Curriculum Development," in *Curriculum: An Introduction to the Field,* p. 246.

17. Ibid., p. 243.

18. Eugene Boyer, *High School* (New York: Harper & Row, 1983), p. 209.

3

Teaching: From Moral Dilemma to Religious Education

In the previous chapter I have provided a comprehensive description of education. Often when education is defined it is looked at from the standpoint of the teacher, or more exactly, from the standpoint of the professional schoolteacher. I have tried to avoid this limitation by describing what a *community* does when it is educating. A group of people who are deserving of the name community reshape life's forms with end (purpose) and without end (termination). The process of education is an interplay of forms rather than the activities of one person.

The tendency to confuse education with the teacher's outlook and efforts is not surprising; education and teaching are inextricably related. But I suspect that people say education when they are really talking about what a schoolteacher does because they are uneasy about the idea of teaching itself. Although teaching is not the whole of education, I think that it is the most important test case of whether we understand what education is. People express little or no ambivalence about "learning," and as a result there is prolific discussion about the learning aspects of education. In contrast, there is very little discussion about the nature of teaching.

60

In this chapter I wish to confront the issue as directly as possible. I am not addressing the topics of education, learning, or teacher but only the meaning of the verb "to teach." My focus is narrowly on the question: "What does it mean to teach?" Obviously, such a question presupposes a context, and the answer eventually has to be resituated in the context of teacher, learner, and education. But to get at the moral dilemma that people sense in the idea of teaching it will be helpful to concentrate on the act or event of teaching. One can say many things about people who are called teachers, but what exactly does a teacher do when engaging in the act of teaching?

The moral dilemma I refer to is evident both in the frequent evasion of a direct discussion of the topic and in the highly ambivalent comments made about teaching whenever it is discussed. An understanding of teaching within the field of religious education is hampered by this failure to get beyond the moral dilemma which people sense in all teaching. My intention in this chapter is to clarify the meaning of "to teach" and indicate how this meaning opens up the area of religious education. These possibilities for religious education will be filled out in the chapters of Part II. We need an adequate meaning of teaching to discuss religious education, while in turn the practice of religious education can throw considerable light on how the modern world has painted itself into a corner with an inadequate meaning of teaching.

THE MORAL DILEMMA OF TEACHING

In the literature of moral education, there is a common skepticism that anyone can teach morality, justice, or virtue. A dilemma thereby arises regarding the contribution of the teacher. Moral education is placed in the school, but schoolteachers are cautioned against trying to teach morality. Although this discussion in the literature of moral education is not the dilemma I am referring to in this chapter, it is a symptom or illustration of the dilemma. The problem in the first place is not whether one can teach morality but whether one can teach morally. Is it morally desirable to try to teach anything? From numerous examples that could be cited, I choose the following three quotations to illustrate the problem.

1. Carl Rogers, in an influential book on education, *Freedom to Learn*, writes of teaching: "When I try to teach, as I do sometimes, I am appalled by the results, which seem as little more than inconsequential because sometimes the teaching appears to succeed. When this happens, I find that the results are damaging. It seems to cause the individual to distrust his experience and to stifle significant learning. Hence I have come to feel that the outcomes of teaching are either unimportant or hurtful. As a consequence, I realize that I am only interested in being a learner."[1]

2. Philip Jackson, in trying to state a consensus of liberal and conservative reform in education, comes up with two points of agreement on what is desirable: a) reduce unnecessary pain in learning and b) increase the independence of the learner. Concerning the latter point, Jackson writes: "Nor would anyone in his or her right mind recommend keeping students dutifully servile to teachers a day longer than is necessary."[2]

3. Leonardo Boff, in describing an international church meeting, writes: "No one wished to be anyone's teacher. All sought to be disciples of all. Bishops and assessors spoke only when called upon to do so, or when they lined up with everyone else to wait their turn."[3]

These three quotations indicate not only a preference for learning over teaching; they imply that teaching is one of the great obstacles to learning. Carl Rogers pits teaching against learning as if they were contradictories. This quotation is fairly typical of what is found throughout adult education literature where the verb "to teach" is avoided as much as possible on the assumption that it refers to childish dependence. That assumption is clearly at work in the second quotation where Philip Jackson accepts the fact that teaching is a necessity for children. The best one can hope for is to shorten the time in which "students are dutifully servile to their teachers." The most remarkable thing about the Jackson quotation is the author's claim that this thoroughly negative view of the meaning of "to teach" is held by both sides in educational debates. The third quotation makes a similar assumption within a church context. Leonardo Boff thinks it desirable that everyone be a disciple (learner) to all but that no one be a teacher. The context of this strange ideal is indicated in Boff's following sentence about bishops speaking only when called upon.

What these three quotations share is an image of teachers and teaching in which one person exercises powerful control over others. Its chief embodiment in the modern world is a classroom. More important than the room is the assumption that the one who is teaching is a powerful adult and that the student is a child or someone who is treated like a child. Teaching becomes confused with a certain arrangement of power (one of great inequality); in addition, the coercive influence is exercised mainly or exclusively through words. The above three quotations assume this single form of education. I wish to argue that this form of education is not the only form. Indeed, far from providing the prototype to understand teaching, it is the most peculiar and paradoxical kind of teaching. Unless teaching of the kind that is found in classrooms has a wider context of teaching, then classroom teaching can indeed become as negative and coercive as the above quotations suggest.

Writers on teaching are presumably aware that one should not equate teaching with classroom instruction. But strangely enough, most writing on teaching gives a preliminary bow to that fact and then proceeds to discuss the activities of the modern professional schoolteacher as the meaning of teaching. For example, at the beginning of Philip Jackson's *The Practice of Teaching* the author writes: "Among the first things to note is how many kinds of teachers there are. Leaving aside the large number of nonprofessional teachers (most parents, for example), we are still left with an impressive variety of types, the major ones well known."[4] Within a sentence that is calling attention to the many kinds of teaching, Jackson dismisses without comment most of the teaching in the world. All of these nonprofessionals are not heard of again after this parenthetical reference on page three. If the book's title were

The Profession of Schoolteacher instead of *The Practice of Teaching* this attitude might be justified. But even then the professional schoolteacher may need parents and others for a meaning of teaching that does not issue in the moral dilemma of keeping students "dutifully servile" for even one day.

THE MEANING OF THE VERB "TO TEACH"

My criticism in the above section is that these writers assume that "to teach" means that powerful people tell powerless people what to think. Is that the meaning of the act of teaching? I cannot deny that the verb "to teach" can have that meaning. In ordinary conversation, many people assume that teaching consists of big people telling little people what to believe. And, in fact, sometimes powerful people know something, convey it in speech, and it is received by powerless or dependent people. On the whole, however, this meaning of teaching is remarkably unimaginative, and it is shocking to see writing on education that simply acquiesces in this meaning. If this is assumed to be the whole meaning of "to teach," then it is almost certain to corrupt the relation between teacher and student. This corruption is the reason for the ambivalence expressed about teaching in quotations such as the above, an ambivalence that ranges from mild suspicion to total opposition.

Although we must acknowledge a common usage of the day in asking the meaning of any term, that is only the beginning of the search. In chapter 1 I said that we must look to both a history of the term and a geography of its usage. The image connected with teaching has not always been the professional schoolteacher. Teaching has included a wide range of people doing a variety of things in diverse settings with various groups. Furthermore, to this day teaching has retained other and wider meanings than the classroom instruction of children. I have noted that most books on teaching acknowledge this fact only to dismiss it. My intention in this chapter is simply to pay attention to the long past and the wide present of teaching.

Etymology is always of some help in tracing the meaning of a term. The root meaning of "to teach" is "to show how."

I begin with the fact that "to teach" in the past and in the present means to show someone how to do something. Everyone is in fact familiar with this meaning and ordinary usage recognizes that each human being can and does teach on occasion. In the Boff quotation above, one group (bishops) were denied the act of teaching so that everyone could be a learner. That is one way to make the point but not a very effective way. The way to avoid coercion by one group calling itself "the teachers" is to have everyone engage in teaching. That requires some imagination about how various people teach and the fact that teaching does not only mean making pronouncements of truth. The only way to safeguard learning is to widen the meaning of teaching.

Teaching is an act performed by every human being—at the least every human being. It is debatable whether the word should be extended to the nonhuman world. Like the word "community," "teaching" is a central characteristic of the human animal. The humans are communal animals and teaching animals. However, the line around the human should not be totally exclusive. Human beings might learn some things about teaching by studying complex nonhuman animals. The gift of teaching is what complex beings do when they show someone (human or otherwise) how to do something.

This description of teaching has no essential connection to children. Teaching can clearly be distinguished from the relation between adults and children. And as to coercive power that may be exercised by adults over children, teaching far from being the same thing is the main alternative. How does one avoid having children be "dutifully servile" to adults? By teaching them. I am not inventing some strange new idea. What I am saying is patent to any intelligent parent. The relation of teaching and learning is a cooperation in power that leads in the direction of mutuality.

I would not, therefore, wish to go so far as Peter Elbow, who in discussing the powerful sexual feelings that are present in most serious teaching, writes: "When the sexuality of teaching is more generally felt and admitted, we may finally draw the obvious moral: It is a practice that should only be performed upon the persons of consenting adults."[5] I am doubtful that Elbow really wishes to exclude children from all teaching. However, his statement provides an interesting shift in perspective. If we were to begin with the assumption that teaching is usually a relation between adults, that teaching as a fully realized activity is directed by an adult toward an adult, then we would be more sensitive as to how those who have less power enter into this exchange. We would examine the peculiar position of children in teaching situations rather than just assume it.

The problem with most books on teaching is not that they are about children. Rather, it is that the writing is about children of a certain age and in a certain setting. Books on teaching have much to say about thirteen-year-old schoolchildren, but little to say of thirteen-month-old children with their mothers. Children should occupy an important part in any theorizing about teaching, especially children under the age of five years old. The basic meaning of teaching has to be tested out against the very vulnerable, those who may not be able to understand explanations. If one assumes, as so often happens, that to teach means to present documentary evidence to support rational explanations, then most of the human race's teaching simply disappears. But if "to teach" is "to show someone how to do something," then that can include infants, some nonhuman animals, and people who are severely handicapped. It is these groups that challenge both the theory and practice of teaching. If we were to reflect on the difficulties of teaching infants or people with severe disablements, we might take a more imaginative approach when presenting documentary evidence to support rational explanations.

If we were attentive to these vulnerable groups, we would notice that "to show someone how to do something" is mostly a nonverbal activity. Showing is done through various gestures and symbols. These means of communication might be called "language," but it is not a verbal language. And the speech that first emerges is not rational discourse. For example, in showing a child how to put food on a spoon, there is little to explain in words although some soothing and encouraging words can be helpful. In teaching a dog to do tricks, words play a small but crucial part; the tone of the command is usually more important than the content of the statement.

I would suggest that the most helpful metaphor for the place of speech in teaching is *choreography*; that is, in most teaching human speech has the modest role of indicating how the body is to move. The learner of dance (bicycle riding, swimming, cooking, sewing, and so forth) receives precise directions. General guidelines or democratic discussions are no help here. The teacher says: Hold your leg this way, raise your arm two inches, press the pedal now, add one clove of garlic after the onions.

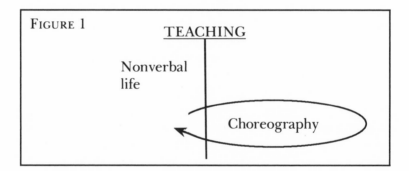

FIGURE 1

TEACHING

Nonverbal life

Choreography

Human beings use speech for many other reasons than choreographed instruction. Speech can be viewed as the center of bodily life. Insofar as teaching is directed toward the learning of something that the body does, speech can be the object of teaching because speaking is a human activity. In other words, one could ask about the choreographing of speech. There can be teaching in which speech becomes the focal point of the teaching. The great danger as speech comes to center stage is that the rest of bodily life may be neglected. Speech can never replace the body; it draws its power by being situated at the center of bodily life.

It is particularly at this point that the moral problem of

teaching emerges. When one teaches physical skills to a child there is continuity between the acts of teaching and learning. The teacher and the learner are engaged in one complex activity; they experience success or failure together. Running down the street with a child learning to ride a bicycle has its frustrations, but there is usually no problem about moral consent. The teacher's evidence that the child wishes to learn is the presenting of the body to the teacher and the willingness to try again after failing. The teacher is trying to teach and the teaching is just what the learner is struggling to get. Philip Jackson, employing a distinction of Gilbert Ryle's, notes that there are "task verbs" and "achievement verbs" (kicking vs. scoring; treating vs. healing). Jackson then writes: "Teaching, as luck would have it, has come to be used in both senses."[6] I think that luck has little to do with it. Teaching is used in this double sense because in most acts of teaching, the task of teaching and the achievement of the teaching are continuous within one act.

It is only when speech begins to be separated from the body that the question can be raised: Is there teaching when there is no learning? Can the teacher be kicking but not scoring? The question often means "can someone be talking and no one listening," the answer to which is obvious enough. Important forms of teaching that concentrate on speech itself as the object of teaching are unavoidable. But before a teacher begins to teach by largely isolating speech, he or she had better ask: Why are these people sitting (standing, lying) in front of me? What kind of license to speak have they given me by their presence? How does anything I say relate to their bodies?

The response to such questions involves distinguishing different kinds of speech. The particular basis on which an individual or group appears before a teacher signifies a moral consent to a particular form of discourse. Sometimes this consent is blurred when people are confused about the nature of the institution or the assembly they are in. Sometimes outside pressure on an individual distorts what seems to be the consent; then the moral problem is the pressure rather than the teaching. A well-known speaker in the

1960s used to say: "The only thing you can be sure of when you see children in school is that they prefer that to jail." The situation has not changed dramatically since then; children are still required by law to be in school. Even changing the law would not automatically relieve the pressure.

Our society has a problem of what to do with many children who do not wish to be in school and who resist being taught. It is obvious that this creates terrible problems for the professional schoolteacher of the young. But much of the discussion of teaching is really concerned with how one keeps people contented who do not wish to be taught. Sympathizing with the schoolteachers of six- to sixteen-year-olds, we ought to give whatever help we can in dealing with social and political problems of schools for children. However, we do no one any good by neglecting to explore the full meaning of "to teach" and the issue of moral consent that is inherent to acts of teaching in which speech is central.

FORMS OF SPEECH IN TEACHING

There are innumerable ways to classify forms of speech. For my purpose in this chapter, I wish to begin with a single, stark contrast of two modes of speech. After that, I will introduce a third form of speech that is on a different level than are the first two. As I have already indicated, speech becomes a moral problem in the act of teaching insofar as speech moves away from a choreographic role and becomes the dance itself. What are the moral limits to speech when a teacher begins to teach in a way that is centered on speech?

I wish to describe two ways of speaking that I call homiletic and therapeutic. The two are opposites in many respects, but each has its appropriate setting. The most obvious example of homiletic speech is a church sermon; the best known example of therapeutic speech in the twentieth century is the work of the professional psychotherapist. However, I am using both homiletic and therapeutic as ways of speaking that include more than the minister's pulpit on one side and the psychotherapist's couch on the other side.

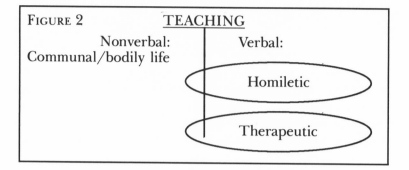

1. A homiletic use of speech is a commentary on a text which a community says that it accepts. The homilist's or preacher's job is both to remind the community of what it has agreed upon and to bring out implications of that agreement. Thus, the homilist is not mainly concerned with providing new *information* to a community. The point of homiletic speech is to rouse people for action beyond the assembly, to inspire people to get up from the seat and change the world for the better. Implied in this use of speech is the conviction that the community knows what it means to improve the world.

Homiletic speech requires a precise set of conditions if it is to be morally appropriate and educationally effective. Lacking these conditions—a community freely gathered, an agreed upon text, a speaker designated by the community to inspire the rest—homiletic speech can be morally offensive and educationally futile. It is not an accident that words such as sermon, sermonizing, preaching, and preachy have such negative meanings. Nevertheless, this form of discourse has its right time and right place. Because today's society assumes that sermons are preached only in church, it assumes that it has escaped this form of speech. In fact, today's society is addicted to sermons of very questionable value.

A homiletic mode need not be imagined as a relentless appeal to the will and a constant badgering of the congregation that they should put a halt to sin. For example, under homiletic speech, one would find storytelling. A community develops stories that embody the agreements of the community about what is good and bad in their past. By telling the story today, the homilist is adding a layer of commentary to a text received from the past. If the story is told well, it ignites the imagination and at least indirectly inspires a reshaping of the community's environment.

Politics would be impossible without the homiletic form of speech. Political discourse is dependent on the existence of a community of people who have made explicit and implicit agreements about how to live together. The politician's words should inspire the best in the community by uncovering deeper levels of that agreement and pointing out the longer-range consequences of today's political activities. A politician who simply follows the will of the people as determined by polls and computers (with an unerring eye on the next election) is not taking the homiletic stance appropriate to politics. He or she is failing to teach people in a way not only allowed but required in a political community.

Many politicians seem embarrassed by the fact that their vocation is to preach homilies. That is one reason why they do it so badly. Sermons that pretend not to be sermons are the most irritating of all. If the politician does not speak to the deeper bonds of community, the usual alternatives are divisive interests of one group or self-serving remarks about the speaker. In the U.S., politics regularly attracts people with a background in church preaching. There is nothing surprising in this fact even though it continually surprises a country that talks endlessly about the separation of church and state. Neither is there anything politically inappropriate provided that the person in U.S. politics preaches on the U.S. Constitution rather than the Christian scriptures.

The most common preaching in the U.S. today is neither in church nor in Congress but in television advertising. Millions of dollars are spent upon fifteen or thirty second commercials whose whole intent is to rouse the viewer from the living room chair and increase the sale of

Crest, Coke, or Cadillacs. Starting from an agreed upon text (I wish to be rich, sexy, clean smelling, or whatever), every attempt is made to get action on the part of the listener. Listeners in the "television community" who do not accept the agreed texts have the choice of turning off the set, finding a noncommercial station, or being morally affronted by the preaching.

In summary, I am arguing that the homiletic form of speech in teaching is inescapable. If there exists a community, it will develop its life by articulating and applying its beliefs in speech. Where community deteriorates into cliques, vested interest groups, or warring factions, then one gets corrupt homilies that inspire vicious activity. Where community disappears into isolated individuals, then one usually gets vacuous sermons with high-level abstractions (democracy, socialist revolution, modernism, national security) that inspire no activity. Often at this point educators, including politicians will say: "We must move from words to actions." Nothing could be more insulting to those who believe that educational speech is a form of action, that politicians are speakers whose choice is to speak well or to speak poorly.

The homiletic form of speech belongs in education; it can be one of the most powerful and effective modes of education if the conditions for its use are met. Insofar as the word "school" can refer to a community in a certain place, the homiletic is one of the school's languages. However, in the special setting of the classroom, the homily becomes peripheral. And when the classroom teacher is engaged in instruction, the homily has almost no part to play. I come back to this point below, but here I just note that elementary and secondary schoolteachers can easily slip into a moralizing attitude, telling students what is right and wrong, true and false. University professors who would be horrified at the idea of moralizing may still have a tendency to give fifty-minute sermons based on scientific evidence or the latest views of the scholarly discipline. Insofar as one lectures or reads at people one usually is dealing in homily.

2. Turning to the opposite mode of speech, I wish now

to describe what I call therapeutic speech. As figure 2 above indicates, homiletic and therapeutic agree in their being rooted in the communal and bodily life. That is, both deal with texts that emerge out of the nonverbal realm of human life. But whereas the homiletic celebrates the text and applies it beyond the community, the therapeutic attempts to subvert the text for the purpose of healing individuals within the community. Instead of trying to agitate people toward external activity, therapeutic speech aims at quieting the interior.

In the therapeutic situation, there are likely to be texts buried deeply in the psyche. The individual has in one sense "accepted" the text although he or she may not have freely assented to the belief. A person may carry a burden of guilt because at some level he or she believes that to break a particular rule means that "my mother will no longer love me" or "God will punish me." Conflicts arise in society because of prejudices (pre-judgments) that "all Jews are _____" or "all officials of this institution are my father."

Therapeutic speech tries to get us to come to terms with our personal and collective conflicts. We need healing within the person and between groups of people. But therapeutic speech has to be a very peculiar form of speech if it is to be effective. It is trying to subvert speech or at least subvert particular texts that are not evident. It cannot go directly at its object as homiletic speech can. Whereas homiletic speech tends to flow in a rushing stream, therapeutic speech often has more silence than sound. It tends toward the minimalist: "Yes, go on." While both the homiletic and therapeutic are personal exchanges, in the homily the preacher does nearly all the talking (except perhaps for an occasional "amen"), in therapy the client does most of the talking. The process of talking can itself be therapeutic, unearthing hidden texts, allowing them to play in consciousness and gradually bringing them into a healing experience.

I am not restricting the meaning of therapeutic to the one image of the psychiatrist listening to the client on the couch in the doctor's office. Professional treatment can involve many techniques, and the treatment of groups not just individuals. Therapy can include a more aggressive method in which the individual screams and shouts or, especially with children, much play and acting out of roles. The individual's treatment may be set in a structural context of family or group therapy. The therapist does not peer into the soul of the one labeled sick but looks for the illness and the potential healing in the pattern of personal interactions.

Far from contradicting what I have said about therapeutic speech, all this variety further illustrates the peculiarity of the therapeutic. It always refrains from pronouncing on how the world ought to be; in fact, it is intent on upsetting all pronouncements about everything. Therapeutic speech is speech that is distrustful of speech and therefore keeps calling attention to the roots of speech. Human speech separates the humans from the other animals; speech is a sign of tragic separation. It is also, of course, the source of human greatness.

In addition to all forms of professional therapy, I refer to the therapeutic as a way of speaking that is found everywhere. While the homiletic is constantly attacked, the therapeutic is seldom criticized. Unfortunately, to be exempt from nearly all criticism is not the most healthful state to be in. If a writer says that all human relations are either violent or therapeutic, then there is not much choice for those who abhor violence. However, in talking about forms of discourse I am suggesting that other contrasts are possible and important.

A number of writers since the 1960s have raised the issue of whether our culture is surfeited with therapeutic speech. Philip Rief was one of the first to enunciate this thesis in *The Triumph of the Therapeutic.*[7] In those situations where people need healing words, the therapeutic is appropriate. One uses speech to soothe, to relieve feelings of anger, guilt, or sorrow. When one goes to a funeral it is customary to say whatever will express affection and sympathy; from peculiar customs like "he (the corpse) looks very natural"—despite being in the casket—to "he (the deceased) was a good man"—despite everyone knowing he was a bit of a scoundrel. In therapeutic speech we temporarily suspend some of our intellectual, aesthetic, and moral standards for the sake of feelings of reconciliation. In therapeutic speech the aim is not achieving an object of choice but reestablishing the ability to choose.

Similar to what was said of the homiletic, a school should not be lacking in the therapeutic. A school (the system, the place, the community) can be a place of healing and reconciliation; occasionally it has to be (for example, when there is a student suicide or when the Challenger spaceship blew up before the eyes of millions of schoolchildren). Schools regularly offer therapeutic service in personal counseling. As with the homiletic, the classroom is the specialized setting where therapy is not at center stage. Schoolteachers are often called upon to say soothing things to students, but if that were all the schoolteacher did in the classroom it would not be schoolteaching or class instruction. What worried Rief and has concerned many critics since is that classrooms turn into "bull sessions" in which everyone shares his or her uninformed opinion.[8] Everyone politely tolerates everyone else's opinion because it is assumed that there is no right or wrong opinion. It is considered less important that truth be insisted upon than that everyone feel better at the end of the discussion.

In summary, therapeutic speech is a peculiar form of speech which undercuts the striving after external goods. At times it is refreshing and liberating; at some moments of life it is an urgent necessity. The danger is in having too much of a good thing, or rather, a good thing in the wrong place. If therapy pervades politics, religion, and academia, then the invaluable resource of speech for human purposes can become clouded. Schools no longer have standards of intellectual excellence; politicians do little except pander to the masses.

Almost everyone realizes that it would be immoral for a therapist to preach at a client ("That's terrible; don't ever do that again"). It is seldom noted that a preacher who makes people feel complacent and self-satisfied is also acting immorally. Sometimes cases of the latter are not immediately evident. Certain television evangelists, for all of their preaching on sin, punishment, and hell fire, use a therapeutic form of speech. They assert that forces outside the congregation (Jews, Catholics, feminists, gays, or whoever) are the source of evil; the congregants can find salvation simply by saying "Jesus is my savior." The effect is a premature reconciliation that leaves out most of the world.

ACADEMIC INSTRUCTION

The third form of speech for teaching is not along the spectrum of homiletic/therapeutic. As figure 3 indicates, the academic overlaps the previous two but is not a simple combination of them.

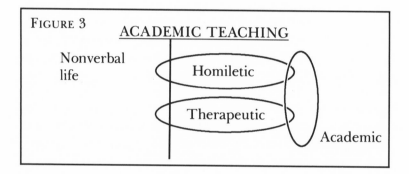

FIGURE 3 — ACADEMIC TEACHING

Nonverbal life — Homiletic — Therapeutic — Academic

The homiletic and the therapeutic mediate communal/bodily life to the academic which is, so to speak, one step removed from ordinary life. Since the academic is not in immediate contact with life on the street, it is always threatened with vacuity. Indeed, to say that a point is "academic" is for many people a way of dismissing its seriousness or even its reality. Preachers are thought of as irritants but academics are considered irrelevant. Often, one hears schoolteachers join in this disparagement of the academic by contrasting the classroom and "real life." But who defines real life? Business executives, military officers, and cynical politicians? The school setting is a peculiar and artificial world outside ordinary patterns of sleeping, eating, walking, earning money, cleaning house, and putting out the cat. It is not, however, outside the real world.

Academic discourse has the important job of examining speech itself in all aspects of reality.

The usual place to find academic discourse is in the world of the school. Like the homiletic and therapeutic, the academic is found in more than one institutional setting. Many books, including this one, use an academic form of discourse. Discussions between colleagues and even between friends may get into questioning the meaning of terms and the presuppositions of arguments. However, academic speech requires a stringent set of conditions that may be difficult to establish outside the school.

As I have indicated, the homiletic and therapeutic get into schools (where they do have a legitimate place), but they may absorb the main classroom activity if the academic teacher does not resist or is unclear about an alternative. The confusion of many academics becomes more evident the closer they get to questions of morality. Harold Howe II in an article entitled "Can Schools Teach Values?" writes: "My wife . . . told me as I was preparing to write this article, 'Remember that you can't preach to kids. Either they won't listen, or if they do, they won't believe you.' I am inclined to agree with her. In my opinion there is a limited return on the direct teaching of ethical principles."[9] Howe follows the advice of his wife (who is a guidance counselor) and spends most of the essay dealing with warm, personal relations. The amazing thing is that Howe here equates preaching with "the direct teaching of ethical principles." And since he feels that preaching is hopelessly ineffective, the only alternative is warm, personal relations, that is, therapeutic discourse.

Both the homiletic and the therapeutic are peculiar forms of speech in which words are attended to at the seeming expense of bodily life. Of course, in these two forms bodily life is not far removed from the discourse; external activity and inner healing are respectively the immediate contexts. Academic speech pushes the paradox one step further. Speech is a given; it occupies not only the center but practically the whole stage. Academic speech neither affirms nor subverts texts; its aim is to talk about the nature of texts and the meaning of particular texts. Thus, it has to turn speech back on itself, creating a contortion of everyday speech. Academic speech is speech about speech. Nothing is more depressing for a person who is speaking academically than to be asked: "But aren't you just talking about words?" If a person is not prepared for academic discourse the question is understandable. Too much of the academic, especially too early in life, can obstruct the release of the power that academic speech contains.

Academic speech overlaps both the homiletic and the therapeutic in their relating of text and community. The homilist says: "We must believe and act upon the agreed text"; the therapist says: "We must be freed from a text that dominates us without our choice." The academic teacher says: "Accept no text uncritically; it might be false. Reject no text uncritically; it might be true." Academic life does not require that a community have *agreed* texts; it does require some knowledge of texts that are part of the community's life.

In most Western countries the Bible is a text or texts that form part of the basis for academic inquiry; that is true irrespective of whether there are any practicing Jews or Christians. Similarly, Greek philosophers, Renaissance artists, modern scientists, and British political theorists provide material for academic examination. The fact that much of the literature is affected with sexist, racist, anti-semitic, anti-gay attitudes is not a reason for excluding it from schools. The point of academically teaching such literature is not to get students to believe what Plato, Machiavelli, Kant, or Mill believed; the point is to understand what has shaped our lives together, seeing texts in all their power and limitations. Of course, schools tend to set up a "canon" of accepted writers. It is therefore necessary to ask who is doing the deciding *today* about which writers are important for understanding the past.

Academic discourse is highly directive in one way, completely nondirective in another. Academic speech can be as passionate as preaching in its urging of change, but the passion is directed at the words themselves. Beyond linguistic advocacy, academic speech is as nondirective as the speech of the therapist. The peculiar key here is "instruction," a word that calls us back to the body.

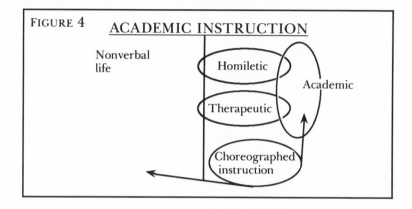

FIGURE 4   ACADEMIC INSTRUCTION

Nonverbal life

Homiletic

Academic

Therapeutic

Choreographed instruction

Instruction is a word used for physical activities. One instructs in swimming, cooking, typing, or kicking a ball. Interestingly, the word returns in the rarified atmosphere of the academic; the word that commonly follows the adjective "academic" is the noun "instruction." Academic instruction is not democratic group discussion but a use of speech that is precise and directive. What saves academic speech from being authoritarian is that the speech bends back on speech. It does not tell people what to think; it is an invitation to examine their ways of speaking.

As a classroom instructor, I ask students to place their words on a table between us; the words include their own personal speech as well as assigned readings. In a classroom, every text except one is subject to criticism. That one agreed-upon text, the agreement signified by walking into the classroom, is a procedural statement. We agree to the value of civility, tolerance, and discourse that is not abusive. My task is to convince them that there are better ways to speak than the ways they now have. What "better" means is, of course, part of what needs discussing and is open to revision from the side of the teacher as well as the student. Since the immediate topic is speech and not the beliefs of the student, there is always some room for the student to step back. I would not attempt to go directly at either the thoughts or the feelings of a student.

The major resources that the academic teacher has for the task are history and geography. Other people have thought about these issues of physics, mathematics, history, or morality. No one's opinion is to be uncritically accepted as the truth; every statement of belief can be improved upon. Neither is a minority view automatically rejected as false; there probably is a kernel of truth in every widely held belief. Academic discourse is neither interested speech (in the sense of self-serving) nor uninterested speech (in the sense of bored detachment). It is disinterested speech insofar as human beings are capable of temporarily suspending their involvements and convictions for the sake of examining assumptions, contexts, and personal blindspots.

TEACHING IN RELIGIOUS EDUCATION

The distinctions concerning teaching in this chapter make possible a richer discussion of the nature of religious education. The next three chapters are needed to play out the discussion of religious education in U.K. and U.S., in schools and other educational forms, in state schools and religiously affiliated schools, in the school and the classroom. Nonetheless, it might be helpful to draw some conclusions at this point so as to provide a framework for the multi-pole conversation. The distinctions of this chapter are subject to revision in the subsequent chapters, but the following three conclusions are immediate and general applications to the area of religious education.

1. Most teaching is nonverbal; this fact is especially true of the moral and/or religious life. As indicated at the beginning of the chapter, most teaching is nonverbal in the sense that the object of teaching is not words. When words play some part, they usually do so in the form of directives for moving the body. Although it is impossible to number the acts of teaching or quantify teaching itself, it does not seem an exaggeration to say that *most* teaching is not a

teaching of words but a teaching of activities in which speech is subordinate. Surely, for a small child most teaching is of this kind, but even as the individual matures and learns to reflect on speech the testimony of life remains stronger than testimonies of speech.

The question has often been debated whether one can "teach virtue." The debate today usually assumes a classroom as the context of the question, a fruitless way to begin the inquiry. Aristotle has sometimes been thought banal for saying that the way to learn virtue is to grow up in a virtuous community. But every religious community knows the profound truth of the principle (as I discuss in chapter eight). Does the child who learns virtue by living in a community learn without having been taught? That is one way to say it, but it is far more revealing and effective to say that the lives of community members teach what it means to be virtuous.

A community life always involves speech—homiletic, therapeutic, and, one would hope, academic. All three come into play in the development of moral and/or religious life. However, none can substitute for religious and/or moral activity that is often in the form of a silent witness. One should recall here the distinction between speech and other kinds of language. Nonverbal forms of teaching the religious and/or moral life can be called language insofar as there is a communication between persons. Thus, in the religious life there is much beyond silence that is not speech. Any attempt at religious education that neglects nonverbal symbols (for example, the posture of the body, the sharing of a meal, the wearing of masks) would miss the center of the matter.

2. All developed religions involve complex uses of speech. When speech does emerge in religious communities, it involves peculiar mixes of the homiletic and therapeutic. I think it is safe to say that any major religion involves some of both discourses, although one may be highly emphasized. Perhaps the extremes in emphasis are Christianity, a very preachy religion, and Buddhism, a very therapeutic religion.

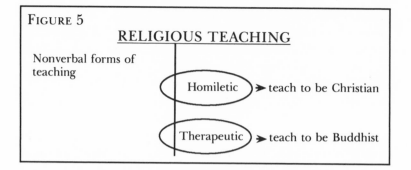

FIGURE 5

RELIGIOUS TEACHING

Nonverbal forms of teaching

Homiletic ➤ teach to be Christian

Therapeutic ➤ teach to be Buddhist

Christianity began with a preacher and quickly issued in a book that became the basis of later reforms. The Christian church developed the sermon as an art form, and it still dominates Christian discourse, not only in the pulpit but in theology books and in documents of the Vatican or the World Council of Churches. Buddhism, in stark contrast, began with the silent one who was moved by compassion to search for the roots of suffering. Speech is used to get free of the illusions of concepts, selfhood, and speech itself.

This contrast of emphasis is not mutual exclusiveness. In practice, Buddhists and Christians use a variety of speech forms that overlap (for example, parable and epigram). Even if we just stay with homiletic/therapeutic as the categories, Buddhists and Christians are not totally different. Christians are not always preaching. They teach by various silent gestures and symbols, as well as by nonhomiletic discourse. To confess one's sins belongs with the therapeutic rather than the homiletic. Even more so, a funeral rite, although it may include a homily, is directed toward reconciliation and inward healing.

On the Buddhist side, a homiletic dimension is usually present. Storytelling, as I have noted, can be seen as a homiletic form. There have been stories and sayings of the Buddha from the beginning of the religion. And within some parts of Buddhism, the homiletic is quite prominent. In a twentieth-century group such as Won Buddhism, most of the "canonical book" consists of sermons by the founder.[10]

3. A proper object for the activity of academic instruc-

tion is religion; a teacher can (academically) teach religion. One preaches the Christian message, but one academically teaches religion.

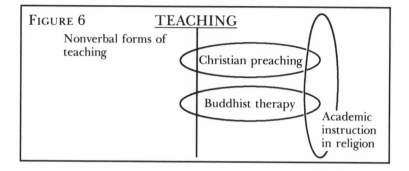

FIGURE 6   TEACHING
Nonverbal forms of teaching
Christian preaching
Buddhist therapy
Academic instruction in religion

Religion as used in this context is one step removed from ordinary life. The academic instructor steps back from the practice of Christian, Buddhist, or other religious life so as to examine the discourse of Christians, Buddhists, and others. The question is often asked in religious circles: "Does religion belong in the classroom?" The answer to that question is: Religion was, so to speak, invented for the classroom; that is surely one place that it does belong. Religion is the name for that one level abstraction from the actual ways that religious people live. Religion is the modern name for an academic subject that fits next to economics, sociology, anthropology, and the like.

Someone who is going to teach religion has to know the texts of one, and preferably more than one, religious group. At least indirectly, that knowledge presumes entrance into religious activities such as meditation, confession of sins, or reception of communion. I emphasize that one's acquaintance need not be by direct participation in religious practice. A direct experience and personal involvement should not prevent someone from teaching religion; neither should that be a precondition of such teaching.

Teaching religion requires that one knows the texts as part of some communal tradition. As is true with reference to all academic instruction, one does not have to agree with the texts or pronounce them true. One only has to agree to the importance of the texts and the value of examining their meaning. And as in history, science, or art, the academic inquiry is suspicious of all canons that establish orthodoxy. A religion teacher in refusing to be orthodox does not become heretical. Academic discourse is simply on a different wave length.

I have offered that the proper object of "academically instruct" is "religion." Is it possible to replace "religion" with Judaism, Christianity, Islam, Hinduism, Sikhism, and so forth? The answer probably varies according to the rough-edged meaning of each of these abstractions. That is, before one asks about teaching Hinduism, one has to wonder whether "Hinduism" is really the name of a discernible object or whether it is shorthand for a great range of things. However, if one takes the example of Christianity, the question is probably a manageable one. Despite the variations within the category and endless debate about Christianity's true form, it is nevertheless intelligible to ask: "Can one teach Christianity?"

Insofar as "Christianity" is an abstract term coined by academics, the answer is "yes"; one can instruct in an academic subject named Christianity. Of course, the phrase "teach Christianity" is often understood differently, namely, as Christians teaching Christians how to live Christianly. But this latter meaning actually conflicts with both the idea of academic instruction and "Christianity," the general name for particular ways of being Christian. If Christians wish to teach their own how to live a Christian life, they will need a far more specific form of teaching than someone teaching Christianity.

A question that must be addressed in later chapters is whether the teaching of Christianity in an academic setting requires the presence of other objects that end in *ity* or *ism*. That is, if there is no comparison to other religions, will teaching Christianity as an example of teaching religion inevitably slide toward preaching the Christian message. Without passing final judgment here, I would just note that maintaining an academic language is usually helped by teaching more than one religion, at least within a department if not always within each course. The topic of religion best fits within an academic department that in most of the English-speaking world today is called "religious studies."

I conclude the first part of this book with a comprehensive diagram that opens the discussion of religious education to its many possible settings and languages.

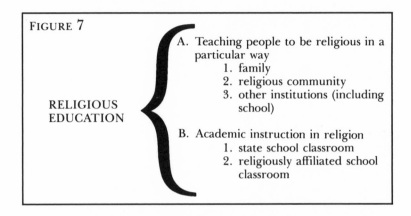

FIGURE 7

RELIGIOUS EDUCATION

A. Teaching people to be religious in a particular way
  1. family
  2. religious community
  3. other institutions (including school)

B. Academic instruction in religion
  1. state school classroom
  2. religiously affiliated school classroom

There seems to be no good reason for excluding either A or B from the meaning of religious education. And there seems to be good reason for keeping the two as distinct though related within a full meaning of religious education; the two depend on each other, at least indirectly. This religious education has existed only inchoately up to the present but it is needed for the future.

The most confusing thing in the above diagram is that school shows up in both A and B. Thus, it will not be enough to refer to the school's part in religious education; further distinctions are needed. Furthermore, within B there are two kinds of schools indicated. Some people seem to think that a religiously affiliated school is incapable of teaching (academically instructing in) religion. But it would seem cavalier to dismiss such schools without even considering what some of them are trying to do. My diagram is not a theory to be imposed on what follows in Part II. It is an interpretive framework for listening to discussions in the English-speaking world about the nature of religious education.

NOTES

1. Carl Rogers, *Freedom to Learn* (Columbus, Ohio: Merrill, 1969), p. 154.

2. Philip Jackson, *The Practice of Teaching* (New York: Teachers College, 1986), pp. 104-105.

3. Leonardo Boff, *Ecclesiogenesis* (Maryknoll: Orbis, 1981), p. 36.

4. Jackson, *The Practice of Teaching*, p. 3.

5. Peter Elbow, *Embracing Contraries* (New York: Oxford University Press, 1986), p. 70.

6. Jackson, *The Practice of Teaching*, p. 80.

7. Philip Rief, *The Triumph of the Therapeutic* (New York: Harper & Row, 1966).

8. For examples of this theme, see Russel Jacoby, *Social Amnesia* (Boston: Beacon, 1975); Christopher Lasch, *The Culture of Narcissism* (New York: Norton, 1979); Allan Bloom, *The Closing of the American Mind* (New York: Simon and Schuster, 1987).

9. Harold Howe II, "Can Schools Teach Values?" *Teachers College Record* 89 (Fall, 1987), p. 58.

10. *The Canonical Textbook of Won Buddhism* (Seoul: Office of Won Buddhist Publications, 1971).

4

Over the Atlantic
and Looking Eastward:
The British Experience

The title of this chapter comes from an experience I had a few years ago at an international conference on religious education. Several of the participants from the United States had spoken of the importance of the family and the church congregation in religious education. Their comments were subjected to harsh criticism by several speakers from the United Kingdom. The heart of the criticism was that U.S. speakers had to concern themselves with family and church by default. Because there is no religious education in the public schools of the United States it becomes a familial and churchy thing, not truly an educational enterprise.

My contribution to this exchange was to say that I felt like I was stranded over the Atlantic Ocean. I thought that the British criticism of the U.S. was too extreme. I granted that it is an academic scandal that religion is not taught in the public schools of the United States. Religious education would be better—and family and church congregation might do their parts better—if the public schools were doing their part.

I was not making an apology for the U.S. In fact, I am generally in sympathy with what religious education means in the U.K., but it has its own problem of narrowness through confinement in the school curriculum. What I think "religious education" should mean—on the basis of logic, history, and present need—is found neither in the U.K. nor in the U.S. Thus, with divided sympathies in both directions I find myself somewhere over the Atlantic Ocean.

One of Winston Churchill's famous quips is the line that the United States and England are two countries divided by a common language. I think that religious education is a good case in point. In the first chapter, I said that almost no one uses religious education as a term of self-description. The clearest exception to that rule is English and Welsh schoolteachers. In the U.K., there is a defined meaning to the term "religious education," a meaning almost completely at variance with the use of the same term in the U.S. Religious education in the U.K. usually means a subject in the curriculum of the state school; in the U.S., religious education never means that.

Is there any way to have a discussion of religious education between these two countries? The answer is yes, but first there has to be a recognition that we do not have a dialogue about a common topic. That would seem obvious enough, but when people use the same term they assume, usually with good reason, that there is some common referent for what they are talking about. When we recognize that we are "divided by a common language," this fact need not stop all conversation; in fact, it can lead to a more interesting exploration of why the term is used so differently. Instead of asking how to make "it" work or why "it" is not working, we are pushed into a truly theoretical discussion, which, if pursued far enough, might revolutionize practice.

To my knowledge there is little such dialogue across the Atlantic Ocean. One has only to check the footnotes and bibliographies of books on religious education. Where there is some movement it is more likely to be eastward.

U.S. books do have some impact in England, although religious educators in the U.K. are more likely to quote U.S. sociologists and psychologists than U.S. writers on religious education. In the U.S. it is not easy to get books from other places and that fact shows in the range of most debates. The discussion of religion and the U.S. public school seldom adverts to British writing, even though that would seem to be one of the most fruitful points of contact.

I wish to argue that some knowledge of the history and the current state of religious education in the U.K. would be helpful in the U.S. This chapter provides a summary that I hope would be acceptable to a British reader and intelligible to the non-British reader. My next chapter is a discussion looking westward, toward the peculiar history of the issue of religion and education in U.S. schools. In some ways these are mirror images, each in need of complementing by the other. I have often thought that if a fully developed theory of religious education ever comes to birth in the English language, it will probably be in Ireland, Australia, New Zealand, or Canada. In those countries, many people combine their own experience with literature from both the U.S. and the U.K.

There are two parts to this chapter; first a recounting of what has been the British experience; second, some points of criticism in regard to that experience. What I hope comes through is an attitude of respect and appreciation. On the whole, I think there is little doubt that British writing on religious education is superior to that in the U.S. The past two decades of writing in the U.K. have been especially fruitful and revealing.

The U.S. likes to think of itself as extraordinarily diverse in religion. Actually, however, the variety has been within a narrow range. In the U.S. one is assumed to be Catholic, Protestant, or Jewish. Jews have made an amazing contribution to U.S. life, despite being less than 3 percent of the whole population. But Jewish religion functions as "the other religion," the non-Christian exception in a country that still talks of itself as Christian. Not surprisingly, religious education tends to get equated with Christian educa-

tion; and ecumenism means Catholics and Protestants talking together, with the conversation sometimes including
Jews.

The U.K. during recent decades has had to cope with a
great religious diversity. Hindus, Sikhs, and Muslims in
significant numbers have brought their own cultures and
religious differences. Religious education in the U.K. has
had to confront this diversity. The struggle over what religion to teach and how to teach it could not help but be
confusing and difficult. But this situation is probably close
to being a microcosm of the world's future. We in the U.S.
need to study this evolution carefully because a much
greater religious diversity may still be in our future. Buddhists and Muslims are the most likely next major religions
that can get admitted as "American" (that is, religions of
the United States). If and when that happens, the meaning
of religious education may undergo drastic change. The
nineteenth-century invention "Judeo-Christian" will no
longer be able to hide the real differences and points of
conflict.

After I try to give a fair account of the British history of
religious education, I have some specific points of criticism. These revolve around one particular use of language
and several others that follow in its wake. My criticisms are
ones that an outside spectator can suggest. They may seem
a bit impertinent, but they are offered with the hope of
giving a new opening to some old standoffs. When debate
in any area has gone on for a long time, it is bound to settle
into linguistic ruts which are so comfortable that no one
notices them anymore. An outsider appearing on the scene
may be startled by the demand to identify his or her position. Are you x or y? Which of the three possible positions
do you hold, a, b, or c? (Are you pro-life or pro-choice? Are
you liberal, conservative, or radical?).

Some categorizing of positions is necessary so that conversation does not become hopelessly bogged down in ex-
plaining everything every time one speaks. Nonetheless, it
is occasionally helpful to step back from our most cher-
ished assumptions. The voice of the outsider can be helpful, not so much for providing an answer as for asking

questions which insiders think are too naive to ask. There is a time for getting on with the details and the applications; there are other times when we need to ask whether a particular distinction, even if not false, could be better stated.

I give one example here which is relevant to this chapter. I was recently on a panel whose topic was "Interfaith Dialogue." I began by saying that I did not believe in interfaith discussion. Until people demonstrate otherwise, I assume that all dialogue is intrafaith. From a Christian, Jewish, or Muslim view, there can only be one faith; a person believes in the only G-d there is or else the person is an infidel.[1] Interfaith is a term that mainly originated from the liberal part of the Christian church for describing conversations with Jews. Since in Christian language Jews were no longer to be thought of as infidels, then the Jews must have their own faith. Jewish organizations sometimes accept this language, although they are more likely to speak of "interreligious," a term that is more helpful and accurate. I suggested on this panel that Jews and Christians might have a different conversation if they began by presuming that they were of the same faith.

At least one person in the audience, a long-time participant in "interfaith" dialogue, became furious at me for trivializing the discussion and failing to say anything practical. I felt, however, that I had stated a serious point which has great practical significance. Of course, I did not expect everyone to agree with me; in fact I would be skeptical if people did immediately agree. I was not saying that everyone else was wrong and that I was right. As an educator, I am interested in asking about the ambiguities of language.

In English, the word "faith" by itself cannot carry the complexity of our differences and similarities. The word "faith" has to be combined with belief, religion, and additional words to take us to an understanding of ourselves and others. My point was that it is at least as true to say that Jews and Christians have the same faith as to say that they have different faiths. Both things can be said in English, but to say "same faith" presses us to think about where the real differences lie and how important they are.

"Interfaith," in contrast, easily conveys the idea that there are two objects called "faiths" and that neither side in the conversation will ever grant that the other has the one, true, saving faith.

In British religious education, it is quite common to refer to "multi-faith" curricula. Here the reference is to Jews, Christians, Sikhs, Hindus, Muslims, and others. Do these people have different faiths or are they all of the same faith? One could say: both. Clearly, there are different patterns of activity embodied in different cultures. These differing religious traditions are now interacting in some new ways in the U.K. and elsewhere.

Within at least Judaism, Christianity, and Islam (in other cases not so clearly), faith is at the center of one's relation to G-d. It refers to the most intimate, interior activity, for which there are no substitutes or competitors. True, in contemporary usage faith can mean other things; no one is going to prevent the word faith from being used in the plural. But if one is going to respect the language of the religious traditions it might be more appropriate to begin with one faith rather than many faiths. Each tradition acknowledges that this one faith is ultimately judged by G-d and not by any human institution. A Muslim is not likely to accept the proposition that Christians are of the same faith, but at least this disagreement might lead to an honest exploration of the differences between Christians and Muslims. Talking about "multifaith" is not likely to get Muslim support either, even though it is presumably intended to be a neutral term. From a Christian and Jewish, and not just a Muslim viewpoint, multifaith is likely to be reductionistic of a very central category.

HISTORY OF RELIGIOUS EDUCATION IN THE U.K.

The history that is most relevant to this chapter begins in 1944 with the passing of the Education Act which made religious education a requirement in British schools. Previous to that time, religious education was tolerated with a somewhat wary eye. The 1870 Education Act had tried to avoid a proselytizing in the schools by legislating that when schools did provide for the teaching of religion it should include "no religious catechism or religious formulary which is distinctive of any particular denomination."[2]

The 1944 Act repeated this proscription and now required that religious education "shall be given in accordance with an agreed syllabus." Coming toward the end of World War II, the Education Act of 1944 showed an idealistic hope of improving the lot of all citizens. The religious education section was guided through the legislative process by Archbishop William Temple, a man of extraordinary intelligence and good will.

"Religious education" was a term chosen for both ecumenical and educational reasons. That is, the aim of the provisions in the Act was not ecclesiastical. This fact was acknowledged by Lord Fisher, one of the participants in the discussion at that time. Referring to the Archbishop, Lord Fisher wrote: "Willie Temple and I were schoolmasters; that tells you all you need to know."[3]

There are two parts to the religious education provision in section twenty-five of the Act. The first concerns worship: "The school day in every county school and in every voluntary school shall begin with collective worship on the part of all pupils in attendance at the school, arrangements made therefore shall provide for a single act of worship attended by all such pupils." This provision laid a difficult burden on the school organizers of such a worship service and perhaps an unfair demand on the school's students.

The second provision of the Act referred to religious instruction: "Religious instruction shall be given in every county school and in every voluntary school." There were no stipulations about the content of this instruction but there were detailed procedures about how to reach an agreement on an agreed syllabus. A syllabus committee consisting of four panels had to agree; any one of the panels representing these four groups had the power of veto: the Church of England, other religious denominations, the local educational authority, and the teachers' organization. Until the 1960s, the second group seldom had representation, while the Church of England had the main say.[4]

Religious education was thus given a prominent and privileged place in the state or county school. Religion was, in fact, the only subject that the school was required to provide. At the same time, a child was allowed exemption from religious instruction. The 1985 Swann Report on multi-cultural education said that the combination of required and voluntary provisions for religious instruction was "anomalous." The report was opposed to the continuance of the provision for worship. However, the Education Act of 1988, which I shall comment on later in this chapter, for the most part reaffirmed the 1944 Act.

Until the 1960s there were few stirrings about religious education. Children went to the morning assembly for worship, perhaps with reluctance but without overt rebellion. Religious instruction proceeded with a content and method not drastically different from what many schools had been doing before 1944. A child should know the Bible and the main teachings of the (Anglican) church. Individual teachers no doubt tried to spice up the offerings, but there was not a lot that the individual instructor could do.

The first great rumbling for change came in the 1960s. University campuses around the world were clamoring for "relevance" and "experience." The pressure was especially strong on religion, and educationally the pressure spread all the way down to the elementary school. The demand for a "with it" Christianity was as strong in England as in the United States. In 1965 Harvey Cox was a thirty-five-year-old professor when he published his church-rocking book, *The Secular City.* England's revolution had started two years earlier with a book by—of all people—a bishop of the Church of England. The respected biblical scholar John Robinson had published his musings, *Honest to God.*

The response to the clamor of the 1960s in religious education was to strip down Christian doctrine to bare essentials and develop techniques that involved the students. Christianity, it seemed, was to be reinvented out of the students' experience; what did not fit that experience was at least temporarily left aside. There was a new element of compassion and sympathy here; it was felt that students have to be helped from wherever they are religiously and not be pressed to accept anything that does not make sense to them. One of the most thoughtful and enthustiastic writers of this period was Harold Loukes who encouraged teachers to give students a good experience in what Loukes regularly calls "Christian education."[5] The "child-centered" approach had made its way into the religion classroom and subsequently found expression in several syllabuses of the time.

What was also happening at this time in Great Britain was an influx of new immigrants from the Middle East and Far East. The assumption that the schoolchildren are Anglican, or at least Christian, whose needs are a more lively Christian worship and more relevant Christian doctrine, began to unravel. Both provisions of the 1944 Act faced a crisis. The requirement of common worship had what was probably an insuperable problem to overcome. The educational inappropriateness of requiring a common worship service in school was starkly revealed. Something might be salvaged out of the idea of a school assembly where ritual could help to distinguish school and nonschool worlds. In her study of U.S. public schools, Sara Lawrence Lightfoot suggests that U.S. schools are in need of some ritual for that purpose.[6] However, worship is not what schools are for, and religious education in a school is not best described as worship added to instruction.

The other element, "religious instruction," faced a different kind of crisis, one which could lead to a strengthening of the school's proper work. If the population of the school is almost all Christian, religious instruction easily slides into being a synonym for instruction in Christian doctrine. Without the challenge of having to compare and contrast several religions, instruction has a tendency to become proselytizing and indoctrinating, two negative terms that everyone seems to agree do not belong in school. If the classroom holds a mixture of Christian, Muslim, and Hindu students, the teacher may still have biases, but he or she is unlikely to confuse the classroom with a factory for producing good Christians.

The British school that was confronted with genuine religious pluralism was in need of some profound theorizing about religious education. Fortunately, there were scholars of religion who were also interested in education. There arose in the late 1960s two contrasting approaches to the question of religious education; these two set the direction for subsequent discussion. On one side, Ninian Smart provided invaluable assistance in developing a curriculum of "world religions."[7] The approach was commonly called objective or phenomenological. On the other side, there was a search for a universal ground of religion that would allow ordinary experience and other school subjects besides religion to be related to religious education. The student's experience was to be tapped for an "existential" encounter with the essence of religion.[8]

Throughout the 1970s the phenomenological approach seemed to have the upper hand, at least among theoreticians and syllabus makers. One has to wonder what was going in the classrooms. How many teachers were prepared to render the fine points of difference between Hinduism and Sikhism? Still, the theoreticians were doing their job of thinking through the requirements and aims of this new approach. It is best reflected in a 1971 document called the *School Council Working Paper #36*.[9] This small book is an admirable attempt to move religious education from where it had been to a "procedurally neutral approach, wherein the teacher is ready to portray sympathetically and without bias any viewpoint which he may be required to teach." The hoped-for result from such teaching? "To create in boys and girls a more sensitive understanding of their own beliefs and the different beliefs by which others govern their lives."[10]

One of the great breakthroughs in the British pattern of religious education was the Birmingham Agreed Syllabus of 1975. The law had stipulated that there was to be a syllabus but neither content nor length were specified. Birmingham is a city that particularly felt the pressures of religious pluralism. A syllabus that agreed on what all the children should know would be difficult to agree upon, and it might not touch the more serious problem of teacher preparation. The Committee in Birmingham took the creative route of agreeing upon a four-page syllabus and then producing a very extensive teacher's handbook entitled *Living Together.* There were some protests against a "syllabus" which was in fact the sketchiest of outlines; however, it did meet the legal requirement. The teacher's handbook, in contrast, is a rather exhaustive treatment of traditional religions. It even covers "nonreligious stances," such as Marxism; these are given sixty pages of treatment, being considered "equally important" to religious stances. The logic of this attitude is questionable. However, once the route is taken of trying to find an acceptable definition of religion and also be factual about all possible choices, the net becomes wide indeed.[11]

The continuity with the 1960s was now thoroughly breached. Studying a multiplicity of religions, each on its own terms, could not be confused with simply improving techniques for "nurture in the Christian faith." There was some grumbling that multifaith was multifact; that is, the student was liable to be overwhelmed by all of this objective data. The phenomenological approach, it was complained, was "rapidly becoming the new orthodoxy for religious education in county schools."[12]

By the end of the 1970s and the beginning of the 1980s, there was some qualifying of this objective approach. The other tradition, the experiential or existential, had not disappeared. It represented a valid concern that religion be intelligible, interesting, and relevant to the student's life. This concern is not for the purpose of subtle indoctrination but because all successful teaching requires an interested and engaged pupil. What is essential to a religion for its own adherents may not be the same as what is essential to a youngster in England trying to get some understanding of it. Put differently, the logic of religion may not be the same as the student's logic; someone has to mediate the understanding. The 1960s were not entirely wrong in their demand that the student's experience and interests be recognized. If one is going to teach religion, the attitudes of today's youth cannot be the curriculum content; but neither can those attitudes be neglected when curriculum designers try to present a particular religion on its own terms.

The most prominent voice in this attempt to bring the competing traditions into conversation, if not agreement, has been that of Michael Grimmitt.[13] His way of formulating the issue is to say that the student should learn *about* religion and learn *from* religion. In the former, the student evaluates "impersonally," asking about the inner logic and meaning of the religious system. In the latter, the student evaluates "personally," asking about the persuasiveness of that religion in his or her life. Grimmitt was not reversing his earlier position but there was a shift of emphasis to acknowledge that on educational grounds, a personal evaluation by the student is part of the study of religion.

Predictably, there are cries of "neo-confessionalism" or "hidden confessionalism" from those who did not wish to have any tampering with pure objectivity.[14] At least in Michael Grimmitt's case, the accusation of a drifting back toward making the classroom a place of Christian testimony is quite unfounded. Grimmitt presents a careful balance in his treatment of the differing elements that make up the curriculum concern. He thinks that Christian theology might be a help in convincing some Christians to go along with the contemporary pattern of religious education. However, he consistently justifies his own arguments on educational grounds.

POINTS OF CRITICISM

As an introduction to my own criticism of these last two decades of British religious education, it will be helpful to note a few points about the 1988 Education Act. The legislative discussion of the place of religious education involved politicians more than professional educators so that one should not expect much educational clarification. However, I think that the discussion and the final provisions are at least symptomatic of how successful the professional educators have been in making their case. The present evidence is not very encouraging.

1. The worship service, which was thought by many educators to be inappropriate, was not only affirmed but given great emphasis. Furthermore, the Act says that this

collective worship "shall be wholly or mainly of a 'broadly Christian character.' " Exceptions and qualifications were added, but the direction that the discussion took is quite clear.

2. When the politicians looked for someone to mediate the debate over whether to name Christianity "the dominant religion," they turned not to a professional educator but to the Bishop of London. Perhaps significantly, the *Times Educational Supplement* headlined the section on religious education: "Defenders of the Faith."

3. Religious education is now part of the "basic curriculum," but it is not a foundation subject; that is, it does not carry the requirement of assessment or testing. There are three core subjects (English, math, and science) and seven foundation subjects (history, geography, technology, music, art, physical education, and a foreign language). Religious education remains important in the curriculum in that the provisions of the 1944 Act were not reversed. But no one yet knows how it will actually fare in the new curriculum, the Act simply specifying that it should occupy "a reasonable amount of time" in every school.[15]

1. Religious Education as Curriculum Subject

I turn now to the one major reservation that I have with this British discussion of religious education; this one point leads to several other uses of language that need examining. My main criticism concerns the way that religious education has become the name of an academic subject, a usage that makes little logical sense and obstructs a wider discussion of religious education still needed in the U.K. I am not aware of a single writer who has consistently and systematically objected to this use of language. Even writers within a church context who sometimes complain about the direction that religious education has taken in the county schools do not speak to this issue. The church people use the term religious education for their concerns, but dialogue does not take place concerning the dominant use of religious education in the county schools.

There is no comparable use of the term "religious education" in the United States. In the U.S. some schoolteachers do teach religion; no elementary or secondary school teacher would speak of "teaching religious education." As a professor in a university, I do teach, among other things, religious education, that is, I teach teachers about the teaching of religion. In the U.K. teaching religion is sometimes used interchangeably with teaching religious education. Writers seem unaware of the logical problem with that and unaware of what a strange use of language it is to make religious education the object of the act of teaching. Does one teach the child education?

I was recently at an international conference where a Dutch professor gave a speech entitled "The Nonidentity of Religion and Religious Education." She spoke in flawless English, but it was British English not U.S. English. What she called "religious education" is what a speaker of U.S. English would call "religion." In the U.S. we have our difficulty in distinguishing two meanings of "religion" (see chapter six). There is a logic and history behind this double meaning of "religion." Granted it would be clearer if we had a word like "religiology" to indicate that what is in the curriculum is religion as an object of inquiry, that a course on religion is a search for the *logos* of religion. It is partly because of the lack of such a word that the British use "religious education" where the U.S. uses "religion." However, the British usage causes more problems than it solves.

The evolution of the British usage is fairly easy to trace. The Education Act of 1944 envisioned two parts to religious education: worship and instruction. Those two words alone may not be able to bear the whole burden of religious education, but they are in the right arena. Religions have to do with worship, or with practices of thanksgiving, praise, repentance, and so forth. Religious education must have some link to this center of religion, although placing a worship service within the school's activities is a questionable way to handle the matter. Instruction, in contrast, is the part of education that is very appropriate to the school's setting. What is the classroom for, if not academic instruction? As I indicated in the historical survey, the worship part of religious education fell into disfavor which left the

7994/

other part of religious education to absorb the whole meaning of religious education. Hardly anyone speaks of religious instruction in the U.K. because it has practically the same meaning as religious education.

Up to this point the story is clear and understandable. With worship effectively excluded, religious instruction in the school becomes equivalent to religious education. The story, however, has one more twist. Religious education as school instruction would seem to mean that religious education is the name of the department or the process of instructing students in religion. Although the British do say that, more often they say that religious education is the object of the instruction. Thus, religious education is not only encapsulated within a school, it is further narrowed down into being one subject taught in the school.

In the U.S. we do have some parallels to this usage even if not in the religion area. When we are doubtful that there is an academic subject and especially when we want a practical result, the word "education" shows up in the curriculum subject itself. Thus, we sometimes have such things as physical education, driver education, music education, moral education, sex education as the names of what is taught. In the next chapter I will analyze what similarities to religion these and other topics in the curriculum have.

The implication here might be that in England, for all the talk about phenomenology and objectivity, the British public (and their politicians) think that religious education ought to have some personal and practical effect. My suspicion is supported by the fact that in the 1980s religious education has had to fight for its independence from a big area called PMSE: Personal, Moral, Social Education. A writer who assumes that the "RE teacher" teaches RE instead of religion should not be surprised that PMSE is absorbing RE.[16]

As far as I know, no one noticed that in the discussion of the 1988 Act the terms of discussion had a fundamental difference from 1944. In the earlier Education Act, *religious education consisted of worship and religious instruction.* The 1988 Act speaks of *worship and religious education.* Someone may wish to argue that the 1988 language is an improvement, but everyone needs to take notice of the fundamental shift in language. The provisions of the 1944 Act could not be reaffirmed because the terms of the discussion were different. Religious education has now become the name of a curriculum subject rather then a process involving worship and instruction.

The use of the term "religious education" as the name of an academic subject obstructs interdisciplinary cooperation within the school. It is bad enough when school absorbs the whole of education; it is much worse when the term education is taken into one topic in the school curriculum. I was once in a discussion group with a woman from England who was complaining that other teachers in the school did not see their academic areas related to religious education. I commented that so long as she used "religious education" as the name of the subject, other teachers could not possibly contribute to the student's education in religion. She became angry and said: "That's just the way we speak here." To which I replied: "I know that but I am saying that so long as you speak that way there is no reason to be surprised at the lack of interest from other teachers." In a school, the literature or history teacher should be able to see a relation between literature and religion, history and religion. In teaching the plays of Shakespeare or the history of the Reformation, teachers can contribute to the student's understanding of religion. However, if religious education is the name of the subject taught by the RE teacher, then every other teacher in the school (not to mention teachers outside the school) is outside religious education.

I am not trying to tell the British how their schoolteachers should work together, nor am I trying to lay out the relation of school and family, school and church. But the conversation on such matters cannot take place at all if "religious education" is the name of a school subject instead of a lifelong process of interacting forms. The failure to notice the peculiarity of the language is reinforced by using the abbreviation RE. After a while, one can forget that RE is not the name of something taught in school, at least religious education is not that in most of the non-British world.

2. The Description of the Debate

The peculiar use of "religious education" prematurely limits the discussion of possible approaches to the carrying out of the work. I indicated earlier that two approaches emerged in the late 1960s and 1970s. The choice between the two reflects, to a large extent, the dichotomy in Western thought that has been with us since the seventeenth century. Are you being objective or subjective? Are you inside the religion or outside? Are you a believer or a nonbeliever? We lack an agreed upon language that can guide us safely from this universe of unbridgeable gaps. The British discussion of religious education has further narrowed the possibilities by limiting a lifelong process to an object of rational inquiry in classrooms.

The two approaches to religious education have their respective logics. The main question becomes which side to join. "Phenomenology" and "existentialism," two rather murky words from twentieth-century philosophy, became the banners under which the debate proceeded. An outsider who arrives late on the scene is sure to ask: Aren't there any other terms for discussing this question?

The phenomenological or objective side insists upon distancing what is studied from the students' lives. Educationally, that does not seem wise unless what is actually going on is an attempt to remove suspicion that there is still a Christian aim in the school. Undoubtedly there are teachers in the U.K., as there are elsewhere, who preach the gospel in the classroom. Instead of trying to solve that problem by imposing a superscientific approach, the needed direction is to get teacher and student alike to begin analyzing whatever religion they know and to place it in relation to any alternative. Granted this kind of thinking might provide only a sketchy syllabus, but after Birmingham in 1975 that is allowed.

In the syllabuses of the 1970s there was sometimes an attempt to treat all religions as equal options and even to include nonreligious stances of life. In the U.K. as in the U.S., Christianity is not one of a dozen phenomena or options. It is what is woven into the history and culture of the place. Churchgoing may have declined and pollsters may report that fewer people are "believers," but the

Christian influence has not disappeared that quickly. The available language to talk about religion, including the word "religion," has a Christian bias. Simply deciding that we are going to study "world religions" instead of Christian theology often has the effect of driving the bias below the surface. If one listens closely to much of the academic discussion in this area, "world religions" actually means everything except Christianity. Christian theology with its own disjunction of "Christian faith" and "world religions" still operates. A new resolve to be more "objective" is not an effective strategy.

In some ways there is not enough Christianity in the curriculum, that is, Christian history, beliefs, and practices as material for academic criticism. That is what is needed in the U.K. and the U.S. so that "religion" can refer to something concrete. For example, in Northern Ireland the most complex and painfully real comparison is between Protestant and Catholic forms of Christianity. Bringing in at least one more party to the discussion can often help, but the focus ought to be religion that the students know.

In Christian surroundings, Muslim or Jewish students look at the concreteness of religion with their own slant; they are quite aware, sometimes painfully so, of the reality of Christianity. An emphasis on Christianity would be the beginning of an interreligious conversation rather than a suprareligious survey. Christianity should not always be at center stage, but it is usually one of the key players. I should note here that most syllabuses in England do give a prominent place to Christianity, that is, about two-thirds of the content of these syllabuses concerns Christian material. That fact is perhaps not well-known, even to British politicians. With the fame of the Birmingham syllabus, it became common to assume that every syllabus gave equal treatment to all religions.

Teachers have to struggle with the logic of each religion, not so much because students are going to grasp the essence or deep structure, but in order that one can start with a few intelligent questions. Christians and Jews often misunderstand one another because the Christians usually start with "beliefs" and Jews with "observance." When one tries to survey Hindus, Sikhs, Buddhists, Muslims, and more, not only the ten-year-old student but the teacher who might have spent twenty years trying to master the language of just one of those religions cannot pretend to understand these religions. Testing the student's relation to one and then several religions at what seem to be a few key points is enough to attempt in a school course. Unless a curriculum on the world's religions is kept very simple it will be intimidating to all but the most avid fact gatherers.

If the terms on the phenomenological side of the argument were simplified, it might become apparent that the split with "existential" or "experiential" is a false one. Or at least these descriptions of the two sides are not the most helpful in understanding differences of approach and emphasis. Once again, because the subject is called religious education rather than religion, all talk of "experience" is suspected of being "confessional." But relating the topic in the school curriculum to the learner's experience is an obvious and unavoidable task in the process of education.

There is also regularly expressed an assumption that the advocacy of an existential or experiential approach implies a theory about a universal essence of religion. Paul Tillich's name is often brought up in this context. People on this side are thought to believe that religion is implied in (that is, "folded within") every academic subject. Thus religion is implied everywhere and every subject in school is implicit religion.

Some people may have such elaborate theories derived from Tillich or elsewhere. However, one need not take over a whole system of philosophy to say that the experience of the student needs to be at the beginning, middle, and end of all teaching. Religion is not necessarily "contained" in that experience, but the student's experience has to be related to other peoples' experience in the past and present. Likewise, religion does not have to be "implied" in history, literature, social science, or ethics, but there are connections which any effective teacher will point out.

I am assuming that "ordinary experience" can be the starting point for "religious experience," unless the latter term is given some technical, esoteric meaning. On educational grounds, what else can one assume at the beginning? In the course of studying a particular religious group, dichotomies that create insider/outsider arise. Then one must try to understand what these categories mean and whether there are any possible bridges. For example, the way Christians usually use the word "revelation" creates a dichotomy whereby a crucial kind of experience is available only to a select minority. But that is a presumption of Christian theology which needs educational challenging. The beginning assumption that there is a continuity between ordinary experience and religious experience does not depend on a theory of universal essences but on the language appropriate to education. "Ordinary" and "religious" distinguish two realms; experience is the educational term expressing continuity.

I realize that the term "experience" has a broader meaning in U.S. than in British English. In the U.S., experience is one of the most likely words for bridging dichotomies rather than being the name for one of the separated pieces. The term can have social and historical as well as individual meaning; it can bind the rational and emotional; it can be active and passive. Recommending this meaning of experience to the British would be presumptuous and probably ineffective; meaning is not easily exported and imported. Nevertheless, British religious education is convoluted around an encapsulated meaning of experience that needs examination. In Ninian Smart's six dimensions of religion that became influential in religious education, "experience" shows up as number five between "ritual" and "social aspects."[17] Of course, one can say that in U.S. English but it would be wiser not to. Experience is far more helpful as the comprehensive category in terms of which ritual, social aspects, and the rest are articulated.

In British writing on religious education, experience tends toward the private and the emotional. It can also be a code word for revealing that the teacher is still trying to stimulate a Christian experience. Thus, it is thought that to talk about experience is to bring in one of the grave threats to objectivity.

The result in much of the educational writing is a peculiar aversion to the student's own experience. In an influential religious education book of the 1970s, the author asks if we should start with the students' experience. She indicates that beyond a certain age it is not wise to do so: "Middle-school pupils are perfectly capable of going straight into a study of the Vikings or the Incas. . . . During this outward period of a child's development, when his curiosity is at its height, an undue emphasis on his own experience may seem slightly precious. For adolescent pupils there is an added reason for not starting with their own experience. This is a highly self-conscious age."[18] The choice, as this author sees it, is attending to facts about Vikings and Incas or prying into the self-conscious interior of students. I suggest it would be simpler and more effective to say that in teaching religion one is trying to relate in an intelligible way the experience of the students and the experience of the religious group being studied.

3. Schools and Religious Institutions

The equation of religious education with the teaching of religion in the state school creates an insuperable barrier to conversation with church/synagogue/temple/mosque. The individual "RE teacher" may not be interested in such a conversation, may in fact still be demonstrating his or her autonomy from any particular religious body. That is understandable enough; however, when one withdraws from a conversation on important matters, one should not take along all the good words. In this case, the teacher of religion in the state school should not claim ownership of the term "religious education." That kind of maneuver not only stops conversation; it precludes new conversation about other approaches to the area of concern.

Writers in "RE" do acknowledge that there is a set of activities in church/synagogue/temple/mosque and that some of these activities are called "educational." Writers in RE draw a contrast between "religious education" and "nurturing faith" in a particular religion. The formula is assumed to be clear; perhaps as shorthand it does do its job. Still, it should not pass unexamined. With a contrast between religious education and nurturing faith, one is asserting that the nurturing of faith is not a part of education in religious life. But the words "nurture" and "faith" taken singly and together need to be within religious education; for their own good, nurture and faith have to be in an educational context. And religious education, lest it shrivel into esoteric facts taught to schoolchildren, needs both faith and nurture.

Nurturing, as I pointed out earlier, is one of the root meanings of education. The rearing, shaping, forming, and parenting that happen early in life are crucially important to a person's lifelong education. Undeniably, nurture particularly connotes the infant or young child; we are nurtured or mothered as infants at the breast; we are surrounded with nourishment, warmth, and affection before we can fend for ourselves. If the church/synagogue/temple/mosque nurtures people, these groups can be proud of that fact. However, when nurture is the only educational term allowed to a religious group, the implication is that they are not up to intellectually challenging any of their members. Instead, the religious body is thought to be engaged in soft, sentimental activities like singing hymns and shaking the hand of the minister.

My suspicion about the term "nurture" is strengthened by the fact that the noun which invariably follows it is: faith. Why always this word? One could argue on the basis of both secular and religious usage that faith is an all important category in human life, that it is wider and deeper than reason. An infant's life is all about faith in the sense of trust. The child begins a lifelong journey of learning to believe in people, believe in causes, believe in life itself.

Despite all the positive things one can say of faith, its exclusive assignment to church/synagogue/temple/mosque arouses suspicions similar to the case of nurture. To people who deal in the rationalistic categories of the modern school, faith usually means something less than reason. The unenlightened masses take things on faith whereas education has to be about critical inquiry and rational explanation.

That the British meaning of religious education is defined in contrast to faith is a loss for education in general, religious education in particular. Faith is one of the most universal religious categories (perhaps even more universal than "religion" itself). It needs study, out of which one might conclude that at least some of the meaning of faith should be encouraged in education. In other words, a result of studying the relation of Judaism and Christianity might be (even if you are a Hindu) a nurturing in faith. I would not necessarily push this formulation which would be one of the ultimate heresies in British writing on religious education. However, my statement is at least as true as its opposite, namely, that religious education and nurturing in faith are totally separate and contrasting activities.

Another term that became a test of orthodoxy in the 1970s was "commitment." Does religious education include commitment? If what in fact we are talking about is a subject in the school curriculum, then "making a religious commitment" is excluded from religious education. If, in contrast, religious education is a lifelong process of interacting forms, then "commitment" is one possible way to describe an important element of education in a religious life. "Commitment" is one of those existential sounding words that has recently attained some prominence in the language. It does not have the rich history of "faith" or even "nurture" in religion and religious education. Still, it is a term that should not be banished from religious education.

Edward Hulmes in his book, *Commitment and Neutrality in Religious Education*, attempted to bring commitment back into the discussion.[19] However, he hurts his case by wildly exaggerating the significance of the term with statements like: "Commitment is not merely *one* of the aspects of religion. It is ultimately what religion is about" and "Commitment is both the point of departure and the final goal of all religious education."[20] More damaging to his case is that he does not notice the cul-de-sac of accepting the usage of religious education as the name of the thing taught in school.

In saying that teachers must be enthusiastic, committed

to what they teach, Hulmes writes: "What is true of the teacher of mathematics is true *a fortiori* of the teacher of religious education."[21] Here and elsewhere in the book he would be able to speak more clearly of commitment if he referred to the "teacher of mathematics and the teacher of religion" in regard to a kind of commitment to what they are doing. Other teachers in religious education (outside of the classroom) may have a different kind of commitment that is intrinsic to their work. There is, indeed, an educational interest, enthusiasm, involvement—commitment, if you like—that the teacher of religion should have. Michael Grimmitt has been helpful in sorting out this educational meaning of commitment from commitment as referring to the enthusiastic involvement in the practices of a religious body.[22]

Hulmes's book is too easily dismissed as reactionary even though he raises several good issues. He speaks with feeling and in some detail about Christianity and Islam, and the need for a religion to be accepted and practiced. He knows that religious education ought to mean something more than gathering facts about a dozen religions. But Hulmes fails to draw the distinction necessary to open a new line of discussion. He repeatedly uses religious education as the name of what is taught in elementary and secondary school. As a result, he is forced to hit from the outside without a chance of success.

4. Education as Lifelong

There is a final, unfortunate result of equating religious education with what is taught in the county school. Without even reading the literature, one could guess that this must follow. Adults are excluded from religious education. The literature on religious education consistently demonstrates this fact. Writers, of course, do not say that they *intend* to exclude adults. British writing pays its respects to adult, continuing, lifelong education. But when authors talk about the nature or aim of religious education, the reference is invariably to children. Consider Hulmes's book and his attempt to broaden religious education to include commitment. He writes: "The aim of religious education is to provide *children* with knowledge and skills which will enable them as they grow into maturity not only to see how varied are the manifestations of religious experience but also how their experience constrains them to consider the implications of a personal commitment."[23] That is a tall order for any person; why cut off religious education with the child and leave the adult who is struggling with commitment outside of religious education? If Hulmes's desire is to bring commitment within religious education, it would seem that on his own terms he should not say that the aim of religious education is to provide something to children.

The U.K. is not very different from the U.S. in nodding toward adult education and then defining education as an affair of children. The U.S. probably has more of an adult education establishment than does the U.K., but their histories of the movement are similar. What makes the British truncating of religious education more illogical is that they have courageously moved toward exploring the complicated world of religions. "Religious education is concerned with exploration of the spiritual life of man so that *children* may begin to discern the relations of ontological independence of a transcending and infinitizing nature which are of ultimate and absolute value in life."[24] This ambitious project would surely take at least a lifetime.

Even writers who have incorporated a developmental idea into religious education do not carry the idea beyond the secondary school. A person in education is preparing herself or himself for disappointment by stating that "the aim of religious education is therefore something to be completely achieved only in the later years of secondary school."[25] The intent of this statement is to liberate teachers from unrealistic expectations too early in education. But pushing up the point of final returns five or ten years is just a start. Why not another fifty years for trying to achieve completely the aims of religious education?

Basil Yeaxlee, in his studies of the early adult education movement in Britain, noted that older people who came to these classes were particularly interested in religious issues.[26] The programs at that time were for the most part inadequate to respond to that need. Neither in the U.K. nor in the U.S. is the situation much better today, and no one has an adequate plan for the future. We need changes on several fronts at the same time to give people who are forty, sixty, or eighty years old a participation in religious education. The very first step on that journey is to stop describing education in a way that excludes adults.

I have tried in this chapter to express appreciation for the British literature on religious education. I have added what I hope are helpful criticisms about particular formulations. The British have, I think, too narrowly defined religious education. That fault is in part due to a clearer focus and greater professionalism than in the U.S. A wide variety of the world's people appeared on the doorstep of the U.K. To their credit, theorists of religious education, syllabus committees, and ordinary classroom teachers have struggled to provide a responsible program. People in the U.S. have the responsibility of thinking through their cultural and religious context. They should perhaps do something different from the U.K., but they dare not neglect the serious debates of the last twenty years in the U.K. on the nature of religious education.

NOTES

1. Here and throughout this book I write the name "G-d." It indicates that religious people are not referring to an object that can be named when they pray to the Holy One or the One beyond names. I use the word "god" only when the reference is in fact to an object discussed in the sciences.

2. John Hull, *New Directions in Religious Education* (London: Falmer, 1982), p. xii; see also, J. Murphy, *Church, State and School in Britain 1800-1970* (London: Routledge and Kegan Paul, 1971); John Bagley, *The State and Education in England and Wales 1833-1968* (New York: St. Martin's, 1969).

3. W. Roy Niblett, "The Religious Education Clauses of the 1944 Act: Aims, Hopes, and Fulfillment," *Religious Education 1944-84*, ed. A. G. Wedderspoon (London: George Allen and Unwin, 1964), p. 22.

4. Edwin Cox, *Problems and Possibilities for Religious Education* (London: Hodder and Stoughton, 1983), pp. 4-5.

5. Harold Loukes, *New Ground in Christian Education* (London: SCM, 1965).

6. Sara Lawrence Lightfoot, *The Good High School* (New York: Basic, 1983), p. 322.

7. Ninian Smart, *Secular Education and the Logic of Religion* (London: Faber and Faber, 1968).

8. J. W. D. Smith, *Religious Education in a Secular Setting* (London: SCM, 1969).

9. *Religious Education in Secondary Schools* (School Council Working Paper #36; London: Evans Methuen, 1971), p. 38.

10. Ibid., p. 18.

11. *Living Together: A Teacher's Handbook of Suggestions for Religious Education* (Birmingham, England: City of Birmingham Education Committee, 1975).

12. Kevin Nichols, *Orientations* (Middlegreen, England: St. Paul, 1979), p. 41.

13. Michael Grimmitt, *Religious Education and Human Development* (Great Wakering, England: McCrimmon, 1987).

14. John Sealey, *Religious Education: Philosophical Perspectives* (Boston: Allen and Unwin, 1985), pp. 49-50.

15. *Times Educational Supplement,* July 29, 1988, pp. 9-12.

16. Grimmitt, *Religious Education and Human Development,* pp. 261-64.

17. Smart, *Secular Education and the Logic of Religion,* pp. 15-18.

18. Jean Holm, *Teaching Religion in School* (London: Oxford, 1975), p. 32.

19. Edward Hulmes, *Commitment and Neutrality in Religious Education* (New York: Macmillan, 1979).

20. Ibid., p. 87.

21. Ibid., p. 37.

22. Michael Grimmitt, "When Is 'Commitment' a Problem in Religious Education?" *British Journal of Educational Studies* 29 (1981), pp. 42-53.

23. Hulmes, *Commitment and Neutrality in Religious Education,* p. 11.

24. Raymond Holley, *Religious Education and Religious Understanding* (Boston: Routledge and Kegan Paul, 1978), p. 141.

25. Holm, *Teaching Religion in School,* p. 10.

26. Basil Yeaxlee, *Lifelong Education: A Sketch of the Range and Significance of the Adult Education Movement* (London: Cassell, 1929), p. 60.

5

Looking Westward:
The U.S. School

This chapter completes the contrast that was present in the previous chapter's image. Still stranded over the Atlantic Ocean, I here examine the issue of religion in the school, especially the public school, of the United States. The U.K. offers substantive material for a field of religious education. Unfortunately, it has located the term "religious education" in a far too narrow setting, namely, the curriculum of the state school. When we turn westward to the U.S., we again find a substantive discussion of religious education combined with an inadequate set of terms for the discussion. Here the linguistic deficiency is almost the reverse. Religious education can mean many things in the U.S., but one thing it does not mean is a subject taught in the state school.

There are historical reasons for the peculiar U.S. attitude toward religion in education. And as so often happens in this country, the historic attitude is entangled in complex court rulings. I will start by trying to untangle a few salient points of that history, leading up to a discussion of two recent documents. Then I will pick up the issue of academic instruction from chapter three, applying this to the area of religion. That will lead, finally, to a discussion of religion within the school's curriculum.

THE U.S. HISTORICAL CONTEXT

Religion in the U.S. public school has always been a topic to stir up fiery emotions. In places where one might hope for thoughtful debate, the discussion is infrequent and abbreviated; and thus there is no readily available language in which to situate the question. A few years ago the Congress of the United States stayed up throughout the night wrestling with the issue of prayer in the school. Congress periodically has these fits of piety because of the popular pressure "to put God back into the classroom." But one has to look far and wide for any discussion of the school doing with religion what schools are supposed to do, namely, teach it and study it. In the several dozen studies of the public schools in the 1980s, there is hardly a word about religion, despite the fact that it is a serious and continuing problem.

One of the exceptions among these reports was Theodore Sizer's book, *Horace's Compromise*. Sizer has only a few comments on the issue, but he brings a listening mind and a respect for peoples' religious convictions. The school is not doing its job, Sizer says, if it merely invokes "the wall of separation between church and state" and then pretends that religion is not a fit subject for intellectual examination. He writes: "By pretending there is a wall between religious issues and their schools, public school people remove themselves from the argument about the ways that religion must properly exist in their schools, and they leave the field open to unchallenged religious enthusiasts."[1]

While leading journals in the U.S. stand at the schoolhouse door to bar religion's entrance, religious enthusiasm and ideology overlay the educational and political systems. Visitors to the U.S. are almost immediately struck by the religiosity of the country. From the saluting of the flag in the public school to the chaplains in Congress and invocations of the Almighty in every presidential address, religious language and imagery shape the life of the citizenry.

Often the religious fervor is called patriotism, but it is not so much love of the country (the United States) as love of the idea about the country (America), a devotion to the sacred cause of liberty. The religious idea of America has profoundly reshaped Catholic, Protestant, and Jewish religions in the United States and to some extent beyond the U.S. This would be an interesting, important, and intellectually provocative theme for a public school curriculum, but it is almost unthinkable that the theme would be touched in a public school.

There is a group of people in the U.S. who have labored over the past three decades to get religion into the curriculum of the public school. I think that their efforts deserve appreciation. In some states, children do have the chance to study religion as a subject, or to study units on religion within literature, social studies, and other subjects. Progress has been slow, which is perhaps to be expected. However, there may be something else to be considered here, and that is the framework in which discussion takes place. The problem is similar to the U.K., but the discussion is within an even narrower range. This is one of the most important educational and political issues in the country, and yet the discussion of it seems to involve only a few hundred people. Surely, there would be a wider interest in this issue if the debate could be opened beyond the fixed formulas that seriously limit discussion.

While the problem in the U.K. is that theoreticians of state school studies have seized control of "religious education," the problem in the U.S. is that theoreticians of state school studies flee from "religious education." The result in both countries is similar: There is no discussion of the various ways that religion and education interact for people of all ages, in schools of all kinds, and in educational forms other than schools. The reason why the problem is worse in the U.S. is because whereas in the U.K. the state school study of religion takes to itself the whole language of religious education, in the U.S. the same discussion is left without a language at all. An excessive amount of Supreme Court language fills the void. And an artificial and convoluted language takes over from there.

At the beginning of the book *Teaching about Religion in Public Schools*, Nicholas Piediscalzi writes: "While the academic study of religion at least at these levels has been identified as 'public education religion studies' to clearly distinguish it from religious study or religious education (which are not constitutionally appropriate for a public school setting), the name is, in a sense, a misnomer."[2] By the end of the sentence, the author is backing away from what is supposedly a clear distinction. The phrase "public education religion studies" presumably needs to be related to some other kind of religious study or else it is without an educational context.

What is most intriguing in the above quotation is that the author is certain that religious education is not constitutionally appropriate in the public school. He includes that point in a parenthesis and assumes that everyone agrees on that. But no court has ever said that religious education is forbidden in the public school. Indeed, the Supreme Court of the United States has explicitly encouraged a study of religion in the schools.[3] So what is going on here? Why does one of the leading authors in this area assume, without bothering to provide evidence, that religious education is forbidden in the public school? The answer is that he thinks that the term "religious education" connotes to many people the work of church/synagogue/mosque/temple. He is right on that point. He also presumably thinks that one cannot change the connotations of "religious education." He may be right on that point, too, although it is a point that at least deserves debate. If he is right that "religious education" cannot be used for what is logically its proper role, then "public education religion studies," lacking an educational area to be in, will remain without much academic footing.[4]

The term "religious education" may not connote the public school to everyone, but the public school is one reason for the emergence of the term in the early twentieth century. The nineteenth-century alliance of nonsectarian religion in the public school and denominational (Protestant) religion in the Sunday school was perceived to be breaking down. The founding of the Religious Education

Association in 1903 was for the express purpose of a new alliance between religious groups and public education. The aim was to provide a professional approach to religious education in both the religious congregation and the public school. The Association and its journal were called *religious* education because the aim was to bring Catholics and Jews, as well as Protestants, into this new alliance in relating religion to the schools and the culture. However, the REA founders had more Protestant bias than they realized so that Jews and Catholics tended to shy away and to form their own educational associations.[5]

Partly for that reason and partly because the U.S. was just not ready to engage the problem, the great dream of professionally prepared teachers of religion in every public school did not materialize. Since the 1960s the REA has become genuinely ecumenical (Canadian and U.S. as well as Catholic, Jewish, Protestant, and Orthodox), but it has not housed the concern for the public school. When public school interest was sparked in the 1960s, it led to the founding of a new association (now called The National Council on Religion and Public Education) that has had little relation to the Religious Education Association. The REA journal occasionally publishes articles on the public school as one of its many sidelights, but not as an issue central to the mission of the REA.

The current status of the question of religion and the public school is indicated by two recent documents. The first is a 1988 pamphlet, "Religion in the Public School Curriculum," published under the sponsorship of fourteen organizations. The second is a 1987 report, "Religion in the Curriculum," by one of those organizations, the Association for Supervision and Curriculum Development.[6] Both documents are hopeful signs of progress, but their particular formulations invite scrutiny.

The pamphlet "Religion in the Public School Curriculum" is mainly eight questions and answers. No one can expect here an elaborate theoretical structure. The great significance of this document is that a consensus was reached among the sponsoring groups, several of which have been suspicious of discussions in this area. Interestingly, the Religious Education Association was not one of the sponsors. It did not oppose the statement, but its support was not asked for.

The first sentence of the pamphlet reads: "Growing numbers of people in the United States think it is important to teach *about* religion in the public schools." The italicizing of the word "about" indicates the authors' approach to the answer of religion in the public school. I doubt, however, that it is an accurate report of how the question is asked by growing numbers of the public. The peculiar phrase "teach about religion" has never gotten far with the public. And the reason, I would argue, is that at best the phrase fails to clarify the issue and at worst it hides the issue.

The distinction between "to teach religion" and "to teach about religion" goes back at least to the 1940s. A 1947 report of the American Council on Education refers to what is "frequently said" about this distinction.[7] The author of the report, F. Ernest Johnson, had little enthusiasm for the distinction. What the report emphasized was "'the study of religion' instead of 'teaching religion' because the latter so commonly implies indoctrination."[8] But that kind of statement is an evasion of the central question here.

The distinction between "to teach religion" and "to teach about religion" was picked up in a Supreme Court decision of the 1960s. Justice Arthur Goldberg in *Abington v. Schempp* offered the distinction as applying to the public school's role in one's education in religion. The phrase was able to stimulate discussion in the late 1960s about religion in the public school. Unfortunately, as a legal phrase "teach about religion" seemed to invite repetition rather than educational examination.

In "Religion in the Public School Curriculum," the first question is: "What is meant by 'teaching about religion' in the public school." The answer begins: "The following statements distinguish between teaching about religion in public schools and *religious indoctrination* [my emphasis]." This is far too easy a contrast to clarify anything. No group—including religious organizations—describes their activity as religious indoctrination. Is the intention here to say that except for "teaching about religion in public schools" all other approaches to religion are indoctrination? In numerous universities, professors "teach religion." Are they all practicing religious indoctrination?

There is perhaps a useful distinction that could be developed here. In elementary school and in the early years of high school, students may not be ready to study the discipline of religion, just as they are not ready for courses in Freudian pyschoanalysis or pre-Socratic philosophy. However, teachers can introduce elements of psychology, philosophy, or religion within the material that is taught in elementary or junior high school. The fifth-grade teacher might then say, "I am teaching about Puritan religion within my history course," while the twelfth-grade teacher might say, "I am teaching a religion course which includes the effects of Puritanism on U.S. history."

One could thus distinguish between "teaching about religion" and "teaching religion" without the implication that the latter is equivalent to religious indoctrination. There is teaching about religion in a history or literature course; there is teaching religion in a religion course. Whether a seventh-grade, tenth-grade or twelfth-grade student is ready for a course on religion is an educational issue worth debating.

Another difficult but educationally rewarding question would be to explore the differences between teaching religion in a public school and teaching religion in a religiously affiliated school. Is there and should there be a difference between the two in the nature of classroom instruction? There is little doubt that the curriculum content will be different. But what is the difference, if any, in what it means *to teach* religion?

I expect that the authors of the pamphlet would say that it was not their task to speak about religiously affiliated schools. However, by contrasting "teaching about religion in public schools" and "religious indoctrination" they are implying a great deal about other kinds of schools and other approaches to religion. By failing to hone out meaningful educational distinctions, the six contrasts that follow employ easy formulas with oppositions of single words.

The first contrast is: "The school's approach to religion is *academic*, not *devotional*." Since what is being contrasted is "teaching about religion in the public school" and "religious indoctrination," then "devotional" is apparently equivalent to religious indoctrination. Could a religious school's approach be academic? This contrast and the five that follow refer to "the school." Is that shorthand for "public school" or is there implied a reference to all schools? Could a religious school be devotional with reference to Judaism or Lutheranism but be academic in its approach to the study of religion?

I will not go through each of the other contrasts, but none of them really clarifies the phrase "teach about religion," which was the question. We are told that the school should expose not impose, inform not conform, educate not promote or denigrate. Everything seems so reasonable that it is difficult to understand why there has been a problem.

I am in agreement with the intention of this pamphlet, and I realize the inherent limitations as well as the advantages when one is trying to reach a consensus statement. Nevertheless, the formulas cry out for examination and some of them may obscure the issue. A group of people who invent a convoluted phrase can build a logical system on it. But that can be at the expense of effectiveness with the public and cause isolation from other scholarly literature.

I turn to the other significant document, "Religion in the Curriculum," which calls for the public school to accept its academic responsibility and place religion in the curriculum. The Association for Supervision and Curriculum Development, a respected professional organization, published the report. Its publication received front-page treatment in *The New York Times*, and its existence is certainly a hopeful sign. The disappointment comes in finding out that the authors of this report uncritically accept standard formulas in this area instead of taking the opportunity to reshape the language for discussing the question. The drawback is manifest in their references to religious education and their attempt to distinguish "teaching religion" and "teaching about religion."

There are four references to religious education in the report, all found early in the document.[9] All four are oblique references; there is no indication that the authors reflected on what the term "religious education" means and what it could mean. There is no awareness of what "religious education" has meant at an earlier period of U.S. history, not to mention what it means in Ontario, England, or anywhere else. Such parochialism cannot get us very far.

The first reference reads: "If moral education is held to be religious education, instruction about morality is constitutionally prohibited." Whatever the meaning of religious education here, its constitutional exclusion from public education is simply assumed. The second reference makes clearer that assumption: "Religious education, or teaching of religion, is the job of parents and religious institutions." Here religious education is equated with teaching religion and then is assigned to parents and religious institutions. The third use of the term is in a statement about people advocating religious education in the public school because parents and religious institutions do not "inculcate any religion but their own." The final reference on the same page reads: "Another questionable assumption is that young people will receive religious education at home or at church, temple, or synagogue. Of course, they might—but rarely about any faith save their own." This last sentence, lacking any other term of reference, seems to imply that there should be a religious education in the public school, a religious education that is wider than that received at home. This implication would contradict the first two statements.

In summary, the report has assigned "religious education" to parents and religious bodies; then it has noted that people should be religiously educated in faiths other than their own. But having barred the available educational term from the public school, it has no way to refer to a legitimate public school concern with religious education. A British reader would surely be amused or confused by a document that calls for religion in the curriculum but bars religious education from the school.

The second weakness of the report follows from its attempt to avoid religious education. The panel of authors adopts the distinction between "teach religion" and "teach about religion." As I indicated above, this distinction has been the legally orthodox way to state the issue; but it is hardly the last word. The authors of "Religion in the Curriculum" could have shown some originality or at least have taken a critical look at the supposed clarity of this distinction. The assumption that one should "teach about religion" is a strange way to talk about both teaching and religion.

The document's title is encouragingly straightforward: Religion in the Curriculum. One might be led to expect that if something belongs in the curriculum of the school, then the responsibility of the schoolteacher is to teach it. But the panel has said that the teaching of religion is unconstitutional. They seem to assume that "to teach," at least in this case, means to proselytize, to indoctrinate, to inculcate. But if teaching religion means inculcating one's faith, what does it mean to teach history, art, or politics? If the school does not know what it means to teach religion, does it know what it means to teach anything else? A good reason for teaching religion in public schools would be that it might force us to reflect on the legitimate aims of all teaching in schools and classrooms.

In "Religion in the Curriculum," the authors do not seem wholly convinced that religion is indeed a topic worthy of the curriculum. There is, as a matter of fact, a problem with referring to religion in the public school curriculum. Instead of confronting the inherent ambiguity of the term "religion," the authors skittishly try to avoid the problem with the phrase "to teach about religion." Their attempted solution only muddies the water.

TEACHING RELIGION

Can one teach religion? Is it constitutionally proper and academically respectable to teach religion in the public schools of the U.S.? Is religion the name of a curriculum subject or not? The answer requires a distinction. "Religion" in twentieth-century English means two very different things: 1) a set of practices that particular communities engage in and 2) an object of scholarly and academic inquiry. The second meaning is as well-established as the first; both meanings arose together out of the Western Enlightenment. "Religion" was adopted as a general and neutral term by which scholars could study particular communities and compare them to similar groups. Does religion belong in the classroom? Religion, as I have earlier noted, was practically invented for the classroom; there is no place where religion more comfortably fits than in the academic curriculum.

Is there still not a danger that the other meaning of religion—specific practices of prayer and other rituals—might crop up with the discussion of religion in the public school? The answer is obviously "yes," which is exactly the reason why the verb that needs to precede religion is "to teach." Even more precisely, what we need is schoolteaching or academic instruction. At present, bits of religion and quasi-religious ideas float mindlessly through the school and its curriculum. The one thing generally not done with religion is to teach it, that is, provide a language for intelligent discussion and thoughtful ordering of what students already know about religion and what they should know for understanding their world.

The distinction between the two meanings of religion may seem too subtle for most people to operate with. However, that is not usually the case in practice. People are quite capable of distinguishing between these two meanings of religion. They recognize which meaning is at stake by the level of abstraction that is operative. For example, Jews, Catholics, and Buddhists do not talk about "practicing religion"; they talk about observing *Shabbat*, hearing Mass, or sitting *zazen*. They know that people do not practice religion in a single, generalized way just as they can recognize that "teaching religion" is a level abstracted from their own or other people's religious practice.

One can compare various religions, out of which one can abstract the idea religion. In the classroom, one can move between religions and religion; one can go from many religions to some idea of religion. After one draws com-

parisons between Jewish and Christian, Hindu and Buddhist religions, one may hazard some generalizations about
religion. People who actually practice a particular religion
are quite capable of understanding the difference between
that meaning of "religion" (the practices) and the abstraction called "religion" whose natural habitat is the classroom.

In the book, *Religion Goes to School*, the authors write:
"The public school will teach no religion, but will study all
religions."[10] One cannot tell here whether their contrast is
between the singular (religion) and the plural (religions) or
between teach and study. Would the authors, for example,
allow the "teaching of religions" even though they are
against the teaching of religion? Probably not, although
"teaching religion" is the phrase that is most anathema.
And yet, both phrases could be applied to the public school
classroom; one teaches religion by examining religions,
and in teaching religions, one is inevitably teaching religion.

The more likely contrast in this quotation is between
teach and study. In literature of this kind, it is quite acceptable to study religion but not to teach it. The students have
an academic subject, the teacher does not. The students
are allowed to study religion so long as no one teaches it.
This contrast is regularly made, as in "Religion in the Curriculum": "The proper role of religion in the school is the
study of religion for its educational value. The task is to
teach about religions and their impact in history, literature,
art, music, and morality."[11] The authors insist throughout
this report on the difference between "teach religion" and
"teach about religion," and the nonacceptability of the former. However, the students are allowed to study religion
not just study about religion.

The most basic problem here is not with the idea of
religion but with the misunderstanding of what teaching
means. People who say that one cannot teach religion in
the public school seem to have a rather primitive idea of
what teaching is. They seem to imagine that schoolteaching is the same as preaching from a pulpit. Thus, this
typical contrast: "One key distinction concerns the differ-

ence between teaching religion and teaching *about* religion. In effect the Court upheld teaching *about* the Bible rather than the direct presentation of the Bible as in the Bible reading practices."[12] The assumption here is that to teach the Bible means to read the Bible in class. Is that what teaching the Bible is? Yes and no. If one is going to teach a text—Hamlet, the U.S. Constitution, the Book of Exodus—presumably one has to read it. Preferably, the students read it at home the night before, although, even if they do, reading excerpts aloud in class is usually a helpful teaching technique. Thus, in order to teach the Bible a teacher is likely to have a "direct presentation," that is, a reading of the biblical text that is being studied. However, this reading is a precondition or, at most, a beginning step in teaching the Bible. The teacher's job is to analyze what the text means, point out its relation to social and literary context, and relate all that to the student's understanding.

Undeniably there are people in classrooms who do not have a sufficient grasp of what they are teaching or who lack techniques of how to teach. They may think that teaching consists in telling children what to think and how to act. The U.S. and other countries have a shortage of qualified teachers; steps are needed, most of them obvious, to attract better schoolteachers and prepare them better. This distinct problem is not a reason for maligning competent teachers. It is not a reason to equate the teaching of religion with the activity of adults telling children what to think religiously and coercing them into specific religious practices.

Reading the Bible without commentary has been a favorite practice of nineteenth- and twentieth-century Christians who wish the public school to turn out "God-fearing and patriotic children." Reading the Bible in a ceremony to begin the school day is still a favorite symbol of such people. In fact, since the Supreme Court declared in the 1960s that such practices are unconstitutional the practice has acquired in some places greater symbolic value in deliberate rebellion against the law. But why should anyone call this activity "teaching religion?" Certainly, the evangelical Christians who agitate for this practice do not. They call it "praying the Bible," "announcing the word," or "spreading the gospel." And there is no logical reason why their opponents should call such ceremonies "teaching religion," unless they are confused about what schoolteaching is and where religion fits in an academic curriculum.

CLASSROOM: ONE LEVEL OF ABSTRACTION

The peculiar phrase "teach about religion" creates a second level of abstraction where there should be only one. To walk into a classroom is to step outside one's ordinary life of cooking dinner, talking to a friend, saying a prayer, or hoeing the garden. School is a privileged moment for considering the language of such ordinary activities. In school, these activities are grouped into more or less arbitrary divisions called literature, art, science, religion, geography.

Schools may fail to supply the needed formality—space, time, materials, competent instructors—to carry the student into the world of reflection, analysis, insight, and synthesis. At the other extremity, schools sometimes break all connection with ordinary activities and create layer upon layer of abstraction; after a while no one notices that the words do not actually refer to anything. The proper place for school to be situated is distinct from but in proximate relation to the non-school world. Teaching religion means talking about the way religious people act; it should not be centered on talking about how philosophers of religion define religion.

A comparison to sex and death might be helpful here. Religion, of course, has a lot to do with sex and death; the two appear frequently in syllabuses of religion. However, people in recent times have tried to develop sex and death into academic areas of their own. Thus, "sex education" and "death education" are hot topics in many educational discussions. Sex education draws passionate conflict between supporters who cannot understand why anyone would object to education and opponents who consider it a horrid evil. Death education does not draw the same fire although death is at least as difficult as sex to treat in a classroom.

The point of my comparison is that dying, sexual intercourse, and worship do not fit in the classroom; yet no one doubts their importance (even the atheist would not deny that worship is an important reality in the world). We need a place for developing a language to talk about these powerful realities and the classroom is the most likely candidate. If we cannot talk thoughtfully in a classroom about these volatile subjects, where can we learn to speak? The school has to deal in sexology, thanatology, religion (religiology). The abstraction to the logic or science of sex, the logic or science of death, the logic or science of religious practice is a deliberate insertion of a language that is not hot with passion, bereavement, or devotion. The schoolroom requires that the emotions be recollected in tranquility, that they be channeled into conversation with other people who directly or indirectly feel the same joys and sorrows.

We all need to learn how to die and, therefore, we need teachers who can teach us how to die. However, that is not what thanatology can do for us. The academic instructor can only provide a language for inquiring into death. If that language is available in a classroom, some students begin to volunteer their experience of the death of a parent or their fears and confusions about their own deaths. Some students will never volunteer such raw data; that should be perfectly acceptable in a classroom. The instructor has to be close enough to the reality of dying so that his or her words are realistic, but not so close as to intrude on this intimate experience.

In actual fact, many if not most students choose a course in thanatology for the purpose of therapy. That confuses the role of the classroom which is not well designed for providing therapy. As a teacher, I would prefer that the students came to death class motivated by intellectual curiosity. In this case, however, the blurring between the therapeutic and the instructional is understandable. If students cannot find therapy anywhere else, it is not the worst of cases that they find it in school. Nevertheless, this fact places an additional responsibility on the schoolteacher not to lose sight entirely of academic inquiry.

A great deal of thanatology does overstep its modest possibilites as a science or logic of death. For example, Kübler-Ross's well-known five stages of dying are often laid out as the way everyone must die; if the patient is not moving through the sequence properly, the implication is that he or she should be pressed to do so.[13] I think that more data, reflection, and linguistic distinctions would restrain a classroom instructor from preaching on how people should die.

What I have said about death could be almost exactly paralleled in regard to sex. The sexology proper to the classroom could be a small but important part of everyone's sexual education. Unfortunately, this is seldom the way the question is posed. The debates and the actual classroom practice can veer wildly: from "sex education" being an intrusion into the intimate experience of a young person where no one, certainly not a schoolteacher, has a right to go, to "sex education" being an abstract exercise in technical terms. Even more than is the case with religion, the best curriculum on sex cannot be a substitute for a prepared teacher.

An academic instruction in sex(ology) should be located at one step back from sexual practice. The language has to be neither that of the street corner and HBO specials nor the antiseptic language of the research project. If the appropriate language is available in the classroom, some students will take the opportunity to volunteer first- or second-hand experiences. Because sex courses are often required in primary and secondary schools, the right of the student to privacy has to be carefully respected. Yes, everyone needs some education in sex as part of his or her sexual education; but the schools have to be flexible in the ways they try to fulfill this responsibility. Although the objections of parents are not a sufficient reason for stopping sex education in school, they are a sign that teachers must proceed carefully with teaching sex in school and that more attention should be given to sexual education outside the classroom.

Probably the greater danger in these two areas is not the intrusion into intimate realms but the opposite tendency.

Sex and death tend to disappear into higher levels of abstraction. After all, if one wishes to avoid messy confrontations with students and with parents of young children the safest route is to ascend toward the sky in scientific or pseudo-scientific abstraction. I have a colleague who calls his course "thanatological study." Since thanatology means the study of death, then his description means "the study of the study of death." And, in fact, that is probably an accurate description of what goes on in school regarding sex and religion as well as death. That second step of abstraction means that our language is about abstractions.

Regarding the "teaching of religion," one can easily forget that the word "religion" is already an abstraction, a term historians and social scientists conceived for the rest of us. It is the right level of abstraction for the activity of schoolteaching. In the next chapter, I take up other forms of teaching whose object is "praying" or "being a holy person." In this chapter my concern is schoolteaching which can be directed to, among other disciplines, religion. Such an activity can be carried out under the auspices of a religiously affiliated school (also to be treated in the next chapter), but it has an entirely appropriate setting in the public school.

A term that has had some success in bridging the public school and the religiously affiliated school is "religious studies." One can find religious studies departments in church colleges, private schools, and state universities. It is the appropriate name for a department, but it is not the proper name for what is taught in the department. Religious studies departments should teach religion courses. Otherwise, there is the same problem here as with "thanatological studies." A course on religion should be a study of how people act; it should not be a study of the study of how people act. Similarly, "to teach religion" is to provide an abstract but useful language to understand people's activities.

"To teach about religion" introduces a second remove. Under that rubric, one does not speak the language of religion, only a language about that language. There is, of course, nothing intrinsically wrong with the phrase "to teach about." Any schoolteacher occasionally uses the phrase ("I was teaching about World War II that morning..."). The problem arises when "teach about religion" is constantly set in logical opposition to "to teach religion." Here there is a deliberate distancing of the teaching from a properly academic subject called "religion."

Although British and U.S. writers approach the issue of teaching religion from almost opposite directions, the results have an underlying similarity. In the U.K. the schoolteacher is "to teach religious education" rather than "teach religion"; in the U.S. the schoolteacher is "to teach about religion" rather than "teach religion." Both shy away from intellectually confronting what people (including the students in class) religiously practice. Instead, the syllabus looks to some philosophical construct about "worldviews."

There is one final twist in both the British and U.S. versions of turning away from the straightforward phrase "teach religion." A large part of the public wants schools to turn out good children, which means boys and girls who morally behave. The public presumes that religion is supposed to motivate, form, and control good behavior. From the beginnings of the U.S. public school a nonsectarian religion was encouraged so that the school could produce morally good children. In the U.K. it is assumed that RE is a partner with PMSE: personal, moral, and social education.

Calling the curriculum topic "religious education" in the U.K. suggests that what is being done in school is "practical," formative of the children's lives and not just ideas. The word "education" in the course title suggests nurturing and formation as in physical education, social education, moral education. Similarly in the United States, "to teach about religion" can suggest that religious influence is getting a foothold in the school, perhaps as a first step to other religious things. When the ASCD report "Religion in the Curriculum" was released, an interview was held with panel member O. L. Davis. One reporter asked Davis: "Are you willing to take the next step and support time for prayer?"[14] In response, Davis patiently explained that that is not what the panel had in mind. Is that reporter especially dense or does he represent a large part of the public? One thing is sure, that the phrase "teaching about religion" is not as crystal clear as its users would like to think; it does not sound to the public like other things that go on in school: teaching math, teaching science, or teaching history.

There is a logical pattern to the British and U.S. usages even though it is a peculiarly convoluted logic. From the side of the theorizers, "religious education" and "teaching about religion" are *two levels* removed from the practices of a particular religion. The writers and schoolteachers wish to leave no doubt about their scientific objectivity. However, from the side of parents, school boards, and politicians, "religious education" and "teaching about religion" may suggest that there is *no level* of abstraction, that the school is doing something about personal and moral formation. These contrasting perceptions can exist together because the teaching is not located where it should be: *one level* removed from religious practice. The religion that belongs in school is that language of how people practice their particular religious convictions. Much of the public would misunderstand the term "teaching religion," but at least there would be only one straightforward issue to clarify.

I am not saying that this confusion is deliberately caused by anyone's bad faith. People make the best case they can for what they think is worth doing. Politicians and school boards are not receptive to academic arguments. If those who are not academics are supportive because they hear something that suggests practicality, academic people understandably accept the support. I sympathize with those who are trying to get a syllabus on religion approved by a state board of regents. I, too, would quote the Supreme Court and shy away from all the phrases that set off alarm bells with state boards of education and politicians. Nonetheless, in the long run religious education, including the teaching of religion, cannot prosper on the basis of confused public support or a language dictated by clumsy legal phrases. In educational journals, we need to reshape a language of education, a better language of religious education than we have ever had. The Supreme Court is almost totally irrelevant to this educational discussion. If school people are clear about what they wish to say, then they can begin educating school boards and legislators.

RELIGION'S PLACE WITHIN THE CURRICULUM

The question always asked in connection with putting religion into the school curriculum is: "Should religion be taught just like every other subject?" The answer to that question is assumed to be either a simple yes or no. I think that the question should be: "Where along the spectrum of subjects in a school curriculum does religion best fit?" Since each subject invites its own particular style of teaching, what other subjects does religion most resemble and which does it least resemble? The general answer to this question is that religion is most like those subjects that involve the human person as a whole, and religion is least like those subjects, that for the purpose of studying an abstract object, prescind from the person's inner life.

Thus, mathematics and much of modern science are at one end of the spectrum. The style of teaching and the means to evaluate what has been learned are appropriately concerned with the student knowing a definite content. While the student's attitudes, feelings, and opinions have to be taken into account by any math or science teacher, no one could ever mistake the student's inner life for the content of the math syllabus.

Toward the other end of the curriculum spectrum are academic disciplines in which the human subject is central. When one gets involved with history, politics, art, and morality, then factual information plays a part but each fact has a context of meaning. In this area, if one wishes to be "objective," in the sense of fair, impartial, evidential, and accurate, then one has to include the "subjective" in the sense of the inner life of human subjects. The classroom's clarity often becomes blurred when we get to this interiority and to personal behavior. Thus, religion is not suddenly the one topic that treads on different terrain. It shares its difficulty of method, and it has its way prepared by similar areas of study.

Before comparing religion to its closest allies, one more

thing must be said about the other end of the spectrum. Math and science cannot be of much direct help to religion (although aspects of modern science have a decidedly mystical slant). What math and science can do is avoid setting up additional obstacles by the way they are taught. A lot of math teaching is in fact a form of preaching ("Copy down these rules and then you can do the problems at home").

Right and wrong answers possess an indubitable clarity, but the teacher who looks only at the answers is not teaching math. Math teaching ought to introduce students to the language of math and help students to think mathematically; likewise, the science teacher deals not in proofs and answers but in the language of science. There are not two kinds of things in the school curriculum, one that is all solid truth, and the other that is mere opinion. It would not be much of a victory for religion to find allies in the curriculum if all of those allies are looked down upon as second-class material in the curriculum. There really is or should be a spectrum in which the continuity of providing academic language is modified by gradual shifts in how each language is related to the student's experience.

If we turn back now to the other end of the spectrum, it will be helpful to draw specific comparisons. The place of art, politics, and morality in the school curriculum provides some of the best examples. In each of these three areas, a larger process of education can be distinguished from a fairly narrow academic study. When the adjectival form (artistic, political, moral) is placed before education, there is implied a formation of the person's life. The purpose of artistic education is either to turn out artists or aesthetically to transform a person's education. The aim of political education is either to turn out politically active people or to transform education in political ways. The aim of moral education is morally good people or an education influenced by moral concerns. In contrast, note how restricted is the school's part: art education does not an artist make; politics education or political science does not guarantee great politicians; and ethics in the classroom may have slight connection to morally good people.

We do, of course, hope that there is some connection in all three cases. These days, the study of art is usually a

necessary but not a sufficient condition for artistic education. While the artist will usually have some school training
in art, he or she will also need other educational experience that does not fit well in a classroom. Most of the
students in an art course (e.g., art history) are probably not
intending to be "professional" artists. Nevertheless, their
art interest, whatever its depth, can be shaped and helped
by studying art in school.

Thus, all three of these areas—and religion is a
fourth—have a distinction between the limited part that a
school can do and the actual practice of art, politics, morality, and religion. When a student of any age walks into a
religion classroom it should be assumed that he or she
wishes to study religion and that the teacher's job is to
teach it. The student's practice or nonpractice of a particular religion should be left at the classroom door. When a
student takes a course on politics, his or her voting record
is not the teacher's business. A political science teacher
who would try to produce either Republicans or Demo-
crats would be acting irresponsibly.

Of course, a teacher may hope that students get sufficiently excited about politics to do something political beyond the classroom. That is not an illegitimate hope so
long as the teacher does not press further. So also an ethics
teacher hopes that the students will act morally even if the
teacher cannot tell them what to do beyond the classroom,
and even though the ethics teacher knows that the moral
education of the home, work site, and leisure are probably
more influential than the ethics course in school.

Although the art course's aim is not to form artists, the
teacher may draw on artistic experience from beyond
school or simulate such experience. Something similar happens in courses on politics, ethics, and religion. In all of
these areas, the line is sometimes unclear as to what is and
what is not appropriate in the classroom. The teacher's
examples may get too personal or the teacher's questions
may pry into the private lives of students. People should
not be pressured in a classroom to confess their intimate
thoughts or to reveal the fine details of their personal lives.
However, even the best of schoolteachers, precisely because
of their attempt to be inventive and engaging, may acci-

dentally cross this line. But responsible teachers in the classroom do not regularly and egregiously transgress the line. And after a very short time in a course even the slowest student can spot the difference between these two kinds of schoolteachers.

Religion should be taught, then, in a manner similar to other subjects with tests, marks, academic credit, and whatever trappings locally apply. The people who are concerned that this approach is not *religious* enough have a legitimate concern in that the teaching of religion is only a small part of religious education. But to ask the classroom to do what it is not designed for is to distort the small contribution that the schoolroom can make. We would do better to ask what teaching can mean within the religious congregation and how students can be taught to act religiously.

In the press release of "Religion in the Curriculum," the ASCD's own newspaper, *Update*, carried the headline: "ASCD advocates teaching about religion as opposed to teaching students to be religious."[15] The latter phrase is a quite accurate description of what the public school should avoid doing. However, in the news story under the headline this contrast does not appear because it is not in the original document. In the document itself, what is contrasted is "teach about religion" and "teach religion." The headline's contrast (teach about religion versus teach students to be religious) is clearer but it would be clearer still if it dropped the word "about." The contrast "teach religion versus teach students to be religious" is the simplest, clearest, and most logical way to put the issue. The U.S. public school, like its British counterpart, has to be concerned with teaching religion rather than teaching people to be religious. It is to the people concerned with the latter issue that we now turn.

NOTES

1. Theodore Sizer, *Horace's Compromise* (Boston: Houghton Mifflin, 1985), p. 128.

2. Nicholas Piediscalzi, *Teaching About Religion in Public Schools* (Niles, Ill.: Argus, 1977), p. 2.

3. Justice Clark, speaking for the majority opinion in *Abington v. Schempp*, 1963: "Nothing we have said here indicates that such study of the Bible or of religion, when presented objectively as part of a secular program of education, may not be effected consistent with the First Amendment" (374 U.S. 225).

4. J. Paul Williams, *The New Education and Religion* (New York: Association, 1946), p. 13. He notes that some people will take his use of "religious education" to be sectarian, but he says he prefers that to having to call his concern "metaphysico-epistemo-ethico-motivationalism."

5. See, Stephen Schmidt, *A History of the Religious Education Association* (Birmingham, Ala., Religious Education Press, 1983).

6. Association for Supervision and Curriculum Development, *Religion in the Curriculum* (Alexandria, Va.: ASCD, 1987).

7. American Council on Education, "The Relation of Religion to Public Education: The Basic Issues," in *Religion's Place in General Education*, by Nevin Harner (Richmond: John Knox, 1949), p. 133.

8. Ibid., p. 164.

9. Association for Supervision and Curriculum Development, *Religion in the Curriculum*, pp. 14-15.

10. James Pannoch and David Barr, *Religion Goes to School* (New York: Harper & Row, 1968), p. 27.

11. Association for Supervision and Curriculum Development, *Religion in the Curriculum*, p. 27.

12. Peter Bracher and David Barr, "The Bible is Worthy of Study as a Secular Book: The Bible in Public Education Today," in *The Bible in American Education*, ed. David Barr and Nicholas Piediscalzi (Philadelphia: Fortress, 1982), p. 167.

13. Elisabeth Kübler-Ross, *On Death and Dying* (New York: Macmillan, 1969).

14. *Update*, vol. 29, October 27, 1987.

15. Ibid.

6

Does Religion Belong
in a Parish?

This chapter turns to the contribution of religious institutions to religious education. In the previous two chapters, I have described what the state school can do in the U.K. and the U.S. The question that I address in this chapter may, from a British point of view, seem anomalous. Although church people in the U.K. use the term "religious education," most theorizing on the topic simply puts the churches outside religious education proper and into the domain of "nurturing faith."

From the standpoint of discussion in the U.S., my argument may seem backwards. Here, religious education is widely assumed to be the domain of church and synagogue. The presumption is that one can teach religion in church but that religious education in the state school is highly problematic. I have proposed that teaching religion is obviously suited to a public school classroom. My question is whether one can and should teach religion in a church. There is a real problem with trying to do so and an answer will require several distinctions.

What I am trying to describe in this chapter are forms of education and modes of speech that can complement academic instruction in religion. I wish to resist any quick and simple division of activity in this area. In the U.K. the division into religious education and nurturing in a particular faith removes the church activity from education and seems to suggest only one kind of church activity. I think it important that churches be related to schools (the relation can be of several kinds) and that at some level of its operation the church engage in serious intellectual inquiry. In addition, there is more than one nonschooling form that the church's educational work can take.

One way of summarizing the church's efforts in education is to say that the aim is to teach people to be religious, or more exactly to be religiously Catholic Christian, Lutheran Christian, or Baptist Christian. The state school cannot have this aim; its concern is the understanding of religion, and it uses the limited though legitimate means of school: instructor, religion curriculum, and all the trappings of secular education. What Michael Grimmitt says about religious educators is clearly true only in reference to teachers in classrooms: "Despite their title, 'religious' educators are essentially 'secular' educators concerned with the educational value of studying religion and religions."[1]

For the most part, religious educators are "religious." They deal with "the whole person," which includes bodily activity and shaping the relation of individual and community. In the modern world, becoming religious usually includes understanding religion, but it surely includes more. A religious teacher (that is, one who is concerned with teaching to be religious) intends to reshape the life of the student, something that a teacher of religion does not have a license to do.

A student in walking into a classroom is *not* saying: "I put my whole life into your hands; I wish to become a religious person and to lead a religious life." The teacher of "being religious" has a great deal more leeway in which to operate. One should also notice that there is more danger of the relation between teacher and student becoming exploitative. The results can be impressive but the risks are great. The freedom of the student to take part or not take part needs careful safeguarding. There can be no required courses in becoming religious.

In the title of this chapter, I use the word "parish," which is usually a sign one is referring to the Catholic tradition of Christianity (Roman, Episcopal, Orthodox). Throughout this chapter I am deliberately using this and other terms of particularity that come from Catholic tradition. If one wishes to discuss the particular contribution from the religious body, it helps to look at a particular case. The Roman Catholic church is an interesting case, and it is also the case I know best. I will refer to other Christian churches and to Jewish practice. However, my main examples and the linguistic framework are Roman Catholic.

The term "parish" gives a particular focus to this chapter. I am mainly concerned with how this unit of the church provides education to its members. "Parish" is a geographic term, a way of dividing up people according to where they live. To this day in Louisiana, parish is the word for the political division of the state. In Roman Catholic theology, parish has several other connotations (e.g., it is presided over by a pastor) that make it the basic functioning unit of the worldwide institution.

Since the word "parish" refers to spatial division and locality, a "nonterritorial parish" would seem to be a self-contradiction. Not quite. A group of people who meet for religious services do need territory on which to stand. However, the people in a congregation may actually come from a variety of places. This fact should be noted because in countries like the U.S., the well-educated and mobile Catholic is likely to go shopping for a parish to join. The phenomenon is not entirely new, although it does seem to be increasing.[2]

Of more importance for the universal church is the transitional form that the worship community has in much of Latin America, Africa, and Asia. There is no building on 233rd street with a rectory next door. Rather, there is a group that meets occasionally with and more frequently without a clergyman, and often without a church building. The situation in many of these missionary areas is viewed with alarm by church leaders. Interestingly, however, this stripped-down version of the institution has been a source of imaginative thinking about what a church really is supposed to be.[3] Any discussion today of education by the church and in the church has to take place with awareness of this great ferment of change.

The question asked in the title of this chapter is intended to be provocative. I would hope that the material in the previous chapter provides some intelligibility to the question. There, I pointed out that "religion" has two distinct meanings: It is a general word for the rituals, beliefs, and moral practices of a community; it is also a word to designate a field of academic inquiry. The first meaning of religion obviously applies to the parish although it does not say enough. A parish is not exactly a place that practices religion; it is a place to practice Catholic Christianity; not ritual, belief, and moral practice so much as Eucharist, Trinity, and protest against nuclear arms.

It is the second meaning of religion that creates a problem for the parish. I have strong doubts that most parishes can engage in teaching religion. Even for those that can, it is not the center of education in a parish. The Christian *church* has a responsibility to teach religion; that is why the church sponsors universities and other schools. Toward the end of this chapter, I discuss what are the conditions necessary if a *parish* is to teach courses on religion. For most of this chapter I am interested in other forms of parochial religious education.

CHRISTIAN TRADITION AND CONVERSION

One does not become religious in a general way nor act religiously outside some ways that have already found shape within human history. The question is often asked: "Why are there so many different religions in the world?" Instead of trying to answer that question, one might turn it around to read: "Isn't it remarkable that there are so few religions in the world?" Religion is a form of language and everyone speaks a particular language. There are thousands of languages in the world, the exact number depending on how one counts dialects. And yet, most of the people in the world belong to a few major religious traditions.

What people do religiously tends to fall within the boundaries of formed traditions. Sometimes people think that they are practicing a religion unheard of in all previous history. Possibly that does happen. More often, however, the people who make such lordly claims lack knowledge both of human history and of their own personal journey. Many are the Christians who think they have "left the church," but in fact their language changes very little; they spend their lives banging on the church wall from the other side.

People who accept the name "Christian" are those who see a value in it for themselves and believe it should be passed on to other people, others of today and tomorrow. Thus, within the present, Christianity has a missionary impulse to "spread the faith," an aspect of the church that can be overbearing and at times insulting to others. I return later to the form such missionary witness might take and the limits that should be observed. As for passing it—the Christian way of life—to the next generation, here we have the question of tradition and the need for education. A Christian education, in the several senses of the term, is necessarily concerned with a Christian tradition.

As I have previously noted, modern education has not spoken well of tradition. The act of "handing on" or transmitting something often seems to be the foil against which the critical inquiry of modern education operates. Perhaps this picture made sense in the eighteenth or nineteenth centuries when a new kind of questioning, doubting, and emancipating was struggling to survive. Tradition, it was presumed, could more than take care of itself; it did not need the help of educators. In the twentieth century we have cause to doubt that tradition carries on without us. The inheritance of centuries of civilizing activity—a Greek, Roman, Jewish, Christian body of materials— could be forgotten. The loss might be not only in the conscious memory but also in the way we carry ourselves as human beings.[4]

What differentiates a Christian education from religious education as a whole is a particular attention to preserve

Christian tradition. The concern may sometimes be exercised in mindless and arrogant ways that are eventually self-destructive. Nevertheless, a Christian education is necessarily "conservative" in the most genuine sense of that term. A conserving Christian education can contribute to a liberalizing religious education. Often in this century church educators have tried to liberalize Christian education. Instead of striving for a complementarity of form, they just tampered with the form that Christian tradition necessarily has, while they failed to bring to bear what religious education should mean.

George Albert Coe was the great theorist of religious education in the U.S. during the first half of the twentieth century. In one of his most famous passages he asks "whether the primary purpose of Christian education is to hand on a religion or to create a new world?"[5] Coe goes on to indicate that he thinks the answer should be the latter: to create a new world. His question was often used, perhaps is still used, as a test to divide liberals and conservatives.

Before one tries to answer the question, there are three things to notice about the formulation of the question. 1) The question is about the *primary*, not the only purpose. 2) The question is about *Christian* education, not religious education. 3) The second aim, "to create a new world," is, to put it mildly, an ambitious aim. Coe calls his question a "practical dilemma," but I doubt that this is the dilemma that confronts parents or Sunday school teachers. The primary purpose of Christian education, they are quite sure, is to hand on the Christian religion. The practical dilemma that confronts parents and schoolteachers is *how* to do that.

A Christian education is concerned with Christian tradition; otherwise, it would not be called Christian. Would the primary purpose of *religious* education be "to hand on a religion?" The small word *a* leads to the answer "no." Religious education is indeed involved with religious traditions in their particularity; one of its aims is that people hand on their particular religion. But as religious education it is also concerned with more than one religious tradition and with comparisons between traditions.

Christian education cannot be entirely separated from religious education; in the very attempt to hand on a (the Christian) religion it has to acknowledge other religions and the Christian relation to them. For example, a Christian education that never recognized Jewish religion on its own terms would not be a *religious* education, and before very long it would cease to be a Christian *education.*

George Albert Coe's formulation has its Christian bias in the alternative that he offers to "handing on a religion." Or we could say that the fact that he is talking about *Christian* education is revealed by the ambitious alternative: to create a new world. A Jew or Muslim might say that, but Christianity and its residual effect in modern culture is the most likely source for this language. Such a phrase has been used so often in recent centuries that we do not blink at the pretentiousness of the claim or its potential for violence. (One of Ronald Reagan's favorite lines as president of the United States was a quotation from Tom Paine: "We have it in our power to begin the world over again." Is there any way to imagine how this could happen other than by nuclear war?) Coe presumably did not mean the phrase to be taken literally; every Christian knows that "creating the world" is the prerogative of G-d.

What kind of positive slant can one put on Coe's phrase? The handing on of a religion should perhaps be conceived in the context of "creativity" and "world." "Create" can be a helpful term to suggest that the handing on is not a mechanical repetition. Effective handing on involves design, reshaping, criticism, and personal response within the process of tradition. Note that one does not hand on the tradition; one hands on the religion in creating anew the tradition, the process of handing on. Coe's use of "world" can be a reminder that besides Christians there are others, both human and nonhuman, that Christian tradition must acknowledge, listen to, and care for. Any claim to be creating a new world has to emerge out of a gentle reshaping of the existing forms that life already has on the only earth we share.

The counterpoint to tradition in the life of the individual is "conversion." As tradition suggests to some people an unbending attitude of attachment to past formulas, so conversion is imagined by some people as a single, divine intrusion into a person's life. However, this is not what the etymology of the term suggests (a turning back) nor what is suggested by the long Catholic tradition of daily conversion of life. A person constantly circles back on his or her past; moments of great crisis need a context of interpretation.

Whether conversion is at the center of Christian education is a question that goes back at least to the middle of the nineteenth century. The liberal wing of the Christian churches has been skeptical of conversion, often pitting education as an alternative to conversion. The conservative wing, for its part, has often staked everything on the one moment of conversion that would make any future education unnecessary. Several of the greatest writers in religious education, faced with what they considered to be mindless and emotional preaching, speak in disparaging or even negative tones about conversion. Coe, for example, writes that "the constant aim of elementary religious education should be to make conversion unnecessary."[6] That is an unfortunate relinquishing of a central religious, in this case Christian, term.

In the idea of development presented earlier, the individual progresses not toward an end point but toward greater integrity of life. The unfolding of this development calls for a constant educational reshaping that deepens the sense of personal awareness and challenges the individual with the wisdom of the past. Personal development includes jolts in our experience that turn us back to ourselves at a deeper level, that is, we experience conversion of life. A question that is frequently asked is: "Are development and conversion compatible?" My answer is that they are not only compatible but they require each other. Without a *conversionary* development, the idea of development self-destructs either by smuggling in idols or by exhausting itself in unlimited growth. Without a *developmental* conversion, a lifelong process of turning toward G-d, then conversion self-destructs by turning some event or doctrine into an idol.

Conversion reminds us that the religious life is based on

experience. The teachings of tradition will not do anything unless there are individuals whose experience is illuminated by those teachings. Conversion of life, the religions believe, is directed toward G-d; however, it finds its embodiment and guidance in the very particular teachings of a religion. Small conflicts between personal experience and the teachings of the tradition are to be expected. However, if one's experience and those teachings radically diverge, then one does not so much "leave the church," as wake up one morning to discover that the tradition no longer shapes one's life.

If a person's experience is thoughtful and reverence-full then he or she may feel justified in appealing beyond a particular teaching to the voice of the "Holy Spirit" within, or to future reform, or to a lost element of the tradition's past. One of the great Christian books that teaches how to be (Christianly) religious is *The Cloud of Unknowing*. Part of its attractiveness, now as in the fourteenth century, is its appeal to common sense, modesty, and trust in experience. The anonymous author, an expert on prayer, says to the novice: "It is best to learn these methods from God by your own experience rather than from any man in this life. . . . Although this is so, I will tell you what seems to me the best of these special ways. Test them and improve upon them if you can."[7]

LITURGY AS EDUCATION

The question in this chapter is: How does one get taught to be religious in a Catholic Christian way? The first context of my response is the parish, the local organization of a few hundred or a few thousand people. The parish's center of teaching is its liturgical service in which the lives of the participants are to be inspired and directed. If the liturgy is formative, then its effect should spill over into social and political transformation within and beyond the parish.

I wish to examine liturgical teaching, or the way in which the liturgical experience teaches how to be religious in a particular way. In choosing to examine the Catholic Christian rather than Protestant Christian way of being religious, my emphasis is on sacramental gesture rather than preaching. I will speak to preaching as an integral element of liturgy; it is an activity generally not done well in Catholic parishes. Protestants are strong on the talking side, Catholics on the nonverbal elements; they have something to learn from each other.[8]

The power of the Catholic liturgy is suggested in an essay that Reinhold Niebuhr wrote shortly before his death. After a famous career as preacher, Niebuhr's last years were restricted because of health to being a "pew worshiper." He describes how he came to doubt the sufficiency of preaching and adds:

> For the first time I ceased to look at Catholicism as a remnant of medieval culture. I realized that I envied the popular Catholic Mass because that liturgy, for many, expressed the mystery which makes sense out of life always threatened by meaninglessness.[9]

The sacramental system of the Roman Catholic church is a system of continuing education that stretches from birth to death. The main teaching is nonverbal; the action is precisely choreographed by directions (rubrics) for the minister. The individual's part is mostly silent prayer, surrounded by communal recitation. At its best, the liturgy allows for the emergence of the full range of human emotion within this fixed communal ritual. For example, the reformed funeral liturgy provides a positive framework within which individual grief has its place. Or, within the marriage liturgy, the couple's hopes and their friends' accompanying joy can find a personal touch.

The center piece of Catholic liturgy is the Eucharist, the ancient ritual that is repeated daily in the parish church. It is a simple prayer of memory, praise, and thanksgiving derived from ancient Jewish practice. The reforms since the 1960s have tried to get Catholics involved in the singing, the responses to the priest, the small rituals within the large ritual. So far the reforms have had limited success. The average Catholic may still talk of "attending Mass," much as one might go to a concert or the theater. Intelligent participation in the Eucharistic service is desirable, although Catholic tradition has never totally discounted the fact of presence, even presence in the last pew.

Despite the erosion of "Sunday obligation," Catholics still come to church in great numbers in the U.S. The priest may have little to say and the hymn singing may be awful but the reenacting of the last supper and death of Jesus is a magnet that draws Roman Catholics and shapes their sense of presence, communion, and mystery. Education in the Catholic church leads to and from this central act of worship. The verbal instruction that surrounds the Eucharist and the other sacraments is called "catechesis."

Catechesis or catechetics is part of the inner language of the Catholic church. Although the root term for catechize, catechetical, catechesis goes back to the beginning of Christianity—and although Martin Luther wrote the first "catechism," the best-known variation on this term—this language is not common in Lutheran or Reformed traditions. The term seems to have fallen into general disuse by Protestants in the eighteenth century. The strong sacramental connotation of the term "catechesis" is probably the main reason why the language is more prominent in Catholic tradition.

If a person is going to participate fully in the Catholic Eucharist and the other sacraments, he or she needs catechizing, that is, some preparation to understand the ritual and to relate it to Catholic doctrine. In a modern recovery of the early church's practice, the adult is taught by a catechist over a period of many months. The person who is preparing to be a Catholic attends the first part of the Eucharist, the "liturgy of the word," and then leaves with the catechist for instruction about the second part of the Eucharist, the more mysterious phase of offering, consecration, and communion. The catechized person is initiated into the church, most preferably during the Easter vigil, the culminating point of the liturgical year. After becoming a church member, the individual needs further instruction in the church's teaching, this too being given in a sacramental context. The sequence of practices just outlined is found in the Rite of Christian Initiation of Adults, which is probably the most important educational change that has occurred at the parish level.[10] Of course, some parishes have not yet heard of such a thing, while for some other parishes the preparation of adults for reception into the church is a powerful example of the continuing education of all the present parish members.

Catechizing (the sounding of a message) is a highly directive affair. The person who wishes to be religiously Catholic has to have the freedom to say: "Yes, I wish to become a new member or a newly reformed member of this parish. Tell me what the tradition's teachings are." The catechist's task is to throw light on practice and convey and explain "what the church teaches."

Although for many centuries the main recipient of catechetical instruction has been the young child, the Catholic church has been trying to shift that focus. The Synod of 1977 said that the "adult catechumenate" should be the model of catechetical work. A young child lacks the freedom to get out of the way of instruction.

The Catholic church, like most of society, realistically acknowledges that children are formed by their surroundings: parents, friends, social position, television, and so forth. Especially in religion, there is no way to be neutral until the child reaches the age of twelve, sixteen, or twenty-one. The church in the form of the congregation can try to be a positive context for the religious and moral formation of the child. This might include a little catechizing, especially when children ask questions of their parents. There is nothing wrong with a Rite of Christian Initiation of Children designed for their own level.

When the major effort at catechetical instruction is directed toward younger children, what is neglected is not so much adults as intergenerational dialogue. Tradition is the process of handing on between adults and children. When adults are neglected so are children. An adult catechumenate at the center of church life is not a disparagement of children. On the contrary, it is an invitation to children to grow up and become part of a community that continues to deepen its understanding and to better its practice of Catholic Christian life. One does not always serve children best by instructing them. The Talmud says that Torah is acquired by forty-eight things: by diligent attention, by proper speech, by an understanding heart, by awe, by fear, by humility, by generosity. . . . These qualities in the community teach the child.[11]

The catechizing of child or adult is one example of what I have called a homiletic mode of teaching. A set text is presupposed; the homilist adds commentary. Preaching a sermon is the best-known example of this kind of teaching. The Catholic parish is often deficient in preaching, which is not to say that it lacks this form of teaching. In many parishes, the catechists make up for what is lacking in the Sunday sermon. Still, an acceptable homily within the Eucharist, at the end of the liturgy of the word, is an educational improvement devoutly to be wished.

Flannery O'Connor, the great southern Catholic writer, recounts in her letters a conversation with a friend who had recently become a Catholic. "What attracted you?" asked O'Connor. Her friend answered: "I once went to Sunday Mass and the sermon was so terrible that I kept going back to find out what attracted all those people."[12] One might draw other conclusions from this story than the need to improve the sermon. Certainly, Vatican II's mandate that a sermon be preached at every Sunday service was, in the absence of any new intiatives to improve performance, a bad idea educationally. A sermon ought to be preached when someone is prepared to do it; otherwise, it becomes an excruciating exercise for both speaker and listeners.

I have great sympathy for the man or woman who tries to preach a sermon in church. It is a daunting challenge, particularly because of the range of age, education, social class, and commitment in the typical congregation. When there is a small and fairly homogeneous group of people gathered around some event or religious meeting, then the homily is a much different affair. As one who has sat through several thousand sermons in Catholic churches, I may be in a position to offer some modest tips to preachers. I do so in a style of writing that here becomes homiletic.

1. *Stick to the text.* The homily is a commentary. It does

need some contemporary references, but it is basically a reflection on what has just been read. And that means the homilist can find most of the sermon in a biblical commentary. He or she may worry about repeating what was said fifty-two weeks ago, but that is a small problem. The preacher who leaves the text behind for original thoughts is often repeating what was said two weeks ago.

2. *Be brief.* The greatest mystery to me is why people who preach badly insist on giving the longest sermons. The best homilies within the Eucharistic service that I have ever heard have usually been under five minutes. When I say that to Protestant ministers (especially black ones) they find the idea very strange. It is one of the differences between Catholic and Protestant traditions. In Protestant circles, the sermon is the center of the service. That does not guarantee an effective service; however, it does throw the whole question of preaching into a different context. Preaching in black churches is really a special art form that deserves separate treatment. My comments here are about the homily between gospel and creed in the Catholic Mass. I can still remember some of the four-minute homilies that Gerard Sloyan preached at Catholic University twenty-five years ago. But I cannot by Sunday afternoon remember a thing about most of the the half-hour sermons I sometimes encounter.

3. *Don't nag.* The sermon is supposed to be prophetic or moving. It ought to say things which challenge the complacency of the congregation and inspire them to act. Some preachers mistakenly equate that with whining, scolding, and generally bemoaning the state of the world. It is particularly offensive when the preacher spends the time complaining about the people who are not there. Why not say something—anything—to the people who are?

4. *Avoid that cloying tone.* There is a tone of voice that is an occupational hazard for preachers (just as there is for university professors, radio announcers, or politicians). If one flips across the television cable channels, the preachers are recognizable by their tone of voice before one hears any content. Some of them screech, some are folksy, but nearly all of them seem to be out of touch with an ordinary

tone of voice. Granted that preaching is not just ordinary speech; it has to be direct, precise, and powerful. But many men and women manage to do that without developing a preachy tone.

5. *Rest the priest.* Requiring the man who presides at the Eucharist to be the one who gives a sparkling sermon is asking too much. Priests and bishops, like the rest of us, sometimes have nothing much to say. It would seem to me an authentic development within Catholic tradition to distinguish the roles of priest and preacher. Not many people are good at doing both; there is no reason why they should have to be, except that several kinds of ministry were conflated in the early church. Some priests would object to the distinction; a lot more of them would rightfully feel relieved. The talent of the whole congregation—including the priest on occasion—could be tapped. Some people could give a good sermon once a month; others might be up to it once a year. This quite simple distinction of ministerial roles would transform education in many parishes. An added bonus would be that it would transform the question of ordination of women away from a simple yes or no. Ordination needs a new discussion, not only for whom but for what.

In summary, the parish's form of teaching is mostly nonverbal. The sacraments, especially the Eucharist, teach by being themselves. They are not *means* to education, a language that liturgical experts rightfully object to; they *are* education. The words that are spoken, including the homily, are specific directives that arise from and return to the mysterious center. The church's main remembrance is not in stone or even in writing but in doing something: "Do this in remembrance of me." In the mystical language of the early church, the people of the congregation are the continuing body of Christ in the world. The Eucharist reminds us that life does not move in a straight line toward a final point; we return each liturgical year to the same place which is yet different. The religious life is a repetition, an asking for each day and a praise of thanksgiving for gifts already received: the daily bread and the earth itself.[13]

REFORMING THE WORLD

Besides the liturgy, there is one other indispensable activity in parish education. It is not an entirely different thing because it is, in fact, the other side of liturgical activity. If the liturgy is alive in a parish it will spill over into acts of compassion beyond the liturgical assembly. The relation is not cause and effect, so much as a rhythm of movement inward toward the quiet center of a community and movement outward to the dispossessed and suffering. One does not need a complicated theory to put these two together. Anyone who stops for a moment and prays to a G-d who is called Father (or Mother) will remember the suffering others who are brother and sister.

In the Hebrew Bible there are two traditions of Sabbath, one that emphasizes doing nothing, the other that gives impetus to action for justice. The one is related to the other in that if there is truly to be a quiet rest, then everyone has to have a share of it, not just a few privileged men. The women need rest from the housework, the oxen need rest from plowing, the earth needs to lie fallow. The Catholic liturgy is designed to be in continuity with this attitude. If the *communion* service is not to be a sham, it has to be a reminder to the congregation that everyone, human and nonhuman, is called to communion.

Parish education in the liturgy is consciously directed to members of the church. It is the nature of a religious community that its language draws a line between inside and outside. The preacher has every right to say "we Catholics" in addressing the audience; it is an assumption based on the fact that this group has assembled for a Catholic liturgical service. Of course, a visitor should be made to feel at home; nothing that is insulting to an outsider should be uttered from the pulpit. Nevertheless, without previous instruction, much of the liturgical service will be unintelligible to an outsider.

When one turns to the parish's obligation to help the poor, the lonely, the sick, the bereaved, the faltering, there should be no line between inside and outside. If someone is hungry and the church has food, the only condition for receiving food should be hunger not church membership. Some Catholic parishes do a remarkable job in being welfare centers. Other parish churches seem to think that this kind of activity is an interesting extra, perhaps for the churches located near slums. The parish, however, is inherently a place for serving the needs of justice; this is not a trendy idea of a few do-gooders. One historian has said that the early church triumphed on the basis of its social security; it took care of the widows, the sick, the poor. Even to the beginning of the seventeenth century, the parish was the distributor of welfare benefits. Some people think it could probably still do a better job of it than the state bureaucracy.[14]

In actual practice, of course, the church's resources are pitifully small in comparison to the state's. For the government to say that in a city like New York the churches and the synagogues should house the homeless and feed the hungry is an outrageous shirking of city, state, and federal responsibility. Nonetheless, the religious institutions do have a part to play here. A parish church in a desperate urban area can feel so overwhelmed by the size of the problem and the limits of its resources as to become paralyzed. What good is it to set up ten beds in the church basement when a city has thirty thousand people sleeping on sidewalks? But by doing what it can, the parish, along with many other agencies, can prod the public conscience and influence the government.

In the richer suburbs where there may not seem to be many poverty stricken it is just as important to have programs of outreach. Other kinds of need surface as beginning efforts take shape. Perhaps as important, some of the congregants who are economically and politically powerful have to become aware of suffering people and at least occasionally lend a hand in the literal sense. Those who spend most of their time at the top of office buildings could use a little education in cooking, cleaning dishes, changing beds, and just being on call.

My description is intended to indicate that the main recipients of education here are the helpers not the helped. The parish is still educating its own in how to be religious in a particular way. That may sound introverted, but it is important to locate properly the educational aspect of action for justice. If people are hungry, they need bread not a sermon. The bread ought not to be served with anything that has the slightest appearance of a hook in it. The only words that should accompany food to a hungry person are: I hope you enjoy the meal.

It is true that, as the church serves those who are in need its life and message become more credible. Over the course of many years such activities will probably draw new members to the church. However, serving the poor for the express purpose of getting an increase of church membership serves no one. The peculiar nature of church witness and mission is that it tries to give something to the nonchurch world without any strings attached. In the modern world, this kind of activity is called "altruistic," a quality that is understandably suspect. Is there not hidden under the claim of self-effacement a devious and compulsive self-seeking? Caryl Houselander describes a woman of her acquaintance as "one of those people who lives for others, and you can always tell the others by the hunted look on their faces."

The church's impetus to reform the world cannot be altruistic. It has to come from a deep personal interiority and the experience of a compassionate community. One protests in the name of justice simply because one can do nothing else. The seeking for justice rather than being altruistic (the other instead of myself), is based on the dawning realization that the person I have thought of as "other"—the stranger, the alien, the outsider—is my brother, my sister, my self. If I start thinking of these "others" as objects needing to be fixed up or as means to my satisfaction and reputation, then it is time to step back from doing good and time to do nothing, except to recover the center from which good activity must flow.

CHURCH RELATED SCHOOLS

The parish's essential contribution to religious education is liturgical experience and its overflow into the struggle for justice. In the course of doing that well, there is plenty of room for intellectual reflection and understanding. As for teaching religion, most parishes are not particularly well-suited for the task. Teaching religion usually requires the trappings of a school. The catechetical instruction of adults and children is essential to the parish. A liturgical setting is the standard sign that catechesis is the issue. Conversely, catechesis is oriented toward liturgy and church life in general; its standard venue is not the classroom.

In August of 1986, the New York archdiocesan office noted in a memorandum to parishes that speakers should not be invited whose "public position is contrary to and in opposition to the clear, unambiguous teaching of the church." The memorandum took on exaggerated importance because of front page treatment in *The New York Times* and follow-up stories that ran for two weeks.[15] Actually, the memo (or more exactly, point twenty-one on the memo) was in all likelihood a routine statement of principle which would be difficult to disagree with at the level of principle. Of course, a rigid or selective application (e.g., applying to abortion but not to nuclear arms) could silence many people who have voiced criticism in regard to any church teaching. However, that an organization should not sponsor people who are working to destroy or undermine it is a fair enough principle. No one's right to speak is denied; just let some other organization pick up the tab. The parish, in contrast to a school, is not set up to handle strident controversy and academic debate.

The more worrisome kind of memo comes from church officials who do not seem to understand what a school is. Official documents often seem to be unaware of the difference between teaching from behind a pulpit and teaching in a classroom. The homilist comments on a New Testament text: "This is what we believe; let us put it into practice." A schoolteacher has a different set of assumptions, procedures, and expectations; certainly, the work is not to tell people what the truth is or tell them how to act. The schoolteacher's modest task is to explore what a text means and to help students to articulate their own convictions.

Is the purpose of a Catholic school to "form the faith" of Catholic children? Perhaps, but the teachers of religion in that school have to maintain the integrity of their own work. One cannot deny that Catholic schools were founded in great numbers because it was expected that such schools would give a well-rounded "Catholic education." All schools socialize students, provide an atmosphere, supply services other than classroom instruction. Catholic parents were willing, and many are still willing, to pay large tuition bills for a school with a religious atmosphere.

Insofar as religion is part of the school curriculum and is taught in the classroom, there is an academic standard it must meet. In the ASCD report "Religion in the Curriculum," discussed in chapter five, one of the recommendations is that educational organizations "explore ways to foster public support for the teaching of rigorous, intellectually demanding accounts of religion in society." The church-related school as well as the public school has to follow this ideal. The child who walks into the classroom of a church-related school has a right to expect not catechizing but "rigorous, intellectually demanding accounts of religion."[16]

The phrase that is often used in official Catholic documents is that teachers must present "what the church teaches." Clearly, that is what a preacher or catechist is supposed to do. Is that what a schoolteacher is to do? If the material is relevant to the topic of the day, the answer is yes. But presenting what "the church teaches" is a preliminary step in schoolteaching. The schoolteacher's questions are: What does the teaching mean? Where did it come from? What are its limitations? How is it changing? and dozens of similar questions. One should note here that "presenting what the (Roman Catholic) church teaches" can be relevant even in a school that is not Catholic. I have on occasion taken a large portion of class time to explore Catholic church teaching in a class that had no Catholics.

An increasing number of Catholic schools are having to think out this question anew. Some of these schools have faculties in which the Catholic teachers are a minority. More to the heart of the issue is the existence of Catholic schools in which a large minority of the students are not

Catholic. A good test of whether religion is being taught to Catholic students is whether the class is appropriate for non-Catholic students. If the school has to exempt the non-Catholic students from religion class, that would be an admission that what is going on in those classes is something other than the instruction proper to a classroom. In actual fact, however, many Catholic schools are able to admit non-Catholic students into both school and religion class without a drastic change. I know of Catholic schools with Protestant, Jewish, and Muslim students in which no one finds it incongruent that a course on religion is required of everyone. The non-Catholic students and their parents generally like the religion teaching, because it really is religion teaching and not an attempt to catechize prospective converts.

The "Catholic school" has in fact become several varieties of Catholic schools. It is even not absurd to imagine a Catholic school in which there are no Catholic students. A legitimate part of the church's mission and witness is to run a good educational institution for anybody who needs educating. Such activity does not require novel justification. Throughout the centuries part of the church's vocation has been to provide needed institutional help. The church started hospitals, supported theaters, ran schools. The educational intent is to influence the world for the better. With its limited resources, the church has to gauge how it can best channel its efforts. The church still sponsors some hospitals, but it has to choose where such institutions make economic and religious sense. A church might, for example, turn its attention to specialized hospitals (or hospices) for the terminally ill. The church might also sponsor specialized schools, for example in poor urban districts where students need intellectual challenge.

It is difficult to imagine a parish having the resources to run a hospital or to sponsor a modern-day high school or a university. Even an elementary school that can serve most of the parish's children at reasonable cost is often not possible. Some parishes are trying imaginative ways to run schools, usually inviting the contributed services of religious orders and parishioners. It may take another generation before it is clear what can survive and educationally should survive from the massive change in the Catholic school system that began in the 1960s. Perhaps there will be no parish-based schools, but undoubtedly there will be a need for church-related schools.

For the academic side of its life the church needs schools. The phrase "church-related school" is better indicative of the appropriate distinction than the phrase "church school." The latter is likely to suggest only the Sunday school and the seminary. The old-time Sunday school has been in trouble for a long time. What is done with children on Sunday morning either needs the context of a real school or else it should not be called school at all. The original Sunday school in England did in fact provide a wider school context. The U.S. Sunday school became too isolated in the nineteenth century. What it has needed in the twentieth century is either closer integration with parish life or else movement in the opposite direction: to a greater distance from the parish where it can become truly a school.

The theological seminary has the practical aim of preparing ministers for the church. It justifies itself as a professional school, in the same category as a law or medical school. It speaks the language of Christian theology much like those other schools speak law or medicine. A broad base of schooling in the arts and sciences is presupposed in such schools; the student is now preparing for specialized professional work.

In the use of church language, there is a tendency for the theological seminary to become the model for church-related schools. That is, Christian theology is assumed to be the language for addressing religious questions. Few people familiar with the history of Christian theology would deny that it contains fascinating material. Modern theological systems like those of Barth or Rahner can be challenging to anyone's understanding. Nevertheless, the student who walks into a religion classroom of a church-related college, is not necessarily interested in the particular language of theology.

The problem here is made acute by the way official

Catholic documents use theology as their instructional language. The mode is properly homiletic if the document is addressed to Roman Catholics. Theology, along with the Bible, fits well here. But just as the Bible can be a book to pray from ("the inspired word of G-d") and also a text that can be critically examined in search of "rigorous, intellectually demanding accounts of religion," so theology can be a homiletic and catechetical instrument or it can be studied as a Christian form of religious language. Interestingly, academic approaches to the Bible seem clearer on this point than academic approaches to theology.

The first step is to place theology in a department of religion or religious studies. For its own intellectual good, theology needs a context of comparison with other religious languages. This is most likely to happen only if seminaries are located in the midst of university life. As for church-related colleges, most of them had theology departments until the 1960s. Under the pressure of losing some tax benefits, most of these colleges changed their departments to religious studies. To most educational boards and legislators in the U.S., the word "theology" connotes sectarian indoctrination. In the U.K. the term "theology" retains a wider meaning, but it could still use the partnership with religious studies.

In the U.S. the pressure to form departments of religious studies in church-related colleges was on the whole educationally helpful. However, if one goes a step further and tries to remove theology courses, then one is interfering with the particularity which is appropriate to a particular group. I once had to write a letter to the state board of regents to explain a course called "philosophical theology" in our private school curriculum. In a course listing of about forty items, one course had the word "theology" in it which was enough to suggest to the state board that the students were seminarians and therefore ineligible for state loans.

Outside of very narrow boundaries, theology does not have much currency in the U.S. Aggressively reestablishing theology departments would be counter-productive. More in the opposite direction, theology needs to be in dialogical situations, at least in dialogue with other religious languages. The presumptuous word "theology" was coined by Aristotle and taken over by the Christian church. This one form of discourse tended to absorb other Christian ways of speaking; in time it became the name for the whole academic discipline when Christianity reigned in Western culture.

In today's world, Jews sometimes use the term "theology," but it is not at the center of Jewish language. Theology tends to be the Christian language. It cannot solve its problem of seeming to claim too much (words from or about G-d) by working more diligently in isolation and constructing grander systems. It needs help from its friends or potential friends in the academic world where every statement is open to challenge, criticism, and reformulation. One can schoolteach theology only by teaching it as religion.

Catholic church officials sometimes do not like what is said in religion classes that are within the church-related school. However, if they try to suppress what they call "dissent," they will only succeed in educationally undermining the school. Any schoolteacher who is minimally competent knows that you do not teach dissent. You teach the subject matter; you teach the students to think; you teach on the basis of evidence. "Orthodoxy" and "heresy" are homiletic terms or terms of theology used homiletically; in the religion classroom of any school, both words are simply irrelevant.

PARISH AS SCHOOL OF RELIGION?

The question posed in the title of this chapter is "Does religion belong in the parish?" My answer has been that although it surely belongs in the church it might not fit in the church parish. The teaching of religion can begin in elementary and secondary school; however, the full range of inquiry into this academic discipline emerges at college and university level. No parish today would try to run its own college but many parishes do try to offer something comparable to college courses on religion for adults in the parish. I think there is considerable confusion about such offerings. More than twenty years of experiencing such programs makes me wonder whether the preconditions are there for effective education.

I repeat that the parish can and should deal with the catechetical as a form of speech. It is a way of educating that can be located in a classroom but has never flourished there. Pre-Cana instruction before marriage, a Bible study group or a refresher course on Catholic doctrine do not usually pose a problem. Particular points of the teaching may cause conflict, but the form of the education is clear enough.

It is different when the parish tries to offer a course or a series of lectures, typically a four to eight week program held once a week for about two hours. The form resembles a college course with a shortened semester. However, the parishioners often come with extreme variations in what they expect out of the course. At the end of the course it often happens that some people are frustrated by getting only a taste of what they wanted and some people are confused because much of what was said conflicts with what they had expected.

The problem is greatly ameliorated if the parish offers a continuing school; those who want more can go back for another course and those who are simply confused may eventually get help. Unfortunately, many parishes offer such programs for four Tuesdays in October or six Wednesdays in Lent; then school closes down. It seems to me that if a parish wishes to engage in school for adults, it has to take on the project seriously. It has to think of its school as permanent even if it is not always in session. It should not say: We will run courses and then decide whether to have more courses. That is not the way a school runs.

I think there are parishes that have the resources to offer academic courses in religion. A parish considering whether it should try to do so might ask questions such as the following: 1. Can we hire at the going university rate an "adjunct professor" for a minimum of a year? 2. Do we have clearly in mind the level of course and the kind of material that will be read and discussed? 3. Is it clear to everyone—clergy, parishioners taking the course, parishioners not taking the course—that the course is not an explanation of Catholic doctrine but rather a study of some facet of religion? 4. Is there some plan concerning what is to follow the first course or round of courses?

Should a parish be spending its resources this way? That is up to the parish to decide. My guess is that in most parishes a proposal of this kind would be turned down. Nevertheless, the discussion of such a proposal might be worthwhile. People might more clearly distinguish between a homiletic mode which does belong in a parish and a mode of religious instruction that may not fit the parish.

But if not here, where? How can the parish serve those who wish to have such academic study? One could reply that this is not the concern of the parish, but I think parishes are not entirely off base in trying to deal with parishioner interest in the study of religion. Several parishes joining their resources might be able to provide the needed conditions; a diocese or regional body would have more resources, but it might also have more difficulty in accepting the academic nature of the enterprise. That, of course, leads back to the reason why colleges and universities exist with their tradition of academic freedom. At the least, a parish should be a place where information is easily available concerning college-level courses in the immediate area. A further step would be providing financial help for some parishioners to attend such courses, an idea I return to in discussing professionalization (chapter eight).

It must be emphasized that the desire for intellectually challenging courses on religion is not the whim of an intellectual elite or the tool of a subversive minority. Neither the Roman Catholic church nor any religious body today can rely upon children acquiring what they need to know and then being content with homilies. One can hope that church officials will gradually come to see that schools necessarily question such things as pronouncements from church offices. The intention of the questioner is usually not hostile. The long-term health of the church requires reverent and open-ended exploration of people's religious questions. Occasionally that leads some people to leave the church, but that is certainly a risk worth taking today. A knowledgeable and free congregation of Christians is presumably the desired ideal.

NOTES

1. Michael Grimmit, *Religious Education and Human Development* (Great Wakering, England: McCrimmon, 1987), p. 258.

2. See, David Leege and Joseph Gremillion, *The U.S. Parish Twenty Years after Vatican II*, Notre Dame Study of Parish Life, report #1, Notre Dame, Ind. (December 1984), pp. 1-7.

3. See, Vincent Donovan, *Christianity Rediscovered* (Notre Dame, Ind.: Fides, 1978).

4. Eric Havelock, *Preface to Plato* (Cambridge, Mass.: Harvard University Press, 1963), p. 291.

5. George Albert Coe, *What is Christian Education?* (New York: Scribner, 1929), p. 29.

6. George Albert Coe, *A Social Theory of Religious Education* (New York: Scribner, 1920), p. 181.

7. *The Cloud of Unknowing*, trans. Ira Progoff (New York: Delta, 1957), pp. 134-135.

8. For a Protestant treatment of the sacraments in religious education, see, Robert Browning and Roy Reed, *The Sacraments in Religious Education and Liturgy* (Birmingham, Ala.: Religious Education Press, 1985).

9. Reinhold Niebuhr, "A View from the Pew," *Christian Century*, December 19, 1984, p. 1197.

10. See, James Dunning, *New Wine, New Wine Skins* (New York: Sadlier, 1981).

11. Judah Goldin, ed., *The Living Talmud* (Chicago: University of Chicago Press, 1957), p. 230.

12. Flannery O'Connor, *The Habit of Being* (New York: Farrar, Straus and Giroux, 1979), p. 348.

13. See, Jaroslav Pelikan, *Jesus through the Centuries* (New Haven: Yale University Press, 1985), p. 87.

14. See, Maria Harris, *Fashion Me a People: Curriculum and the Church* (Philadelphia: Westminster, 1989), chapter 8.

15. *New York Times*, August 22, 1986, p. 1.

16. *Religion in the Curriculum*, p. 36.

7

Is Religious Education Moral?

This chapter takes up the question of "moral education" which most people view as closely related to religious education. Indeed, the words "closely related" are not strong enough. In some places, moral education has been located within religious education. In other places, religious education is thought to be part of moral education. There is no agreed upon logic to discuss this relation. I do not claim to have any simple formula that will clear up this confusion. However, I think that some of the distinctions introduced earlier in this book can throw some light on moral education in its relation to religion and religious education.

It hardly needs saying that the issue of moral education is one of practical urgency. People generally uninterested in religious education perk up when the moral aspect is raised. The press, the television, experts on society, not to mention right-wing preachers, talk about a moral crisis. No one is sure that human beings on the average are more immoral today than they were in the past. But the interconnectedness of today's actions, the reverberation of an evil act across a continent can magnify the effects of moral acts. Telling people to be good or threatening them with punishment if they are not seems less and less effective, in part because there is little agreement about what "good" means. One person's terrorist activity is another person's act of national liberation; one woman's right to choice about her pregnancy is another woman's horror at murder.

No doubt there have always been disagreements on the fine points of the law. That is why there are courts of appeal in the legal system today and why religions developed talmudic commentary and jesuitical casuistry. Our problem today seems to be more deeply rooted, a confusion about what to talk about as morality and how to talk about it. I agree with Isaiah Berlin that "one should be able to distinguish between good, bad, and downright awful," and yet that often is not happening. Allan Bloom says that when he asks college students today "What is evil?" the only response they can come up with is: "Hitler." And since Hitler was obviously an aberration, one need not pursue the question of evil.[1] The students have been taught to believe that every question has two sides, that everyone has a right to his or her opinion, and that no one should judge another's moral actions. The word that Bloom uses to describe today's college students is "nice." That may be damning with faint praise, but the students are trying to get along the best they can in a world infested with drugs, AIDS, nuclear arms, and a volatile economy under the control of no one.

When one turns from the confusion of youngsters to the expert opinion of their elders, the level of debate about morality and moral education often leaves much to be desired. Take, for example, an exchange between the then U.S. Secretary of Education and the President of Harvard University. At a Harvard symposium, Secretary William Bennett began the volley by saying that if students happened to get a good education at Harvard "it is a matter of chance." President Derek Bok said that Bennett had not noticed changes under way such as Harvard's requirement that students take courses in moral reasoning. Bennett replied that courses in moral reasoning are not the same as moral education. "That's about dilemmas, lifeboat stuff. I don't mean theory. I mean getting drugs off campus." Bennett's comments drew hisses from the audience. In response to a question from a student as to whose morality they should be learning, Bennett said: "Most people agree on what's right or wrong."[2]

This exchange is unfortunately all too typical of discussions about morality and moral education. William Bennett knows that he is playing the reactionary in this debate, but he is confident that he has popular sentiment on his side. Most people think that a moral education should turn out moral people, which means not people who reason well but people whose behavior is moral. Neither Harvard nor any other school can guarantee that their graduates will be people who morally behave. Bennett can therefore punch holes in the claims of moral education, but his own conclusion that "most people agree on what's right or wrong," could suggest that there is no need to study moral issues.

THE RISE OF MORAL EDUCATION

The twentieth century has been the century of moral education. Like the term "religious education," the words "moral" and "education" had existed for centuries and sometimes found themselves next to each other. However, people did not think of "moral education" as a well-defined world within which scholars offer theories on how best to do "it" and doctoral candidates do research on whether "it" is succeeding. One emerging tradition of moral education cast the question in social terms; a second and eventually stronger tradition spoke psychological language.

Whether the emphasis was sociological or psychological, inherent to the rise of a field called moral education was a distrust of religion. The distrust has sometimes meant an attack on religion as an immoral fraud or, sometimes more benignly, a doubt about religion's continuing effectiveness as a motivator of moral actions. Certainly, from the seventeenth century onward, Western philosophers and scientists thought that morality should not be based on religion. They thought that morality could and should be derived from reason alone. Nonetheless, they acknowledged that some people are not capable of such reasoning; fortunately, for those people, wrote John Locke, "there needs no more but to read the inspired books to be instructed; all the duties of morality lie there clear, and plain, and easy to understand."[3] While a totally secular morality was still getting on its feet, the help of religion as a motivator of the masses was gratefully accepted. As Voltaire cynically phrased it: "I want my steward, tailor, and valets to believe in God; I imagine that then I'm less likely to be robbed."[4]

By the beginning of the twentieth century, it was believed that the reasonable basis of morality was stronger and that the effectiveness of religion was weaker. It was time for a strictly moral education to be launched. The tone and direction are well captured in Emile Durkheim's announcement at the beginning of his *Moral Education* in 1903: "We decided to give our children in our state-supported schools a purely secular moral education. It is essential to understand that this means an education that is not derived from revealed religion but that rests exclusively on ideas, sentiments, and practices accountable to reason only—in short, a purely rationalistic education."[5] Later theorists of moral education, such as Jean Piaget and Lawrence Kohlberg, are equally insistent on distancing themselves from "revealed religion."

I think that the project to have a distinct field of moral education is a desirable one. Moral education is not simply a subdivision of religious education; even less should it be conceived of as being under ecclesiastical or theological control. However, one does not get a divorce by merely announcing the separation. The obstacle to an autonomous moral education is not religion or religious education so much as the particular language of the discussion and its institutional control. By announcing total and immediate separation from religion, moral educators leave behind a whole area of life, and yet there is no guarantee that the assumptions of a Christian theology have been eliminated.

I was at a meeting for parents one evening at a suburban public high school. It was the first meeting to explain the moral education program being introduced in the school. The speaker gave an excellent presentation of the need for moral education, and he went over the works that would be read by the high-school students, starting with the trial of Socrates. After the talk, he asked for questions and when the first hand went up I correctly guessed what the woman's question was: "What has this program got to do with religion?" I knew what the speaker's answer would be, but I hoped that he would agonize a bit on his feet and take the question seriously. Instead, his answer was: "None at all. This moral education has nothing to do with religion."

It seems to me that for that woman, for her sophomore son, and for everyone else in the hall, not excluding the speaker, morality and religion are always related. At least since Amos came down from the mountain denouncing injustice almost three thousand years ago, Jewish and Christian religions have been immersed in the morality of Western culture. If moral education is going to get at the real life and the whole life of the student, the existing relation of morality and religion cannot be denied. If the relation is acknowledged, then one can begin to draw some careful distinctions.

In concerns of morality—warfare, economic oppression, medical technology, abortion, and almost any moral issue one can name—religion has had a lot to do with the way the question is posed. Neither teacher nor student can step outside of that history. What they might be able to do, one case at a time, is to distinguish between religion as a presumed source of answers and religion as a rich field of experience. If one does not make such a distinction and goes down the route that Durkheim announced, the only alternative to his "revealed religion" is "a purely rationalistic education." Moral education on that basis can mean picking over the dry bones of philosophical rationalism.

Moral education and religious education deserve to be close to one another, distinguished from but related to each other. Some of the material in religious education could show up in a discussion of moral education. And religious education should have reverberations in the moral formation of people. Of course, I am not referring here to religious education and moral education as things taught to youngsters in school. Moral education and religious education are lifelong processes that involve the whole person. Both of them concern the body, the emotions, external activity, the formation of character, and the dedication of a lifetime. Only a small part of either religious or moral education can be provided to youngsters in school.

The main task of the school in religious education is to teach religion. I think that one can best describe the school's main contribution to moral education as the teaching of ethics. The term "ethics" has a long and honorable history. It refers to a branch of philosophy in which one thinks about issues of moral practice. Students in elementary school do not need a separate course called ethics. However, as soon as a child can think about right and wrong, good and bad, it is not too early to have ethical discussions as the need arises. In schools, discussion of ethical issues may be needed within the study of history, social science, art, religion, and the rest. Like religion, ethics as a systematic course of study belongs in the later years of secondary school, college, and professional school. The push these days to introduce ethics into business, law, and medical schools would be more encouraging if the subject were not so completely neglected previous to graduate school.

The school does in fact convey some moral education, whether or not it teaches ethics in the classroom. Even more clearly than in the parallel case of religious education, schools are always acting morally or immorally. Every written and unwritten rule in the school implies an attitude toward the student's dignity and selfhood. How children line up for the bus, eat in the cafeteria, get permission to use the toilet, and get spoken to over the public address system have an effect on the student's (and the teacher's) moral sense. If the school cannot teach the student to act morally, it can at least refrain from violating the developing moral sentiments of the young person.

The school ought to be properly modest about its part in moral education. If society were to transfer the guardianship of morality from the clergy to the professors, that would at best be a small improvement. Schoolteachers do not know how students are supposed to turn out; what the teacher can do is help students to think about the differences between "the good, the bad, and the downright awful." That is not much, but in these times it can be a crucial contribution to the moral education of young people.

I find scary this statement near the beginning of Bloom's *The Closing of the American Mind:* "Every educational system has a moral goal that it tries to attain and that informs its curriculum. It wants to produce a certain kind of human being."[6] The first sentence is not bad; insofar as education is a reshaping "with end," then one can say that there is always some goal at stake in every form of education. However, Bloom's conclusion in the second sentence could have frightening implications if school staffs thought that they had license "to produce a certain kind of human being."

I find more encouraging Theodore Sizer's description of the high school's modest part in moral education. Sizer says that the school's moral concern should be "decency," a term that captures the demand that human beings be treated with respect and dignity.[7] The school's teaching of ethics is not going to make much impression in an atmosphere of indecency. The school's staff need not spend their time examining how each rule will teach a particular virtue. It is enough to clear the atmosphere of flagrant violations of decency and then let the administrators minister and the teachers teach.

About every two months, *The New York Times* headlines a story: " 'X says that we should teach values to our children." The 'X' might be anyone from the president of the United States or the pope to the local head of the school board or the latest commission on some social problem. So why does it not happen? Probably because no one knows how to do it. The phrase "teaching values" is a particularly vacuous way to address the burning moral issues of the day. Hardly anyone attacks the teaching of values because it does not actually touch any real activities in the public arena.

I say "hardly anyone" disagrees because there have been court suits brought against the "values" language of some textbooks. In one Alabama case, a book entitled *Homemaking: Skills for Everyday Living* was attacked as un-Christian for saying: "Values are personal and subjective. They vary from person to person. You will be able to understand and get along with other people better if you keep an open mind about the value judgments they make."[8] The right-wing Christian group that brought suit was the butt of ridicule for objecting to such passages. I think that the group was wrong in trying censorship; however, they were not wrong in being upset at such vapid advice being given to youngsters in the context of school where intelligent discussion is called for.

The passage begins with the assertion that "values are personal and subjective." One has to admit that this is usually true—by definition. Value is the standard modern word for locating ethical issues in the inner recesses of each individual's mind. It creates instantaneous tolerance, or at least the demand for tolerance, as the rest of the passage demonstrates. Morality is put beyond the realm of discussion; everybody "makes his or her value judgment" and no one can say that he or she is wrong.

What is clear about the whole passage is that it is based upon the subjective values of the textbook maker and the nineteenth-century philosophy which underlies this language. If that bias were acknowledged, perhaps there would be less of a preachy tone in such passages. Right-wing Christian groups accurately perceive that what is preached in this textbook conflicts with what they are preaching.

One cannot actually have academic instruction on values. Since they are personal and subjective, the schoolteacher has nothing to examine. The verb that often accompanies the word "value" is "to clarify." In recent years students were asked to list their values and "to prioritize" them; but the teacher was warned against trying to teach values. Some of the discussion that went on in this context may have helped students to understand real moral issues. For the most part, however, debate on real problems and advocacy of one position as morally better than another were discouraged.

Ironically, the form of discourse that sneaks in with value talk is the homiletic. If people cannot intelligently advocate a moral position, they are eventually forced into preaching. While being told in textbooks that values are personal and subjective, young people are preached at endlessly. The messages that are preached contradict one another: incitements to sex, selfishness, and greed are overlaid with pious admonitions to live like a monk. And when the sermons fail, society goes to external restraints and punishment as the final resort. Lawrence Kohlberg shocked his followers in the late 1970s when he wrote a brief essay on the fact that his moral education seemed to have little success with some youngsters.[9] Kohlberg expressed consternation that little boys still lie and cheat. After twenty years of ridiculing religions for indoctrinating their followers, Kohlberg said a little indoctrinating might not be a bad thing.

The moral education that flees from what are supposedly the terrible tactics of religion—preaching, discipline, indoctrination—invariably ends by having to adopt some of these tactics. No major religion in human history has ever failed to notice that people lie and cheat. Neither has any religion thought that "clarifying values" is an adequate moral education. Religions do not suddenly import new rules and methods to shore up unrealistic moral techniques. Religions are nothing if not painfully aware of the moral failings of human beings and the need to confront moral deficiencies in a thoroughly realistic way.

The field of moral education is still at an early stage of development. Like religious education, it is still threatened by an illogical reduction to a course in a classroom or some particular technique. The base needs to be broader both in regard to *how* one teaches morality and also *what* constitutes morality. Moral education's headlong flight from religion cuts it off from a major source of material on both counts. For illustrating the fruitful relation that should exist between religious education and moral education, I turn to these two questions: What does the religious experience of centuries have to offer regarding *how* to teach morality? What does that same experience have to say about the *what* of moral education?

HOW TO TEACH MORALITY

Across the major religions of the world there is great diversity in their rituals and practices. And yet, what strikes me about the manner of teaching is the remarkable similarity that one finds in these diverse systems. Not all the major religions fit perfectly the characteristics I enumerate, but all of them have some of the flavor and the general direction of this description.

1) *The Teacher.* There is, first of all, the teacher; not just a teacher hired to do a job, but the leader, the guru, the master, whose life is an inspiration. Very often there is no greater title bestowed upon the founder of a religious community than: teacher. A religion like Hinduism may not have a single, great teacher as the fount of all, but great teachers have arisen within the tradition. In some traditions, such as Judaism, teacher is just about all. Moses was the great teacher and Jewish history is the story of teachers ever since. In Christianity, Jesus of Nazareth arose as a teacher; "rabbi" is the least controversial title applied to him in the New Testament. As can happen in any religious tradition this utterly central characteristic became obscured by polemics. "To the Christian disciples of the first century the conception of Jesus as a rabbi was self-evident, to the Christians of the second century it was embarrassing, to the Christian disciples of the third century and beyond, it was obscure."[10]

One of the most striking things about religious teachers is that they appeal to something given in the workings of the universe. In Eastern religion, that is usually to some suprapersonal law that governs all life, such as *karma.* In the West, it is usually to God's will written in the very nature of things. Not that facts, reasoning, and demonstrations are cast aside; it is simply that the ultimate source of authority is beyond human control. The teacher is not the source of the authority; he or she is an embodiment of that authority. Without constantly calling people's attention to it, his or her person becomes an extraordinary source of inspiration to sustain people in bad times. Gorky said of Tolstoy: "As long as this man is alive, I am not alone in the world." The same thing can be said of every great religious teacher. They convince not by their arguments so much as by their presence.

2) *A Few Disciples.* The religious teacher provides moral

guidance to a small community. Seemingly in disregard of all the world's great problems waiting to be solved, the focus is on the daily life of a handful of people. A few disciples (students) gather around the master and share a way of life. One of the major studies of religious conversion describes this phenomenon as "coming to accept the opinion of one's friends." That is not bad for a sociological description of conversion. A person joins a community, participates in the activities of the group, and gradually comes to see the world in the way the community does. The teachings or doctrines are acquired more by osmosis than by indoctrination.

So-called "cults" in the United States strike terror in the hearts of rationalistic leaders. These religious groups are accused of all sorts of brainwashing techniques and coercive restraints. Although these things occasionally are used, the success of religious communities has a much simpler explanation. Intelligent and goodwilled young people, who feel themselves to be in a morally rudderless world, encounter religious groups who live with a clear, consistent, and cohesive pattern. The initial attractiveness is confirmed by just a few days of immediate experience. As many people discovered in the 1960s, the "experience of community" can be intoxicating. Of course, if one tries to live in a tightly knit community for months, years, and decades, one runs into some very bad days when one would prefer to be somewhere else.

Within a religious community, the homiletic mode is the standard form of teaching. The master or guru gives very direct instructions to the community. What modern scholars often miss, however, is that the preaching is always a secondary element. It is commentary on how to live out the way of life already being lived. The preaching is directed toward those who have already agreed to live within this covenant or brother/sisterhood. St. Paul did not address the world at large; he told the folks at Corinth or Galatia exactly how they should act—given the fact that they had already agreed to live in the Christian community.

3) *Living within a Discipline.* Religions teach morality by the imposition of rituals that at first glance have nothing to

do with morality. What do the time of rising in the morning, the food one eats, or the clothes one wears have to do with the great moral issues of the world? "Discipline" means teaching, and it is still used in the academic world today for an area of teaching. However, the modern world more often thinks of discipline as harsh restrictions or external punishment.

If one asks non-Catholic parents in urban ghettos why they send their children to Catholic schools, the most frequent reply is: discipline. Are these parents simplistic in thinking that strict rules and frequent punishment will save their children, or do these parents correctly sense that discipline as teaching is necessarily connected to discipline as a well-regulated way of life? Their thinking may be a little simplistic, but what they know with certainty is that without moral discipline, achieved in one way or another, their children will make a mess of their lives.

Often there is an unrealistic burden placed on the school and its teachers to deliver this discipline. In religion, discipline comes out of community experience and the thousand daily rituals that weave the fabric of community relations: respect, care, compassion, courtesy, gratitude, patience. Eventually the moral life may require heroic courage and magnificent love, but most religions let those moments come as they may. If one observes all the little virtues, the big ones will be there when they are called for.

Religion is regularly accused of being "legalistic" because it insists on obedience to the rules even when there seems no point to the observance beyond the rules. Liberal Christianity often sides with modern experts who think that we should act only from motives of love and that we should get rid of all rules whose usefulness to us is not obvious. But long before Freud and Jung helped to clarify this question, religions recognized that we are the seat of competing forces, that we regularly flimflam ourselves about what is good for us, and that we need routines, fixed rules of conduct, to protect us from forces that are part of us and are too strong for the center to cope with.

4) *Toward the Unity of Self and Cosmos.* Despite the prominence of rules, religions view morality as going beyond

rules of behavior. Religions move beyond obeying rules not in the sense of being concerned with motives so much as looking at the direction of human actions. The human search for a unity is played against a backdrop of a cosmic fissure. The humans will find rightness only when the universe is healed.

What dominates modern ethics are rights of the individual and equality of treatment. Religions offer a necessary reminder that human beings are not the only individuals that have rights. Each thing in the universe has some right to be itself by the fact that it exists. The word "right" is used here in a simpler, more common sense meaning than the legal concept of "right." It is right that things are, that they stand in relation to all the other things that constitute a universe. The only alternative is to think that human beings know what is right, are smart enough to know how the universe should be arranged.

Equality is the category that has become an obsession in the modern world. It is a word that best belongs in mathematics where the negation of qualitative differences (e-qual) is appropriate. Equality as the bearer of all moral consideration leaves much to be desired.[11] As directed toward all human individuals, it is a legitimate beginning; insofar as an individual is human, he or she calls forth a certain level of respect and appreciation. But the moral life is mainly one of "discriminating," that is, of perceiving differences between human beings and nonhuman beings (who deserve another kind of respect and appreciation), among the particular human beings who call forth a wide range of response depending on whether the person is parent, spouse, child, friend, stranger. Every human and nonhuman being equally deserves that we should care, but only the precise context can specify how.

The modern idea that justice is the supreme ideal and that justice means "to treat each man equally" is a terribly truncated view. The sexual bias in the phrase is no accident, but adding the word "woman" is barely an advance in this idea. The human beings have to discover their relation to everything else and to realize that we are all of a unity. Either there is cosmic unity or there are no whole

human beings. Justice, in the Hebrew Bible, is a reconciling unity; the world will be redeemed by the everyday
deeds of men and women who recognize that they are a
microcosm of the universe.[12] Eastern religions have their
own variations on healing or reconciling; they, too, never
separate the moral activity of human beings from the great
drama of the cosmos.

5) *Moral Education is Lifelong.* Religions are very realistic
in understanding that moral education begins at birth, if
not earlier, and continues at least until the last breath.
Moral education does not begin when the child is able to
discuss dilemmas and clarify values. The infant's life is
shaped morally by the whole physical and social environment. Piaget called the young child "pre-moral" because
the child cannot yet handle certain concepts, like equality.
However, moral education for young children has to do
with the care they receive and the cultivation of moral
sentiment.

The child's sense of unity with the nonhuman world
should not be dismissed as magical. For example, some
children object to eating meat on the ground that animals
are not for eating. Is the child's attitude here merely primitive or could it be postmodern moral thinking? Often, a
child with the barest of conceptual apparatus is capable of
profound moral insight. Frederick Douglass writes in his
autobiography: "I was just as well-aware of the unjust,
unnatural, and murderous character of slavery when nine
years old as I am now. Without appeal to books, to laws or
to authorities of any kind, I knew to regard God as 'Our
Father' condemned slavery as a crime."[13]

The religious reference in Douglass's statement is hardly
an accident. The stark, simple clarity of the slave's perception is not likely to arise from the kind of exercise that the
twentieth century has equated with moral education.
There, only the bare bones of the child's capacity to compare concepts is attended to. Of course, if the whole point
of moral education is to get children to see the value of
equality, then the nearly exclusive concern with a logical
kind of thinking may be justified. If in contrast the point is

action for a reconciling unity, then what is commonly called moral education is only one small step along the way. To Piaget's credit, he did recognize that there was a whole world of moral language that went beyond his studies of pre-teenage children. When the child discovers that equality does not govern the world, where does he or she turn? Perhaps, speculated Piaget, to a sense of morality in which terms like care and compassion are prominent.[14]

One of the clearest points of conflict between religion and modern theories of moral education is the question of "backsliding." According to Kohlberg's theory, progress is "hierarchical, sequential, invariant." One needs elaborate explanations for any seeming regression. Once gained, the "higher" stage is secure forever. If one can reason at stage four, one will not return to stage two. The accuracy of this claim only reveals the gap between what passes for progress in modern moral education and the contention of religions, supplemented by overwhelming evidence, that people sometimes regress morally. People whose lives had been admirable become corrupted by power or money or pride.

Religions constantly warn that the greatest enemy of the moral life is complacency with one's virtuous achievement. Maimonides speaks for more than just the Jewish tradition when he says; "Let him not be overconfident and say: 'This virtue I have already mastered successfully, it can never leave me.' There is always the possibility it may."[15]

What should be particularly noted here is not merely the need for continuing improvement. There is a bigger paradox that is captured in religion and is embodied in the world's great dramatic tragedies. The great person can be brought down by a moral flaw. The most virtuous are the most in danger of moral disaster. "The more excellent the man," writes Thomas Aquinas, "the graver the sin."[16] The moral life is not a question of getting better ideas; it requires a kind of "conversion," a reversal of the attempt to make ourselves better, an acknowledgement that we are permanently vulnerable to self-deception, which is why we need teacher, community, discipline, and acts of reconciliation.

THE SEARCH FOR WHAT TO TEACH

I turn to the second of my questions: *What* is the morality that needs teaching? In describing *how* religions teach morality I have already covered much of the ground. That is because part of their effectiveness in how they teach is that they never entirely separate the how and the what.

In summing up this what of morality according to religion, my interest is not to convince people to accept religion. Rather, it is to call attention to the moral substance that most religions converge upon. Moral education in fleeing from religion cuts itself off from its roots in an everyday sense of what is right and wrong. I would not endorse without reservation the William Bennett statement at the beginning of this chapter: "Most people agree on what's right or wrong." The statement can easily be interpreted in an anti-intellectual way ("there is no need to think about these things") or as a reduction of morality to public opinion polls ("whatever most people agree upon, that's what is right"). Religion can unwittingly give support to the first of these interpretations with its own brand of anti-intellectualism. But religions would be extremely suspicious of the second, that is, public opinion polls on morality. A majority of people in one place at one time can be dead wrong about morality. Lynch mobs have a total consensus; voting majorities in some countries can be, in the longer sight of history, morally obtuse.

Religions, nonetheless, do lend support to the belief that "most people agree on what's right or wrong." At least, if people could get in touch with a real self, if they could penetrate the shell of illusion they have built, they would find deep down a sense of good and evil. People feel guilty, and rightly so, when they fail to live according to their sense of what is right and good. To be conscious is to have a conscience, even if its workings can be almost entirely blocked out of mind.

Philosophers, such as John Locke who thought that religion is morality for the masses, were not far off. Philosophers understandably develop complicated theories of philosophical ethics. But morality, like religion, lives in the practice of ordinary people. The foundation of morality has to be uncomplicated and immediate. The fragile human being, vulnerable to being crippled or annihilated at any moment, works from primitive signals of good and evil. "The food smells rotten, don't eat; the stove is hot, don't touch; the night is cold, bundle up." Whatever the meaning of "morally good," it cannot be completely at odds with these basic perceptions.

In the attempt to establish rational certainty, modern philosophy has carried out a dangerous escape from the organic world. The body is disparaged, an attitude, ironically enough, that is often attributed to religion. Although all religions have a disciplining of the body, the aim is usually to bring the warring members under governance from the center. That is different from neglecting the body. "If your eye lead you into sin, pluck it out," is a frightening saying which only the demented take literally. It is a far cry from "treat each man equally," something that lacks all moral passion and yet is still preachy. Treating each man equally is best analyzed and applied if the "man" is just an abstract agent of thought and choice.

Timothy Cooney's *Telling Right from Wrong* is a novel attempt to cut through modern ethics to the ultimate basis of morality. If the author were not so bitterly antireligious he could have devised a stronger case. I do think, however, that his criticism of the basis of modern ethics is persuasive. The seventeenth-century philosopher, Descartes, set much of the direction for what followed in history by his method of systematic doubt. He came finally to his one certainty: "I think, therefore I am." Cooney suggests that if Descartes had stayed at his task for six or seven more hours on that day in 1620, he might have discovered a different truth: "What I know most certain is: I'm hungry." And then the second truth would have been: "I can satisfy the hunger with food."[17] Cooney argues that good and bad do not arise later in the philosophic quest. The good is implicit in our first judgment about to be and not to be. The ability to satisfy at least some of our desires is our most certain link between mind and world.

Most of contemporary ethics goes through the imposing

figure of Immanuel Kant. Picking up the pieces from Descartes and his more immediate predecessors, Kant tried, as he put it, to establish a rational basis for the pious beliefs of his ancestors. Justice as equality became the secularized survival of Christianity; the golden rule reappeared as Kant's categorical imperative: Act in such a way that your action could be a universal guide of conduct. None of the sayings of Jesus is more often quoted than the golden rule: "Do unto others as you would have them do unto you." It is one of the least original lines of Jesus, found in most religions. The Jewish version, attributed to Hillel is cast in a negative formula: "What is hateful to you, do not do to your neighbor."[18]

Placed at the very heart of a religious tradition, this rule of mutuality can be a helpful summary of the moral life. But like sayings out of the fourth gospel ("love one another") this golden rule can be a vapid formalism. Kant was still supported by the Christian inheritance that kept men and women at their ordinary tasks under the vault of heaven. Nietzsche rightly called Kant "the great delayer," the one who temporarily obscured the fact that the substance of moral thinking was no longer there. Given the growing confusion about what was good "in the nature of things," Kant simply bailed out and located the good in the human capacity to choose, or more exactly in the capacity to make things good by choosing. "It is impossible," writes Kant, "to conceive anything at all in the world, or even out of it, which can be taken as good without qualification, except a good will."[19]

This reduction of the good to the narrow confines of the human will is the amazing principle on which so much of philosophical ethics and moral education is erected. In Kohlberg's dilemmas it does not matter whether you think something is good or bad; what counts is your procedure for getting there. The seemingly neutral procedures are not exactly neutral in regard to what is judged to be a higher morality. Formal principles that lead to equality rank above any attempt to root morality in physical need, familial affection, or ecstatic delight.

The legacy that Kant left us is the long list of dichotomies that patter across the pages of ethics books: is versus ought, fact versus value, description versus prescription. Underneath these commonly cited oppositions is the less evident one: the human will versus an abstraction called "nature." There is no bridge for connecting these separate pieces, which is not to say that one must be content with them. It is constantly intoned that "you cannot derive an ought from an is"; but one need not try to do so if one's beginning point is not bare fact. A meal is neither a fact nor a value; it is a human good. So is a symphony, a mother's smile, a warm house on a cold evening. As for knowing what we ought not to do, murder, rape, or torture are not facts, they are recognizable evils.[20]

WHAT THE RELIGIONS TEACH

I come, then, to what I think is the ultimate foundation of morality from a religious view. As in *how* to teach, there is a remarkable convergence on *what* to teach, despite the great variations across religious traditions. There is a fundamental difference between religions, and that difference shows up almost immediately. Nonetheless, I venture to offer that most, if not all, of the world's religious traditions testify to the belief: "What is unnatural is immoral."

This moral statement is appropriately in the negative. Religions, despite the arrogance of some of their spokespersons, do not have a plan for how the universe should be arranged. They are much better at saying how we should not act. Not that religions are morally negative. As religions they are generally positive, celebrating what exists and praising what is good. But when it comes to moral *statements*, the clearest thing they say is: Don't destroy it. You don't own the world's goods, so pass them on unscathed.

Here is where the division of East and West quickly arises. While they agree on the immorality of destroying the texture of life on earth, they disagree about the efforts to transform the world, to alter fundamentally the relation of human animals to the rest of the cycle of living beings. The Eastern emphasis has been on conformity with nature.

The traditions of China, India, and Japan differ, but on this point they stand together in contrast to the West.

In Western culture, there developed an alternative to either "living in conformity with nature" or "acting unnaturally." There is a realm of the non-natural, the transforming of the natural that can be good if it does not involve the contortion, violation, and destruction that the term "unnatural" connotes. Can anyone be sure of the difference between the unnatural and the transformation of the natural? As individuals we can be blind to the reverberations of our actions. For example, it is difficult to believe that a can of hairspray is destructive of the ozone layer, which is indispensable to life on earth. What seems to be a harmless activity may in time be revealed as contrary to nature; conversely, what has in the past been thought to be contrary to nature is often revealed as an imaginative variation on human possibilities. Polluting a river is surely an unnatural act, even if our moral vocabulary lags behind. In contrast, homosexual love, it seems clear today, is a variation within the human condition and not something "contrary to nature."

There will always be disagreement about the limits of human action vis-á-vis the nonhuman world. At one end of the spectrum is the Jain monk who, based on the desire to avoid all harm and killing, refrains as far as possible from moving, digging, lighting, and bathing. The Jainas offer dramatic reminder to the rest of us; but short of us all becoming such monks, we must try to refrain from adding violence; after that, we can try to reduce violence by re-channeling the passions that lead to violence.[21]

The terms "natural/unnatural" used here do not refer to the abstraction "nature" that has been pitted against "man in modern science and technology." Men thought they were discovering the "laws of nature," scientific rules of activity for everything in the universe. This belief gave rise to a language whereby "man" is outside nature, defying nature; human activity was proclaimed to be unnatural. David Hume in the eighteenth century can say: "If I turn aside a stone which is falling upon my head, I disturb the course of nature."[22] Even at present, our language reflects this peculiar arrogance of thinking one knows enough about G-d and has sufficient power to interfere with some supposed plan of the universe.

Joseph Fletcher, in pushing a medical ethic that does not "leave things in God's hands," writes: "For the fact is that medicine itself is an interference with nature. It freely cooperates with or counteracts and foils nature to fulfill humanly chosen ends."[23] Contemporary medicine is painfully learning the lesson that it cannot "counteract or foil nature for humanly chosen ends." The trap here is the assumption that if one does not fight nature, then one must submit. But this warrior image is built on the huge fiction of Hume's "laws of nature." There are a lot of other images for the human being gently responding to all the other beings on earth and to the earth itself.

Religions have little to say about "the laws of nature." They have a lot to say about the law of natures, the respect due to each organism in its brief lifespan. Each nature— including each human nature—is born, grows, declines, and dies. Its nature is to occupy some place in a texture of life, whose complexity outstrips every human imagination. There are scientific facts to be discovered so we will know what helps and hinders each of the natures. But the search for factual information needs the context of a morality grounded in a religious appreciation of particular and concrete reality: this snowflake, that goldfish, these children who are my offspring, those friends from my childhood.

One of the great religious figures of Western history is Francis of Assisi, the unofficial patron saint of ecology. Those who think of Francis as a sentimental singer of hymns are not familiar with the harsh discipline that goes along with his words of love. Furthermore, as Chesterton notes in his lively biography of Francis, "He did not call nature his mother; he called a particular donkey his brother and a particular sparrow his sister."[24] A religious morality is not based on a love of nature but on a care for natures, for each organism in its uniqueness. That is the human vocation, one that cannot be abandoned in the name of an egalitarianism of the species.

In the ecological crisis that is upon us, Christianity (or

the abstraction "Judeo-Christian" tradition) is regularly thrashed for being the cause of our ecological problems.[25] Jewish and Christian religions do have to bear partial responsibility for the ecological mess. Christianity, in particular, did prepare the way for the ecological problem of recent times. But one should note that the ecological problem surfaced as Christianity's power receded. In the Christian scheme of things, "man" was at the center of creation, receiving power from G-d above. Unfortunately, it was all too easy for modern philosophy and science to take over this image and simply replace "G-d" with "man." If Christianity had resisted a sex-biased language, the relation of men, women, and nonhumans would have been imagined differently. The modern world could not then have simply replaced "G-d" with "man." I think that it is unlikely and perhaps undesirable that ecologists will start talking about "god." But ecologists badly need to rediscover the distinctive nature of human responsibility which Jews, Christians, and other religious people have understood. If writers in ecology were not so harshly anti-Christian, they might have a more imaginative language to work with.

Christian and Jewish religions do in fact recognize a superiority to human life; the human beings, as far as we know, are the only morally responsible earthlings. The Book of Genesis places the man and woman in the middle of a garden with plants and animals. The human vocation is "to dress it and keep it." The man and woman have to listen to everything else and then respond according to their best lights. At the minimum they should not destroy the world; at best, the man and woman might gently transform some things for the better. The humans own no power of their own; they have only an extraordinary capacity to receive. The human is the teachable animal who starts from near zero.

It is constantly said that the ecological problem is caused by "anthropocentrism," a result of Judaism and Christianity exalting the human.[26] But the ecological crisis is caused by an image that puts man on top; this is a fundamentally different image from one of man and woman at the center. The worst disease one can have is one in which the name of the cure is given to the disease. One cannot even begin to look for the answer. The only way to get "man" from the top is to put the *anthropos* at the *center*. What is assumed to be the answer—an equality of species—is an implicit evasion of human responsibility. The humans have to accept their burden of superiority; when it comes to responsibility, the humans are the greatest.

There is a "human community" that has its own distinctive relations; it is from this moral community that human beings can respond to the organic relations of the biotic system.[27] Each organism has its right to exist, its condition and length of life being fairly well set within an order of natures. There are species such as dolphins and chimps where each member has its own individuality. There are species such as cockroaches and mosquitoes where individual life is barely discernible. In all cases, the humans have the vocation not to destroy the earth, including species that seem disagreeable. If one does not romanticize nature and if one recognizes that natures compete with one another, even eat one another, then human action can be seen to have some leeway. The human vocation includes competing and sometimes killing. To bathe, to walk across the grass, to breathe is to be a killer. The humans also have to eat, not necessarily steak, but something that has lived.

Religions here are simply realistic although they often prescribe rituals to restrain the killing of nonhuman animals. If humans do take the life of an animal, it should be done with a minimum of pain and a maximum of gratitude. This is a dying/rebirthing universe; we cannot spend our moral passion trying to defend the life of every individual in every species. Better to stand against flagrant violations such as insecticides that destroy the cycles of life. Humans have to accept with gratitude and a tinge of guilt the power to transform and, therefore, to kill on a wider scale than any other species. "In the case of food, literally, and in the case of much else metaphorically, we die into one another's lives and live one another's deaths."[28]

A MORALITY OF MEN AND WOMEN

One final note that links ecology, religion, and moral education. I noted above that much of ecological literature is still oblivious of its sex-biased language: man and nature. In the dichotomy of man/nature, women tended to get placed on the side of nature, that is, with the organic, the passive, the hidden interior. Man is conceived of as being just the opposite: the rational agent, who "makes decisions," who, among other things, is likely to elaborate a system of ethics. However, the moral life as a whole, especially when this is identified with sentiments and ideals, has usually been associated with women.

This split along gender lines is an unhealthy one. Christianity did not cause but neither did it heal this split. Nor has twentieth-century moral education really faced the issue. "Moral education" has almost always been in reality a male ethics with no attention to the moral formation of young children and with a bias against women. The person best known for blowing the whistle on this bias is Carol Gilligan who began in the 1970s to analyze the gender bias in Kohlberg's scale of moral development. I think it is doubtful, however, that Gilligan's own concepts, such as justice and responsibility, get free of the philosophical tradition she is trying to criticize.[29]

There is another basis of radical criticism rooted in nineteenth-century romanticism, a body of material brilliantly explored in Marilyn Massey's *Feminine Soul*.[30] Although this tradition has its inbuilt distortions—mostly writings by men about women—it is nonetheless about *moral education*, not just ethical systems. It deals with passion, blood, bodiliness, emotion, protest, care, family, and all the other elements in living and dying morally. And, as one could probably guess, it is very much rooted in religion; more exactly, it springs from a radically reformed tradition in which G-d is imagined as feminine.

One should retain a little suspicion of German philosophers waxing romantically about their mother's religion. Nonetheless, buried deep in writers such as Pestalozzi is a way to think about moral education that does not prematurely divide morality and religion, reason and emotion, method and content. Pestalozzi provides a far more convincing picture than does Kant of the origin of moral duty; it takes its beginning from "the first faint shadow of the feeling that it is not right to rage against the loving mother, the faint shadow of the feeling that the mother is not in the world altogether for his sake . . . the feeling that he himself is not in the world for his own sake only."[31]

Moral education ought to be a distinct field of its own. It should not be dictated to by any religion or by religious officials. But religion and morality have had and continue to have an intimate connection, so intimate that any simple division of territory is impossible. One thing religions have always been is practical. They have sometimes been morally obtuse but they know where the moral question is: in the bodily activities of a human community in an earthly setting. Moral education's attempt to cut all ties with all religion is suicidal. It cuts itself off from most of the practical side of morality, leaving moral education to be the ethical discussion of hypothetical dilemmas or the clarifying of subjective viewpoints. Moral education needs religious education neither as lord nor servant but as thoughtful colleague.

NOTES

1. Allan Bloom, *The Closing of the American Mind* (New York: Simon and Schuster, 1987), p. 67.

2. *The New York Times*, October 11, 1986.

3. John Locke, *The Reasonableness of Christianity* (Stanford: Stanford University Press, 1958).

4. Albert Plé, *Duty or Pleasure?* (New York: Paragon, 1986), p. 60.

5. Emile Durkheim, *Moral Education* (New York, Free Press, 1961), p. 3.

6. Bloom, *The Closing of the American Mind*, p. 26.

7. Theodore Sizer, *Horace's Compromise* (Boston: Houghton Mifflin, 1985), pp. 120-130.

8. *The New York Times*, October 19, 1986. The case is *Smith v. Board of School Commissioners of Mobile County.* For commentaries on the case, see, *Religion and Public Education* 14 (Spring, 1987), pp. 123-144.

9. Lawrence Kohlberg, "Moral Education Reappraised," *The Humanist* 38 (November, 1978), pp. 13-15.

10. Jaroslov Pelikan, *Jesus through the Centuries* (New Haven: Yale University Press, 1985), p. 17.

11. See, Michael Walzer, *Spheres of Justice* (New York, Basic Books, 1983).

12. See, Walter Brueggemann, "Voices of the Night - Against Justice," in *To Act Justly, Live Tenderly, Walk Humbly* (New York, Paulist, 1986), pp. 5-28.

13. Thomas Webber, *Deep Like the River* (New York: Norton, 1978), p. 80.

14. Jean Piaget, *The Moral Judgment of the Child* (New York, Collier, 1962), p. 323.

15. Judah Goldin, ed. *The Living Talmud* (Chicago: University of Chicago Press, 1957), p. 86.

16. St. Thomas Aquinas, *Summa Theologica*, I-II, 73, 10.

17. Timothy Cooney, *Telling Right from Wrong* (Buffalo: Prometheus, 1985), p. 25.

18. Jakob Petuchowski, *Our Masters Taught: Rabbinic Stories and Sayings* (New York: Crossroad, 1982), p. 51.

19. Immanuel Kant, *Foundations of the Metaphysics of Morals* (New York: Harper, 1963), p. 1.

20. See, Wayne Booth, *Modern Dogma and the Rhetoric of Assent* (Notre Dame, Ind.: University of Notre Dame Press, 1974), p. 139.

21. See, Christopher Chapple, "Noninjury to Animals: Jaina and Buddhist Perspectives," in *Animal Sacrifices: Religious Perspectives on the Use of Animals in Science* (Philadelphia: Temple University Press, 1986), pp. 215-217.

22. David Hume, *Ethical Writings*, as cited in James Rachels, *The End of Life* (New York: Oxford, 1986), p. 163.

23. Joseph Fletcher, in *Voluntary Euthanasia* (London: Humanities Press, 1986), p. 66.

24. G. K. Chesterton, *St. Francis of Assisi* (Garden City, N.Y.: Image, 1957), p. 87.

25. See, Paul Taylor, *Respect for Nature* (Princeton: Princeton University Press, 1986), p. 115.

26. See, Richard Watson, "A Critique of Anti-Anthropocentric Biocentrism," *Environmental Ethics* 5 (Fall, 1983).

27. Cora Diamond, "Eating Meat and Eating People," *Philosophy* 53 (1978), pp. 465-479; Jim Cheney, "Eco-feminism and Deep Ecology," *Environmental Ethics* 9 (Summer, 1987), pp. 115-146.

28. Lewis Hyde, *The Gift: Imagination and the Erotic Life of Property* (New York: Random House, 1983).

29. Carol Gilligan, *In a Different Voice* (Cambridge, Mass.: Harvard University Press, 1982).

30. Marilyn Massey, *Feminine Soul* (Boston: Beacon, 1985).

31. As quoted in *ibid.*, p. 78.

8

Religious Education Profession

The title of this chapter is deliberately ambiguous. I wish to deal with a two-way relation between religious education and profession. The more obvious of the two issues here is: In what sense is religious education a profession? But from the opposite direction the question can be asked: How might the idea of profession be thought through with the aid of religious education?

The title "Religious Education Profession" is a parallel to the title of one of my books: *Religious Education Development*. In that book I explored a similar two-way relation. Religious education has to understand and use the idea of development if it is to engage in serious dialogue with the contemporary culture. I also argued, however, that development needs both religious and educational meaning if it is not to self-destruct. The reciprocity of the relation does not doom the discussion to being a closed circle. Development has more than its religious and educational meaning, and religious education is more than a discussion of development. The reciprocal relation could strengthen both development and religious education. I think that something very similar can be said about religious education and profession. Both development and profession are examples of what I said are ostensibly secular terms whose religious roots need retrieving.

It had been my hope that after publishing *Religious Education Development* I would be able to publish a complementary volume entitled *Religious Education Profession*. The moment passed and I did not have the time to do so. I still think that such a volume is needed, although I do not think I am in the best position to write it. Someone who has worked in various professional capacities within a religious institution and in the secular educational system might have the experience to address the whole issue.

What I am trying to get at in this chapter is, in a sense, the other half of religious education. We tend to think of religious education as divided into the two halves of theory and practice. But my reference to profession as the other half of religious education is to something within theory itself rather than to the practical. Writing on religious education typically addresses a range of issues such as teaching, curriculum, course content for different ages, audio-visuals, and the like. There is, however, another range of theoretical issues that are generally missed. These issues eventually have to be addressed if religious education is to have standing.

When the Religious Education Association was founded at the turn of this century, its hope was to establish a twofold meaning of religious education: 1) as a field of serious, academic inquiry and 2) as a profession of educators in churches, schools, and elsewhere. I have acknowledged throughout these pages that religious education is still a fledgling among academic disciplines. As a profession, religious education is even more of a beginner. Although one could rightly blame such things as economic problems for retarding this profession's development, the theoretical exploration of the history and current state of professionalism does not depend on economic good times.

I can easily envision not just one book but a dozen books that are needed on this issue, studies that touch on history, organization, authority, politics, and economics. The two main questions in this context are: What is a religious educator? How is the work of religious education related to institutions? The religious educator shares with other educators a confusing relation to the modern idea of the professional. The fact that it is *religious* education compounds the problem because religious organizations have their own somewhat peculiar notion of professional work.

The most that I can accomplish here is to present a sketch of the history and present situation of professionalization insofar as it is related to religion and education. That includes suggesting some possible directions for the present and future. To lay out the details of professional organization, one would have to go into all sorts of differences according to culture and country. Once again, even in British and U.S. history there would be considerable differences, for example, in how schoolteaching is viewed professionally or how schoolteachers are professionally prepared.[1]

Although it is impossible to paint a universal picture of "professional religious educator," a few statements of principle, both negative and positive can be offered. In positive terms, the professionalizing of religious education probably has to result in some kind of hybrid. Religious education has elements that cross the boundaries of existing professions, as do forensic medicine or medical law. Negatively stated, religious education has to resist being subsumed too easily under an existing category. In the U.S., the profession offering its embrace is church ministry. When religious education as intellectual inquiry is assumed to be a part of theology, then quite logically religious education as professional work is thought to be a part of church ministry.

In the U.S. we have one big religious category called "clergy" which includes Catholic priests, Protestant ministers, and Jewish rabbis. And anyone else who is visibly religious, such as Catholic nuns, gets lumped into this category. The ordination of women has not changed this perception much, the assumption being that some women have moved from being minor to major clergy. The Christian educator, often a woman or a young man fresh from the seminary, is presumed to be lesser clergy, even if in church language the person is "lay."

In Judaism the situation and the language are particularly anomalous. The Jewish rabbi is called a clergyman (or clergywoman) and is in charge of a congregation. There may also be a Jewish educator for the congregation. This person may have gone through another track in the seminary or received training elsewhere. Thus, the professional standing of the Jewish educator can have an ambiguous relation to rabbi, seminary, and congregation. I think that the pattern for Jewish congregations (at least Reform and Conservative) is similar to the Christian. But the professional tension between the term "rabbi" and "educator" is more paradoxical than, say, between priest and educator.

In speaking about professionalization, the U.S. Catholic church offers a remarkable case study in the several thousand people who are parish Directors of Religious Education (DRE). I have closely followed this idea and the people involved since DREs began in the mid-1960s. (The title did not actually get established until the mid-1970s with the publication of Maria Harris's fine study, *The DRE Book*).[2]

Since the Second Vatican Council there has been no more positive a sign in the U.S. Catholic church than the DRE movement. Many of the best and the brightest of the Catholic church's educators moved into this work. Many highly competent nuns, and former nuns, provided the backbone of the early DRE group. Later, there were middle-aged women who had reared large families and were looking for a new outlet for their talents and energies. Despite the generally high quality of the men and women in DRE work, the very idea of the work has remained shaky from the beginning. The exodus of talented folks is also a hallmark of this group. The idea of the DRE still needs theoretical study and development.

Over the years I have written a series of essays trying to provide theoretical underpinnings to the DRE movement.[3] I have tried to bring in some historical backdrop and to point out what lessons are to be learned from other groups who are also struggling to be recognized professionally. Many DREs did not take kindly to these ideas, and I can readily understand why. For example, pointing out that the idea of professionalization has become captive to the idea of big money may be generally true. But it can sound like a cruel joke to would-be professionals who are struggling to get up to the government's poverty level.

There is, however, a worse kind of joke that is often played with the idea of professional. As Harold Wilensky pointed out in a famous essay twenty-five years ago, the idea of becoming a profession seems alluringly simple.[4] Innumerable groups go through a series of steps (a name, a journal, an association, an accrediting process, a code of ethics, and so forth) before announcing that the group now constitutes a profession. But steps of that kind do not guarantee any of the benefits that accrue to the professional class in our day. To put one's energies into making your own little group "a profession" may merely succeed in isolating the group from much larger groups that do have some prospect of benefiting from a process of professionalization.

Thus, in the present instance DREs in the Catholic church do not constitute "a profession." DREs in the Roman Catholic church of the U.S., like many educators in the religious area, find themselves caught between the two worlds of religious institutions and secular education. Both of these groups can conceivably offer leverage, status, and protective cover to the DRE. An individual who wishes to be recognized as a competent religious educator could say that his or her profession is either church minister or secular educator. But it would be self-defeating to say that "my profession is parish director of religious education." There is no disparagement in this comment. One can prepare to do the specific job of DRE and can be proud of doing it well without claiming that the work is "a profession."

The greatest significance of the DRE struggle for professional recognition may be that it focuses attention on the two possible routes of professionalization. Is church minister (or, more precisely, Jewish and Christian clergy) a well-designed profession as currently conceived, or is there still a need for major reform? And what are the strengths and weaknesses of a "teaching profession"; is there anything special that teachers of religion bring to that professional identity? The unifying question in this area is whether there are any inherent links between religious work and educational work.

THE PROFESSIONAL IDEAL

We have a strange situation today in that few terms are more attractive than "professional" just at the time that the very idea of being a professional is in crisis. Although the U.S. government classifies about one out of seven jobs as professional, a survey of any high-school class will reveal that the vast majority of students hope to be professionals. Exactly what kind of professional is not the important thing. (I have heard at least one young man express the desire to be a "professional criminal.") The difference between the number of professional jobs available and the number of people expecting to occupy these jobs is one kind of crisis in professional circles.

There is a deeper crisis that affects the professional ideal itself, a problem brought on whenever something good is democratized. The democratizing process attempts to widen the circle of people who enjoy a good. Some people resist this process because of snobbish elitism. Others do not necessarily resist sharing the good but worry about whether there is need for other kinds of change than simply distributing a good. The City University of New York two decades ago opened its doors to every student with a high-school diploma. As experience showed, it would have helped the university and the students if the greater attention had been given to improving the elementary and secondary schools.

In the 1850s, James Baldwin Turner of Illinois College noted the fortunate division of all civilized societies into 5 percent of the people who are capable of being the professional class, and the other 95 percent of people who are fit for industrial work.[5] Naturally, in a mobile society like the U.S., individuals became intent on proving that they are in that upper 5 percent. Turner's particular numbers proved to have nothing natural or necessary about them. The percentage of jobs that in anyone's classification are called professional increased to well over 5 percent while the number of industrial jobs has fallen. However, if 5 percent is not the limit, is 15, 35, 85? Could everyone in society become a professional? I think that this question is a good test of the idea of professional. I wish to suggest that the extension of the word "professional" to everyone is imaginable, even if unlikely. However, in the meaning that Turner was using in the nineteenth century and has come down to us today there would be an inherent contradiction in the indefinite increase of professional jobs, whatever the exact percentage of the limit may be.

It is this threat of self-contradiction that forms the deeper crisis in the idea of professional. In the late nineteenth century, the idea connoted a good that a lot of people wanted. As increasing numbers did get some share of that world—at least a share of the language and the external trappings—a disillusioning process was almost inevitable. A high-school diploma in the late nineteenth century was a great dream of millions of people; as millions realized the dream, a diploma became devalued.

The word "professional" is still most often used in a positive sense. But in a culture of professionalism where everyone is making claims for their own profession, the word raises suspicions. A typical backlash in the meaning of professional is illustrated in a *Time* magazine special issue on the crisis in education: "It has been argued that teaching needs to be more professional. But in some ways it is too professional now—too encrusted with useless requirements and too tangled in its own obscure professional jargon."[6] So does *Time* think that the schoolteacher should be a professional? It is difficult to say because of the confusing overlay of meaning now connected with the term.

Consider another example, a book on child abuse in which the authors strongly urge the use of "lay therapists." They write: "The essence of their relationship is that it is not 'professional'; it can cover whatever time and activity the parent wants or needs."[7] Ironically, what the authors describe here as *not* professional, is just what professional might have meant in another era.

The use of the word "lay" in the above quotation, brings up one of the two words most often contrasted to professional. In asking the meaning of a term, it helps to know what people are trying to exclude by its usage. The opposite of professional is assumed to be either amateur or lay. The conceptual contrast between *amateur* and professional is usually clear. Frequently used with reference to athletes, the amateur plays the game for the fun of it; the professional is paid and makes a living at it. The contrast of professional to *lay* is usually more severe; the lay person is not in the game at all. A lay person is one who lacks skill or training, while a professional person is one who is competent.

In regard to the question whether everyone could turn professional, the answer depends on what is the opposite. If amateur means you do not get paid and professional means you do, then there will always be a division between amateurs and professionals. Suppose, however, that one goes back to a deeper meaning of amateur as one who loves to do something. Then one could be an amateur and a professional at the same time; indeed, the two meanings tend to converge. If an amateur loves to do something and a professional does it well, could anyone doubt that Ted Williams and Mickey Mantle, Magic Johnson and Larry Bird are amateurs *and* professionals?

Obviously, all of us cannot be as competent at basketball as are Magic Johnson and Larry Bird—but neither are the other two hundred fifty professional players in the NBA. That is, professional can refer not to one dividing line (between paid and unpaid) but to degrees of competence. If sports programs were widely available, everyone could become a professional athlete, that is, reach some degree of competence. My example is not a trivial inflation of the word "professional." The education of boys and girls in some athletic skills and the continuing reshaping of those abilities throughout life are central to education and religious education. The assumption that only 5 percent of us, or less, are capable of being athletically competent is a wedge that divides people even down at the lower grades of school.

As to the other contrast, lay versus professional, the self-exclusion of the two sets is clear, but one must be careful of the application. "Lay" (or "laity") is almost always a simple negation. One tries to become a professional in order to leave behind lay status. Clearly, the desirable ideal here is that there be no lay people; education as a whole could be imagined as a journey into professional competence. One can conceive of a world in which everyone is becoming professional, a world in which lay people are on the decrease.

The Christian church may be the only prominent institution that still tries to give a positive meaning to "lay" and "laity." A historical connection is drawn between the word for "laity" and "the people." Laity could be a way of expressing the communal character of the church. If that were the case, the relation could be similar to the one between professional and amateur, that is, one could become a professional without ceasing to be a lay person. Some Christian groups try to say something like that, but I do not think it has been with much success. When a line has been drawn between a clerical class and a lay class for a long time, the line may be unhelpful but it cannot simply be erased.

Splits do develop in the church as in any large institution. The way to avoid a two-class system is to have many gradations in the way one can belong. There are degrees of competence in being a church member and these variations need to be admitted and sometimes publicly affirmed. Most church people will always be lay in the sense of being a noncleric, but that is not the same as being a lay person in the church. Cardinal Newman made the famous comment that it would be a very strange church if there were no laity. Strange perhaps but not impossible or undesirable. One could imagine a church of professional Christians, everyone having a degree of skill and competence in practicing their religion.

In my book *Education Toward Adulthood* I traced the existence of two conflicting ideals of adulthood through various institutions. These two ideals are:

A. An ideal of adulthood that glorifies the rational, independent, and secure man.

B. An ideal of adulthood in which there is an evolving integrity of rational/nonrational, dependent/independent, living/dying in the lives of men and women.

The last chapter of that book is on how these ideals are embodied in our idea of profession. I considered dropping that chapter as being too far from my main focus of education, religion, and adulthood. Eventually, however, I came to the conclusion that the power relations manifest in our notions of the professional are at the heart of the conflict about adulthood. And without an acceptable process of professionalization, our educational and religious institutions will not liberate people into an adulthood that includes childlikeness. Rather, education and religion will turn out a laity childishly dependent on a few experts.

What I have called ideal A of adulthood correlates perfectly with the professional expert of recent times. The physician, for example, became the prototype for this man of near godlike knowledge and control. The "doctor" or learned one is the only man who can write prescriptions for what ails the human race. The patient or lay person can only place himself—or more often, herself—into the hands of the professional expert. It was this relation that inspired G. B. Shaw's famous line in *The Doctor's Dilemma*: "All professions are conspiracies against the laity."[8]

What meaning of "professional" correlates with ideal B of adulthood as described above? Here the single dividing line between a class of experts and an uneducated laity would be missing. There would be recognized a great variety of skills. Everyone could become competent to some degree in the most important areas of life. At the same time, it would be readily acknowledged that everyone has something to learn from others. A professional would, therefore, be someone who works in a team of knowledgeable men and women, someone who invites people into participating in the knowledge. This notion of professional involves recognition that we live in a dying and rebirthing universe; technique will not save us from dying. Acting professionally is based upon a wisdom born of confronting mortality.

Is there any hope for such a meaning of professional or is my description an idyllic dream? I do not expect a sudden and total change in this direction. Much of our society plunges headlong toward ideal A of adulthood and to a securer conspiracy against the laity. At the same time, however, there are rumblings of protest and some signs of practical change. As the nineteenth-century medical profession led the way to the total split of doctor and laity, so in the late twentieth century we have the rise of a "health profession," based on teamwork, teaching, and the patient's body as chief healer.

The doctors did not sit down one day and decide to make this change; in fact, many physicians resist this shift in the meaning of their profession. The medical profession is changing because of several kinds of pressure. The most striking sign of change is the malpractice suit and its necessary insurance; it represents the final split between the expert who is supposed to guarantee success and the helpless client who can only shout foul. The majority of physicians are probably happy to be relieved of godlike status even if it takes them a while to learn how to be team member, teacher, and acceptor of mortality.

The technical training of the doctor a few decades ago seemed crystal clear. But no one is now certain about educating the health professional for tomorrow. Some new balance of technical training and humanistic education will have to be devised. Leon Kass has written that the professional in health can be neither proud master nor servile technician. Referring to the physician, Kass writes: "The professional bears witness to the being of something higher and more enduring, participation in which can only be called a blessing."[9]

Kass's description of the professional attitude of the physician has a religious overtone. That is not an accident. In most cultures the priest and physician are closely related, if not the same role. These cultures have men and women who learn the art of healing in the context of religious rites and a religious attitude toward life and death. One need not romanticize the effectiveness of the healing arts in the premodern world, nor deny that the modern world has made astonishing discoveries in the treatment of illness. Nonetheless, the dismissal of the religious roots of medicine in the nineteenth century is having to be reexamined today. The relation of mind and body is more complex than the nineteenth-century thought. The body heals itself in part because of the expert knowledge of the physician and the technology of medicine, but in part because of other forces and other kinds of knowledge and technique. The nurse, the counselor, the chaplain, the family, and the friends of the patient can all be part of the "blessing" which the body must have.

HISTORICAL PATTERNS

Our term "professional" has its origin in the medieval monastery with Christians who made a profession of vows. Or, more exactly, in language used to this day, people are "professed" in vows. They con-fess their faith and thus they are pro-fessed as a grace or blessing. A person does not lightly enter such a profession; he or she experiences a calling or vocation. The person is then tested by community living to see if his or her dedication is genuine and enduring. The profession to live in the community is received by the whole church in a public ceremony. Henceforth, the professed have privileges and duties that go beyond ordinary labors.

In medieval and early modern times, the professional dealt in a kind of knowledge and dedication that were not for sale at any price. The three vows of the religious order—poverty, obedience, and chastity—were the extreme embodiment of the ideal, but physician, lawyer, soldier, or statesman were supposed to live according to the same essential code. To be professional meant: 1) readiness to live in poverty, 2) obedience to the life and goodwill of the community, and 3) availability for what has to be done, when it has to be done.

Besides a special dedication, professional has always meant a person with special knowledge. What is widely assumed today is that this special knowledge means specialized "expertise," the mastery of a body of abstract knowledge. Thus, anyone whose training requires the acquisition of a maze of complicated bits of information (e.g., tax accountant) is considered a professional. In premodern times, what constituted the knowledge as special was that it touched on the mystery of life and death. Robert Herrick describes professionals as having "guilty knowledge," dangerous insight into the most intimate sphere of life and death.[10] The physician, the priest, the statesman, or the soldier, were thought to live at the edge of ordinary existence, privy to secrets about the deepest level of human existence. This kind of work was not a job, occupation, or employment; it was not the means to "making a living," but living itself. The work was doing what is right and good for no other reason than it is right and good. This is the "right livelihood" in Buddha's eightfold path, it is the seeking of the kingdom in Jesus' teaching.

Throughout the past century, while the claim to special knowledge and dedication continued to be voiced, a near reversal occurred in the meaning of the professional ideal. The economic possibilities of having a knowledge that others badly needed began to be emphasized. Professionalism became entangled with the sexual, racial, and age bias present in the society. Having a professional career meant going up the narrow ladder of success. To be a professional now came to mean: 1) the possibility of earning big money, 2) independence from any and every community, and 3) control of time, place, and conditions for the exercise of one's highly specialized knowledge.[11]

Being a professional has thus come to be something highly desirable. The problem is that in the late twentieth century we can no longer afford this ideal. Until recently, the modern ideal of professional could be sustained because it was realized by only a small minority in the population and because it retained a residue of earlier attitudes, such as belief that one should put in a good day's work at whatever one's job. When too many people are simply interested in big money and maximum independence, society cannot bear the strain. But it is hopeless to offer a variation on poverty, obedience, and chastity as a working ideal for today.

What might be possible is to work out a new synthesis that recovers some of the premodern attitude while retaining the real advances of the last century. The key to success here is to keep at the center of things that professional still means skill and service. An increase in knowledge and training does not detract from the meaning of professional. On the contrary, the heart surgeon of today can be as much or more the dedicated professional as the country doctor with his black bag. But we do need some checks on the human propensity to greed, sloth, envy, and the desire to be in total control of one's life.

Thus, one can imagine a professional ideal in which: 1) The individual is able to support a family but has chosen work worth doing over the biggest paycheck possible. 2) The individual is capable of acting like an entrepreneur but chooses to work in a community or team of peers. 3) The individual's technical skills are highly trained but are set within an attitude of reverence for living things and a recognition of human finitude.

This description of a "postmodern" professional is not an unrealistic dream. I have noted previously that the professionals in the health area are going in this direction, some out of conviction and others out of necessity, sometimes with the ideal clearly perceived and at other times blindly stumbling forward. In addition to health care people, there are lawyers, clergy, social workers, psychologists, police, schoolteachers, and others who are at least wrestling with the problem. Patience is needed and misunderstandings are inevitable. One person's luxury is another person's necessity; one person's group support is another person's invasion of privacy. The professional ideal is necessarily one of discriminating choices.

One of the key changes in this move from modern to postmodern professional is the relation of men and women. The modern professional man had to scramble up the career ladder, but women were not allowed to join the ascent. Inherent to the idea of the modern professional was that women stayed at home with the children. Someone had to console the tired professional man at the end of his day on the higher plane; someone had to do all those ordinary chores that the professional man does not have time for.

Women were allowed only one profession: motherhood. Catherine Beecher and other reformers in the nineteenth century tried to have motherhood recognized as a profession. The case can be made that motherhood involves guilty knowledge and dedication. The trouble was that the meaning of professional was changing and to be a mother did not require mastery of a body of technical abstractions. So women became professionals of one kind just when that kind was being relegated to the past.[12]

The two subprofessions into which women were allowed in great numbers were nursing and schoolteaching. Women were thought to be experts at these professions because these two were imagined to be an extension of motherhood. Certainly, the dedication needed for nursing and schoolteaching is obvious. As for the mastery of a body of abstract knowledge, the nurse and schoolteacher were thought to be better off if they relied on their (male) superiors. The nurse was to do nothing except carry out the orders of the doctor. The schoolteacher was the servant of the schoolboard and administrator, those people who most insistently referred to professionalism and thought of themselves as the true professionals in education. Separated from the advanced training in technical knowledge and the control over their own work, the life of the nurse or schoolteacher could be miserable. But among the ranks of schoolteachers and nurses one can probably find great wisdom. The ones that found a way to survive and blossom retained an older meaning of professional while they endured the narrowness of the modern idea.[13]

The religious professional has something of the same problem as these subprofessions of nursing and schoolteaching. Until the nineteenth century, the dedication of the clergyman was assumed. So, too, it was assumed that the clergyman had secret knowledge of this life and beyond, gathered from a life of prayer, discipline, and study of sacred texts. The clergyman typically pastored in one or a few communities. There was no salary but there was a stipend as well as other benefits: a house, a garden, contributed skills, and the support of local clergy. However, when the complex knowledge of "divinity" was put in question, the clergyman had to scramble in what became a career more than a vocation. One now became a professional minister with the hope of getting a large congregation or becoming a part of the high-level governing board of clergy. Like nurses and schoolteachers, however, the clergy still represented some link to an older meaning of professional. The clergyman is one of those people who are "on call" at times of need and tragedy. A few television preachers flaunt their wealth; most clergy live on very modest means. They are still largely paid in ways other than salary.

What the modern crisis of the clergy should have revealed is that becoming "professionally religious" is not the same as being a clergyman. In fact, the term "profession" comes out of a different strand of church history; the religious order which dealt with the professedly religious was often at odds with the clergy. Professional at being religious means taking up a discipline and learning a wisdom born of dedication and service. The training of the rabbi, priest, and minister in the modern seminary has often been out of touch with this tradition of spiritual discipline. Even the Catholic religious order seems to have lost its bearings. A new kind of "order" may arise, helped by conversation between Eastern and Western religions. In the pattern of the future, there is unlikely to be a two-class system of professed and nonprofessed, monk and layperson. Rather, there will be various ways to be professionally religious and a series of concentric circles where an individual can find profession in some kind of order.[14]

The Protestant Reformation's dream of a universal vocation could finally be realized in a more complex pattern than could be imagined in the sixteenth century. Luther and Calvin were surely on the right track in wishing to open the idea of "religious calling" to every church member. As many Protestant writers acknowledge today, Luther and Calvin overreacted to the corruption of the monastery by including everyone *except* monks in the idea of vocation.[15] There is something to be learned from the history of monasticism and from people who have tried to be "professionally religious." But the church—both Catholic and Protestant—still needs to think about and experiment with diverse forms so that people's religiousness can find expression in different ways at different times in their lives.

PROFESSIONALIZING RELIGIOUS EDUCATION

In saying that we need new syntheses and people who are connecting links, it is not farfetched to propose religious education as a work of professional importance. If one tries to describe a professional ideal for today, one can hardly avoid either religious or educational language. The professional is someone who discovers work that is worth doing, whatever the money; that is the language of mystical traditions East and West. The professional is someone who is necessarily a teacher; in a sense all professions are either educational or anti-educational. The professional is also someone who discovers the reality and importance of community; that is, the language of both religion and education.

The professionalizing of religious education, therefore, need not mean a drastic shift into a foreign set of characteristics. Many people in religious education may already be more professional than they realize. While they may be lacking in technical training of one kind, they ought not to overlook strengths (e.g., a sense of community) which they do have and which are often lacking in other professions. In the drive to get professional recognition, some of these desirable qualities could get undermined. With just a little attention to both sides of the issue some big advances are possible.

Take as an example, a particular group I mentioned above: middle-aged women who have become Catholic DREs during the past decade. The potential for professional contribution from this group is enormous; most of them are intelligent, well-organized, and highly dedicated. Since their husbands have professional salaries and their children are now older, they can work for the low stipend which the church institution offers. But this willingness to work for little money is a source of friction in a group wherein many individuals are struggling to get a living wage.

It would be tragic if the dedication and good will of

these women undercut the "professionalizing" effort of the rest of the group. In actual fact, the gap here is not so great as it may first seem. These women are willing to work for a low stipend, but they are not happy with it.[16] They do not need big money, but they, like any self-respecting workers, resist being economically exploited. They are united with their colleagues who badly need the money when it comes to being treated with a sense of dignity and fairness. The institution's leaders who may think they have discovered a new source of cheap labor are deluded. They will be brought to their senses soon, but perhaps not soon enough to keep alive the present movement to professionalize religious education in the Catholic parish.

THE TWO BASES FOR PROFESSIONALIZATION

As I have acknowledged throughout this book, there is a rather sharp line down the middle of religious education. On one side, there is the teaching of religion; on the other side, there is the teaching to be religious. In the world of professional organizations, the divide is usually between the school and the religious congregation. One's professional loyalty as religious educator is likely to be rooted in the one place or the other.

So distinct are these approaches that some people might conclude that the term "religious educator" is an equivocation. I do not think the difference is that severe; however, it is wise to acknowledge how great is the difference, rather than referring to the "professional religious educator" as if there were a single, clearly defined profession. If a conversation can take place, then there can be some closing of the gap, a movement that does not presuppose that the gap should ever entirely close.

The closest one might come to a single profession would be in the religiously affiliated school. Here the institution and its staff may accomplish both parts of religious education, the teaching of religion and the teaching to be religious. Of course, it is no secret that the attempt at a premature union of these two tasks can result in mere confusion. The products of some religiously affiliated schools may know almost nothing about religion, while despising religious practice. I am not saying the whole record is that dismal. But such schools must clearly distinguish the two different parts of religious education and allow them both to live within the school, even if they are not always amicable partners.

Given my description in chapters four and five of the contrasting use of religious education in the U.S. and the U.K., British religious educators generally form a closer identification with schoolteaching whereas in the U.S. the religious organization's meaning of professional tends to dominate. As I also indicated, however, this split of language is not total. There are British religious educators in church/synagogue/temple/mosque. And in the U.S. there are teachers of religion in private and in religiously affiliated schools as well as in public schools.

Furthermore, there are in both countries professors of religion in the university. As that very name "professor" suggests, here is one of the main sources for stimulating a professional religious education. Unfortunately, those who talk about a professional religious education generally exclude the professors, which suits many professors quite well. Many of the professors think of themselves as being *neither* schoolteacher nor minister of religion. They might improve their performance as professors if they paid some attention to both.

1. *Schoolteaching.* This is the more modern of the two professional routes to religious education. It has some of the marks of the modern professional—independence, critical inquiry, a limitation of hours—but it has never been fully accepted as a distinct and complete profession. New York State, for example, lists thirty professions, including beautician and masseuse, but not schoolteaching. As a woman's extension of motherhood, the image of the schoolteacher has been subprofessional, taking orders from the head of the school family.

The professional association in the U.S., the National Education Association, always talked about a "unified profession," meaning teachers and administrators togther.[17] It was a unity in which the teachers often felt at the bottom of a bureaucracy. Schoolteachers eventually turned to the model of the labor union, organizing themselves against educational administration. Until the 1960s there had never been a strike of schoolteachers; now annual strikes are a way of life. After a perilous decline in the 1970s, schoolteachers' salaries and working conditions were appreciably improved in the 1980s. The issue of professionalism remains cloudy.

The teacher of religion has no magic wand to wave in clarifying the professional character of schoolteachers. Still, from a lifelong conversation with religion and religious people, the teacher of religion might have some helpful insights and sensitivities. For example, one of the most striking characteristics of schoolteachers is their isolation. In John Goodlad's fine study, *A Place Called School*, one hears teachers repeatedly say that they are interested in their colleagues' work but have no real knowledge of it.[18] The religion teacher is not the only one whose interest is community. However, he or she is at the end of the curriculum spectrum where personal involvement and communal experience are most significant. One cannot professionally teach religion (or art, politics, ethics, literature) in a school that is insensitive to the bonds of community between student and student, teacher and teacher, student and teacher.

The world of elementary and secondary schoolteachers needs a closer link to the university, not simply as a place to get credentials but as a place of colleagueship. This link has historically been present in the British preparation of teachers; it is almost nonexistent in the U.S.[19] One reason for the importance of this connection is simply age. So long as schoolteaching is confused with adults tending little children, a profession of schoolteaching will not be given much credit. But if schoolteaching (including university professors) is understood to be an intellectually challenging venture with people from five years of age to seventy-five, there might be a boost of morale and dignity for schoolteachers as well as more money. Schoolteaching ought to be thought of as a conversation between adults into which children are admitted on their way to becoming adult.

The university professor, in a comfortable professional position, is able to identify with his or her field of inquiry. When a professor of religion attends a conference on religious issues, no one suspects that he or she is becoming a proselytizer for a particular religious group. The professor of religion is likely to have religious interests beyond the classroom. As a professor, that presumably enhances rather than detracts from classroom instruction. In the U.S. literature on public school, it is constantly asserted that one cannot "teach religion" because that connotes proselytizing and indoctrinating. And yet, the phrase is regularly used in the university without contortion or apology. In other words, it is allowed to a professor to have a rhythm of associating with artists and teaching art, of associating with political causes and teaching political science, of associating with a religious community and teaching religion. There is a difference in each case between the former and the latter, but intelligent people can distinguish within the unity of a life.

When we come to elementary and secondary school teachers it is often assumed that such distinctions are impossible. The teacher in the religiously affiliated school is often assumed to make no distinction; he or she must teach as a "believer." The teacher in the state school is asked to make a total separation. He or she is supposed to manifest total neutrality in regard to religion, saying every day: "I am a secular educator not a religious educator." A good reason for closer ties to the university is to break down this strange dichotomy. And if professors of religion would identify more with schoolteaching to describe their work, they could be an example of the postmodern professional.

2. *Religious Organization.* The person who approaches the professionalizing of religious education from this side faces a different set of obstacles and has other lessons to teach. Here one often needs some immediate protection from an overly personal style of operation. ("If you need anything to do your job, just let me know. We don't bother with budgets.") The religious congregation is sometimes, if not in the Middle Ages, at least somewhere before 1850. That can actually be a help to the full meaning of professionali-

zation today. Understandably, however, the lack of organizational apparatus can be a hair-raising experience for the individual.

Take the example of a contract. Many Jewish and Christian educators seem to think that a contract is the mark of a professional. It is not; nonetheless, a contract might not be a bad idea on the way to becoming a professional. If I worked for a church I would want something in writing; more on what I am not expected to do than how to do my work. I would be most interested in knowing how the resources of the congregation are being used so that I as professional educator could coordinate what already exists.

As my description in chapter six indicates, any religious congregation that is at all alive educates its members in various ways every day. The person hired as educator has two main tasks; first, to be a coordinator of a team of ministers whose place is at the center (not the top) of the congregation. The second essential task is to keep looking for ways to tap the educational possibilities of every member in the congregation. The ultimate aim is the professionalization of everyone and the elimination of the laity. Every individual has to be invited to have a genuine share in the life of the congregation.

Here is where the old-time sense of community can be helpful and sometimes be a corrective to a tendency of the religious institution merely to imitate other institutions. The professionalizing of religious education should mean increasing the competence of everyone, drawing on the dedication of each community member. Some of the needed skills are not listed in university catalogues. Taken alone they could not be sustained, but within a community of workers they might be. For example, some urban congregations provide an ombudsperson for the elderly. While the city provides services for the aged, you have to know how to get them and be persistent. Is an ombudsperson who provides the mediation between city and elderly a professional religious educator? There is no doubt that the work requires knowledge and dedication. A master's degree in gerontology might help, but it would probably be put to better use elsewhere.

The chief coordinator or director of congregational education does need connection to the world of books and ideas. Where a congregation runs its own school, there is a marvelous opportunity to experiment with new forms of organization. The director of the congregation's education might be department chair of religion in the school or at least work closely with the chair and the school principal. Or a separate entity might be invented, an organization that supplies teachers to both the school and the congregation.

The adults in the congregation also need intellectual stimulation from a library, discussion groups, courses. At the least, the congregation through its educational leader can channel information of what is available at a nearby college. One Catholic parish in New Jersey (St. Mary's, Colt's Neck) has made scholarships available for parishioners to study in summer programs of religious education. Instead of trying to find one overworked and underpaid person to solve everything, the congregation decided to distribute the educational money it had available. Now after fifteen years of such scholarships, the church has dozens of professionally educated people, not experts in theology but people who have an intelligent stake in their local church and the wider church.

Another variation on this approach has been taken by a well-known Protestant church in Washington D.C.: the Church of the Savior. Members of the community prepare themselves for participation by study, they dedicate time to work in the church, and they become ordained as "non-professional ministers." Other people join in particular projects of the church, but being a member of the church community refers to a level of knowledge and dedication.[20]

Religious educators who coordinate or direct the religious institution's education need solidarity with others in similar work, both within their own religion and across religious boundaries. A "profession of religious education" cannot be housed under one religion. It needs to include a multiplicity of religions as well as several kinds of secular institutions. The full blossoming of this profession is not likely to happen soon; certainly the economics of such a profession are unclear. But that does not mean that each person who is in religious education must operate in the isolation of a single institution. There are several ways to contribute to the overall work of religious education, and if our language does not blind us to potential allies some fruitful conversations are possible and some professional associations can be established. Religious education is an idea and a profession whose time is still coming. Many small contributions from several directions will help to shape its complete emergence.

NOTES

1. R. K. Kelsall and Helen Kelsall, *The School Teacher in England and the United States* (London: Pergamon, 1969).

2. Maria Harris, *The DRE Book* (New York: Paulist, 1976).

3. For example, "The DRE: Choosing Between Professions," *Living Light* 19 (Fall, 1982), pp. 233-241; "The Professions and the Family: Healing the Split," in *Family Ministry*, ed. Gloria Durka and Joanmarie Smith (Minneapolis: Winston, 1980), pp. 94-113; "Some Professional Concerns: Money, Community, Skills," in *DRE: Issues and Concerns for the 80's*, ed. Thomas Walters (Washington, National Conference of Diocesan Directors, 1983), pp. 5-24.

4. Harold Wilensky, "The Professionalization of Everyone," *American Journal of Sociology* 70 (1964), pp. 137-158.

5. See, Arthur Wirth, *Education in the Technological Society* (San Francisco: Intext, 1972), p. 6.

6. *Time*, June 16, 1980, p. 63.

7. C. Henry Kempe and Ruth Kempe, *Child Abuse* (Cambridge, Mass.: Harvard University Press, 1978), p. 76.

8. Cited in Daniel Maguire, *Death by Choice*, 2nd ed. (Garden City, N.Y.: Doubleday, 1984), p. 153.

9. Leon Kass, "Mortality and Morality," *Toward a More Natural Science* (New York, Free Press, 1985), p. 223.

10. Cited in Darrel Reeck, *Ethics for the Professions* (Minneapolis: Augsburg, 1983), p. 17.

11. Burton Bledstein, *The Culture of Professionalism* (New York: Norton, 1976).

12. See, Barbara Harris, *Beyond Her Sphere: Women and the Professions in American History* (Westport: Greenwood, 1978).

13. Daniel Lortie, "The Balance of Control and Autonomy in Elementary School Teaching" and Fred Katz, "Nurses," in *The Semi-Professions and their Organization*, ed. Amitai Etzioni (New York: Free Press, 1969), pp. 1-53; 54-81.

14. See, Susan Walker, *Speaking of Silence* (New York, Paulist, 1987).

15. Michael Walzer, *The Revolution of the Saints* (Cambridge, Mass.: Harvard University Press, 1965), p. 216.

16. Thomas Walters, *National Profile of Professional Religious Education Directors/Coordinators* (Washington: United States Catholic Conference, 1983).

17. Dan Lortie, *Schoolteacher* (Chicago: University of Chicago Press, 1975), p. 18.

18. John Goodlad, *A Place Called School* (New York: McGraw Hill, 1984), pp. 186-187.

19. Kelsall and Kelsall, *The School Teacher in England and the United States*, p. 3.

20. Elizabeth O'Connor, *Call to Commitment: The Story of the Church of the Savior* (New York: Harper & Row, 1963).

9

Toward a Wider Conversation

In the previous chapters I have tried to make a case for a comprehensive and consistent meaning of religious education. I have also acknowledged that neither I nor anyone else can simply establish such a meaning by logical argument. The best that I can hope for is to convince some people that my meaning has a historical basis and some current plausibility. If many people were to become convinced that this meaning is the most desirable to use (or at least better than others that get assumed today), then the actual meaning in practice would, over a period of years, change to this new meaning.

There is a "catch 22" phenomenon at work in arguing this way. As I described in chapter one, key terms in our language tend to exclude minority or unpopular groups who might bring some needed creativity to the discussion in the area of the term. Religious education, on that account, is the poorer for excluding many things that have elements of the religious and educational about them. For example, much of the current interest in "spirituality" is not heard from in religious education. One cannot get the benefit of a particular point of view if the conversation is so defined that it excludes that point of view. The contribution of books like this one is to call for a wider conversation

216

and demonstrate some of the steps toward actualizing the conversation.

In a real conversation—as opposed to many exchanges that only pretend to be conversation—a person listens to another point of view and thereby undergoes a change. Seldom does that change mean giving up one's own convictions; most often the change is in the direction of enriching the convictions that one started with. One responds to the point of view that has been introduced into one's prior convictions and the same pattern is repeated by one's partner. Only after each partner has had a chance to speak twice is the conversation fully in process. And after that there is no preordained endpoint; all good conversation is endless.

In this chapter I wish to describe the needed conversation in religious education with four adjectives, each beginning with *inter*, an appropriate prefix to describe conversation. A person cannot always be attending to all four of these dimensions. Nonetheless, all four have to be implicitly there or, at least, not be denied as one goes about daily tasks in a small slice of the world. Some people make significant contributions in one or two of these aspects of the conversation. They need not be criticized for not being equally master of all four. The four aspects or qualities of the conversation are: international, interreligious, intergenerational, and interinstitutional.

Before proceeding to discuss each of these four terms, I think it is helpful to pull together the language I have used in this book within a single diagram. I construct the diagram in two parts.

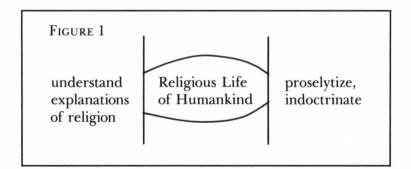

FIGURE 1

| understand explanations of religion | Religious Life of Humankind | proselytize, indoctrinate |

Religious education has to do with the religious life of the human race and with bringing people within the influence of that life. The word "education" indicates some restraints on how that influence is exercised. The words to the right in figure 1 indicate where the boundaries of education would be violated. The two terms, proselytize and indoctrinate, do not flatly contradict education (as, for example, the modern term "brainwashing" does). Nonetheless, there are negative connotations that have long been associated with these two terms. I think that it is fruitless to argue for their usefulness in educational discussion.

The phrase to the left—understand explanations of religion—has a different kind of unsuitability. It refers to an activity that is beyond the boundaries of religious education because it is two steps removed from the religious life. In an academic course in which the aim is to understand the explanations of religion, we have sociology of religion, psychology of religion, philosophy of religion, and the like, but not religious education. At its worst, this approach simply explains away religion, reducing it to something else. However, the left line of itself is not meant to be a negative judgment. Religious educators need to be in touch with such studies as psychology or sociology of religion. But authors and teachers in these fields do not think of themselves as religious educators; their sense of who they are and what they do should be respected.

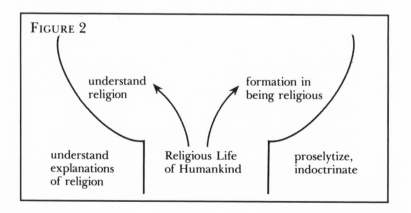

FIGURE 2

understand
religion

formation in
being religious

understand
explanations
of religion

Religious Life
of Humankind

proselytize,
indoctrinate

The two distinct parts of religious education are indicated in figure 2 as understanding religion and formation in being religiously Christian, Jewish, Muslim, Buddhist, or the like. The two activities are related but distinct from the two activities that I have said go beyond the boundaries. The part on the left is what happens in academic books, classrooms, and those modern settings where a special discourse of religion and religions has developed. The problem of student consent here falls under the general problem of whether anyone should be forced to undergo schooling. If we legally require pupils to sit in a classroom and try to understand algebra, then on the same basis we can require them to understand religion. I am not arguing for a law that requires a youngster to be in school, although I think a good case can be made for one. Nor am I saying that school requirements should be rigidly applied so that everyone in the same ninth grade must study algebra and Hebrew Bible. My only point here is that a course on understanding religion for youngsters does not require a special justification beyond the typical things required of young people.

Religion is one of the many areas in the school curriculum where options should be available. At least in the secondary school, youngsters should have some say of when, how much, and what aspects of religion they wish to study. Certainly in the university and beyond, we should work with the assumption that people know what they wish to study. At most, a university might have a requirement of a certain number of credits in a broad area that could include religion courses.

The right side of the diagram brings up a different question of consent. Religious education, similar to artistic, moral, and political education, includes more than academic study. The possibility for having one's life formed by one's own religious experiences ought to be available. Of course, religious education should also include the possibility of simply saying no to religious formation by any group or institution.

For those people who give their unforced consent to participation in a religious group, education consists of all the verbal and nonverbal elements that gradually shape people's lives in relation to a tradition. Here the education is very particular; one does not become generally religious. One becomes Roman Catholic, Lutheran, or Jewish. More particularly, one becomes a New England Irish Roman Catholic, a Missouri Synod Lutheran, or a U.S. Reform Jew. An adult should have the choice to what extent he or she wishes to participate.

The fact that such education presupposes consent raises what is truly an insoluble problem in regard to children. Just as with morality, art, and politics, there is no way to shield the child from religious influence, even if one were convinced that the best policy would be no influence at all. In actual fact, parents who are religiously inclined will wish to pass on their religious beliefs and practices to their children. I think that a sharp distinction should be made here between the family influence, which simply cannot be postponed or avoided, and the school whose mandate is much narrower.

Does the family's influence on the infant and young child qualify as "religious education" or is it across the boundary to proselytizing and indoctrinating? That depends on the quality of the religious influence. If one of the tenets of the particular religion is respect for freedom of choice, then the influence of family practice on the child need not be a violation of individual choice. Of course, there is a difference between a group "holding a doctrine of freedom to choose" and a particular family living that way. But I think many parents do sense this dilemma and they try to prepare the child for an exercise of free choice that can only come years later.

Traditional Christian battles over baptism of infants versus baptism of adults were indicative of this dilemma. The battle seems to be on the wane with the recognition that each side had a part of the truth but not the whole truth.[1] Neither practice by itself guarantees members who know their Christianity and freely practice it. A formation that begins at birth (or earlier) and continues throughout life is what makes possible an intelligent, responsible, and dedicated Christian life. The formation could include important rites in infancy, teenage years, young adulthood, middle age and old age.[2] Such formation must also include the possibility of escaping from Christian church influence, if not entirely during childhood then in later years.

This last sentence leads into consideration of the situation in elementary schools, particularly religiously affiliated schools. The elementary school, certainly in the lower grades, is in continuity with the family. Parents usually send their six-year-old to a Jewish day school or Catholic parochial school because they wish to have a "religious atmosphere" for the child. This atmosphere is part of the issue discussed above, that is, the religious group tries to provide positive experiences so that later the young person can choose for or against religious practice on the basis of experience.

The elementary school, however, should not forget that it is a school. It is a community that nurtures (a word related to "mothering"), but it is also a place whose reason for existence is supposedly academic. The healthy tension between school as a nurturing community and school as a place of critical inquiry should not be entirely absent in the religious area. The first six or eight years of school should not be bracketed as religious nurture before critical questioning takes over. The intellectual criticism can be introduced gently, but it should start about five minutes after the child's school career begins.

I think that this issue deserves frank discussion, carried out mainly by teachers who work with the young but allowing in a few outside voices. Those teachers who work daily with elementary school children know the problems and possibilities, the practical difficulties of teaching the young. Their closeness to the scene, however, could cause a blindspot to the worldwide rebellion against any particular religion being imposed without the individual's consent. This development is quite new at least in its intensity; one can trace its roots back several centuries, but a dramatic increase in the reaction seems to have occurred in many parts of the world in the decade of the 1960s.

I am not celebrating this legacy of the 1960s. The intense concern with individual freedom of religion may or may not prove to be a good for the human race; or a good for such places as Ireland, Quebec, Norway, the Netherlands, and the United States. What is certain is that schoolteachers of the young are cast in a more difficult position than ever. They cannot be blamed for failing to solve a problem that goes far beyond them.

I would say, nonetheless, that a bigger revolution than has yet taken place is needed with elementary school programs of religious education. Occasionally, I am asked to examine a syllabus or a textbook series that claims to be a new approach to teaching religion to youngsters. Although I try to approach each case with an open mind, my usual response is to find the material not very different from what I was given to teach thirty years ago or even what I was taught in elementary school more than forty years ago. In these new books there are all sorts of references to current affairs; they are usually colorful with lots of pictures (although the art is often as bad as ever). What most strikes me is that the religious assumptions go unchallenged, particularly that the child is already a practicing Christian who is interested in all the fine details of Christianity. I am not claiming I could write a better textbook; I am skeptical that the kind of curriculum material that keeps rolling off the presses of Catholic and Protestant publishers is the right direction. Perhaps one simply should not try to teach religion in elementary school every day and every year. The religiously affiliated school can be defended on other grounds than what goes on in the religion class.

At the secondary school level there have been significant changes in some places. In fact, what is clear in many places is the firm line which has been drawn between the approach of the elementary school and that of the high school. I refer here particularly to Catholic school systems in Australia, New Zealand, Canada, the U.S., and elsewhere.[3] I think the same can be said of Protestant and Jewish approaches in these countries although I do not have such extensive data. In many high-school curricula today the intelligence and free will of the student are respected. In this kind of approach, the religiously affiliated school and the state school might have the possibility of some cooperation. I would not expect the same material to be used in the two systems, but I do think the same attitude toward teaching religion can be shared.

What I think must be questioned is the firmness of the line that exists between elementary and secondary schools. I am suggesting that instead of one division there should be many gradations, that the acknowledgment of critical intelligence and free choice should work its way through the whole school system for young people. It is no longer adequate to say that in the elementary school we take a "community of faith" approach and in high school we teach them religion. I am not in favor of teaching a "world religions" course in the third grade. But already by the third grade there can be an appeal to the child's critical intelligence where religion appears in the curriculum. For example, a school under Christian auspices could acknowledge the limitations of Christianity and its relation to other religious possibilities.

For further summarizing my argument of what religious education does mean and can mean, I turn now to the four headings of international, interreligious, intergenerational and interinstitutional.

1. INTERNATIONAL

As indicated at the beginning of this chapter, my modest aim here is to indicate the kind of conversation we need. I cannot provide an international survey, let alone draw the threads of international discussion into a unity. In one respect, this international aspect is only the obvious; every field of study today has to take account of what is happening worldwide. Biological researchers in Paris are aware of Berkeley; no economist in New York is going to neglect Tokyo; anthropologists study culture worldwide. Beyond the fairly obvious need for religious education to be aware of what is happening in the world, some special factors must be noted.

Religious education in most places is closely related to national governments. Many religions are *transnational* in character; a world conference of a particular religious group could have but does not necessarily have the character of an *international* discussion. But partly by reason of historical accident and partly by reason of education's institutional relation to government, religious education usually does denote some relation to the nation and its governmental bodies. Thus, a discussion of religious education worldwide need not always refer to national particularities but there is strong reason to do so.

While there is some advantage in being able to name the participants in this conversation as Dutch, German, English, Japanese, Brazilian, and so forth, the disadvantage is the lack of a common language. I do not only mean the United Nations problem of translation between German and English or English and Spanish, but that there is no direct translation possible in religious education. That is, the very term "religious education" has no exact equivalent in many languages. When biblical scholars meet anywhere in the world, they have a common text which (with some variations) they agree to discuss. An international meeting on religious education is a much more confusing discussion because it is by no means clear that the meeting has even a general area for discussion that everyone agrees on.

The discussion in this book is biased by the fact of being written not only in English but in U.S. English. Instead of trying to do an international survey, my main effort has been to try to call attention to differences within the English language so as to open a conversation between the British and U.S. meanings of religious education. If the discussion stopped at a dialogue between the U.K. and U.S., that would not be much of an international conversation. My hope is that this opening of an exchange would quickly lead to inclusion of other parties. The British influence on education and religious education extends to Canada, Australia, Ireland, New Zealand, the Carribean, eastern and southern Africa, and parts of Asia. The U.S. influence is of a different kind, but in the last forty years it has worked its way into numerous nations. Coming into a U.S./U.K. discussion of religious education is not entirely foreign territory for many people.

The nations that might have the most to say would be

those that have been strongly influenced by both the U.K. and the U.S. Places like Canada, Australia, New Zealand, and Ireland, rather than being just satellites to the dialogue, may hold the key to thinking through a developed meaning of religious education.

Canada and Australia each have complicated patterns of religious education due to variations at the provincial and state level.[4] Their international voice has to be complemented with intranational discussion. Their language of religious education is strongly influenced by the developments in England/Wales during recent decades. However, Australians and Canadians are very conscious of the U.S. scene through books, television, and movies. Some new variations on relating education and religion may emerge in Canada or Australia.

In Ontario, to take one Canadian example, the recent history of religious education has striking parallels to England. A similar law in 1944 required religious instruction and worship in the public school. Similar to the English history that I traced in chapter four, Ontario discovered a new diversity in the 1960s that complicated both religious instruction and worship.[5] Actually, Ontario's discovery came a little earlier and it appointed a government commission in 1965. The Keiller Mackay report from this commission in 1969 recommended that the 1944 program be abolished. It proposed instead the "incidental" teaching of religion in elementary schools, world religion courses in secondary schools and an emphasis on moral education.[6]

The Ontario government quickly moved to produce guidelines for world religion courses, and it supported studies on moral education through the Ontario Institute for Studies in Education. The elementary school's incidental teaching (which might best be imagined as units within other courses) has not been attended to. Over the past two decades the Ontario government has been rather slow to further the implementation of the 1969 report. The educators have looked to England for help in developing curriculum.

A complicating factor in Ontario is the influence of the religious institutions. The historical pattern of separate school systems funded by the government makes Ontario (and with variations, all of Canada) differ from both the U.S. and the U.K. The presence and influence of church groups, especially a large Catholic school system, complicates matters and slows progress. An optimistic view might see the cooperation of churches and government as bringing about a more stable and realistic pattern. Thus, it is an ecumenical commission of the churches that has been advocating a teaching of religion (as distinct from Christian instruction) in the public school. I think that it is unlikely that there will be a situation similar to England where the Bishop of London was suddenly called upon as mediator in the midst of the effort to make religious education in the schools "mainly Christian."

Australian states would offer other variations around these themes. One does not have the parallel of a 1944 Act requiring religious instruction and worship in the public school. But there is some similarity in the fact that Australia had talked of itself as a "Christian country." Then, in the 1960s it discovered that religiously the world had changed and so had Australia.

Australian state governments established commissions in the 1970s that proposed having religious studies in the state or government school.[7] Sometimes this process involves church bodies working directly with state schools, as in Queensland; sometimes the model is closer to England, as in South Australia (at least since 1972).[8] The term "religious education" is fairly common in Australia, more so than in the United States. While its usage strongly reflects developments in England, there is room for avoiding the British tendency to equate "RE" and the subject in the state school.

Some fine work in Australia is being done by Roman Catholic educators who are trying to combine the Catholic use of religious education that is found in Ireland or the U.S. with the British conviction that religious education should refer to a classroom. In general, there is cooperation among Roman Catholic, Anglican, Uniting Church, and Evangelical churches on educational matters. The churches in turn are willing to work with governmental agencies. With its connections to Asia, Europe, and North America, there is probably no place better suited than Australia to work out a comprehensive meaning of religious education. As in Ontario, the progress may be slow but the work may be lasting.

The above discussion of international is about the English speaking world. There are conferences that bring other language groups into this conversation (the Netherlands, West Germany, Sweden, Norway, Denmark, Belgium, Korea, Israel), but the translations are mostly one way. Do these countries and others further afield in Eastern Europe, Asia, Africa, or South America have religious education? Most countries have a term, very often several terms, that cover some of the territory. Perhaps if people in the English-speaking world were more conversant with other languages there would emerge a better term than "religious education" as the focus of an international discussion. However, I am unaware of what that might be; at least at present in English, I cannot see a serious competitor.

It is interesting that the second half of the term "education" is as much of a problem as "religious" when one looks for international equivalents. Germans, for example, are willing to translate *Religionsunterricht* as religious education although the second half of that term indicates instruction in a classroom more than does "education" in U.S. English. There are other German words that can translate "education" but they do not easily go with "religious."[9] In European languages there is usually a distinctly church language (the Catholics, a catechetical language; the Protestants, an evangelical language). Alongside this language is something that might get translated as religious education. But this religious education does not get into the secular arena; it is usually the religious instruction in the church-related school.[10]

Whenever I speak in another country, two things usually strike me: 1) In most ways we are remarkably similar. 2) In a few ways that may take a long time to discover, there are some startling differences. I always have the fear that in speaking of religious education no one will have any idea of what I am talking about. It is always a pleasant surprise to find that they are usually struggling with problems similar to those in the U.S. The first time I had a conversation with a religious educator in a country where 95 percent of the people are members of the state church, I did not expect to have anything in common. To my amazement, his description of the problems, the attempted solutions, and the results were not at all foreign to my own way of thinking. In fact, the danger in such conversations is that we rapidly translate everything and assume that the situation is the same. We need conversations that are without end so that gradually we may discover where our true agreements and disagreements lie.

2. INTERRELIGIOUS

While the international aspect of religious education can be seen as a historical accident, the interreligious aspect is inherent to religious education itself. That is, "interreligious" is simply a more emphatic way of saying "religious." If the education were not a conversation across some religious boundaries, there would be little need for the existence of the term "religious education." The need for a religious education has arisen in the twentieth century as each religious group and individuals within each group find themselves in a world of religious pluralism. That does not mean that every course has to be a survey of the world's religions; in fact, that is seldom the best way to initiate conversation. The *inter* in an interreligious approach means understanding one's own religious position in relation to other religious possibilities. Similar to the problem with an international conversation, an interreligious conversation begins by being limited to those who can realistically be interlocutors. From the start, however, the conversation has to be in principle open to all.

As I pointed out in chapter five, "interreligious" is a more accurate term than "interfaith"; certainly, it is more helpful in thinking about education. While Christians, Jews, and Muslims may think that faith is ultimately more important than religion, it is the visible, tangible, socially available elements called religion that can be dealt with educationally. A Christian, Muslim, or Jew, may believe that education is successful when it has reached a "formation in faith." They are right to contend that religious education has to include more than the study of religion in classrooms.

The teacher, nonetheless, has to work with what the student presents: speech, rituals, moral practice, posture of the body, breathing, diet, imagination, chant, story, and so forth. In the case of teaching someone to be religiously formed in a particular community, the teacher can only try to teach religious practices, not faith. More obviously, if a Christian is trying to understand Islam and Muslims, the understanding is of the religion. Perhaps if I understand the religion I may get some glimmer of what faith means but faith is not the object of study. Only by reducing faith to a set of beliefs can one directly study faith; and no Christian, Jew, or Muslim accepts such a reduction when it comes to his or her own faith.

Not everyone will agree with my analysis of how to use the word "faith." But at the least, the terms "interreligious" and "interfaith" should not be casually interchanged. If someone believes that interfaith is preferable in educational discussions, then I think the case has to be argued, not simply assumed.

A world of "religious pluralism" is not just a world of multiplicity. There would be nothing new in the fact that there are many religions; the Roman Empire had already achieved that. But when there have been many religions in the past, one of two outcomes was likely: Either one religion asserted itself as superior and tried to suppress the others, or none of the religions was taken seriously so that more religions meant less religious life. The attempt at a religious pluralism today is the demand that each religion be affirmed as important but only in relation to the others; that is, the plural and the relative are understood positively. That is not an easy position to affirm; some people would say it is impossible. It certainly will fail unless there is genuine education within each group and between groups. Thus, religious pluralism has been the condition that led to religious education, but religious education is the condition for sustaining religious pluralism.

Religious education seen within this context has two aims: 1) a better practice of one's own religious life and 2) a deeper understanding of the other's religion. These two aims are not parallel; the latter is intrinsically related to the former. One cannot intelligently and freely practice any religion today without some understanding of the other, some backdrop of comparison. "Other religions" is not a coda to be attached to the handing on of one's own religion. In the other direction, I have said that one's intelligent and free exercise of religious practice is what one brings to the task of understanding religion. That would exclude some people as not competent to teach religion. However, that lack of competence is not based on someone's failing to attend church or on a classification of oneself as agnostic. Such people may have a rich experience to bring to the understanding of religion. My objection to people who call themselves atheists teaching religion would be the same as I would have toward fundamentalists. They are usually so certain they know the answers that I would be suspicious that they cannot address the questions with an inquiring mind.

The two parts of religious education can be clearly distinguished, but there is not a total dichotomy between (understanding) religion and (being) religious. For example, if one is trying to form the religious life of a Christian person, the understanding of Jewish religion is an issue. To become Christian is to take a stance toward things Jewish. Every statement and practice of Christianity has to be thought through in its Jewish implications. Given the history of the two groups since the first century C.E., for a Christian not to consider the issue is to perpetuate many beliefs that need changing. Granted that the relation in the other direction is not so dramatically necessary, Jews still need to think out their religious life today in relation to Christianity. As soon as possible, the relation to Islam on the part of both Christianity and Judaism should also become part of the conversation. Some small steps in this wider conversation have been taken in a few places but that journey has barely begun.

There have been repeated attempts over the years to define the relation of Christian education and religious education. I think this question is important, but I have given up trying to find acceptable definitions of the relation. The main thing to be said is that Christians should not preempt religious education by using it interchangeably with Christian education. And neither should people interested in religious education try to make Christian education (or catechetics) a simple subset of religious education.

I doubt that any religious body accepts a definition of its relation to religion as part to whole. The modern, scientific mind may insist that obviously Christianity, Judaism, Islam, Buddhism, Sikhism, and the rest are *parts* of a whole called religion. In a classroom, that assumption is practically inevitable. But in educating a person to be religiously Lutheran or religiously Jewish, one does not have the sense of dealing with a part of religion. The particular religious life at issue fills the stage; for the moment, it is Christian forming Christian to be Christian; and similarly with Jew, Muslim, or Buddhist. Implicit in this reality is a relation to the other, but this relation is more aesthetic than logical; the whole is embodied in each of the particulars.

Ludwig Wittgenstein, in trying to explain human understanding, uses a helpful example of what it means to appreciate music. If I wish to provide someone with an understanding of Beethoven, it involves comparing the sixth and ninth symphonies. Do you see (or hear) what he is doing here in the sixth? Look now at the ninth. Now turn to the fifth. Eventually, the person understands what Beethoven is doing by listening again and again to the symphonies and noticing variations on possibilities. A further step to understanding may come in placing Beethoven in relation to Mozart, or more exactly, revealing the relation already there. There is no need to disparage Mozart for the sake of Beethoven, although those concerned with the appreciation of Beethoven may say little of Mozart. Some people appreciate Beethoven by listening to almost nothing but Beethoven; some people come to a better appreciation of Beethoven by sometimes listening to Mozart.

Religious education is not music education, however, the

language of music may provide a better analogy than does the language of the sciences for religious understanding. A Christian (or Jewish) education is religious education in concrete expression. A Christian (or Jewish) education is concerned with the history, teachings, and ritual of Christianity (or Judaism). How these elements are approached will determine whether the process is really educational or whether it is an attempt to fix the mind on an established body of material that bears no further development.

Education is "with end and without end." A Christian, or Jewish or Muslim or Buddhist education has to fulfill both conditions. The first is usually the more obvious in a religious group; there is a way of life to be conveyed. However, every major religious group also recognizes that there is a truth beyond whatever it has formulated. In every pronouncement, in every ritual, in every gesture toward the outsider, the religious group has to acknowledge its own incompleteness. The universal is embodied—but not completely—in the particular. The seeds not only of tolerance but of religious pluralism lie within the religions themselves. Without a religious group having to retract its belief in the way, the truth, and the life, there can be acknowledgment that other people have a particular way, truth, and life. The opposite of a logically true statement is a logically false statement; the opposite of a religious way of life can be another religious way of life.

Is "religious education" an unbiased umbrella term for conversation between Christians and Jews, Christians and Buddhists, Sikhs and Hindus, Muslims and Jews? Hardly. But all terms in this area are biased in their origin. A term like "ecumenical" began as a Protestant Christian term; in the 1960s it incorporated the Roman Catholics (with their own term "ecumenism"). Many Christians today intend the term ecumenical to embrace more than Christian; its root meaning of "world" suggests that it could and maybe some day it will. But Christians should not be surprised if Jews, not to mention Muslims and Hindus, shy away from ecumenical embrace.

A similar limitation has to be acknowledged about "religious education." The term has little currency in the East. In most Western countries it has possibilities for being the aegis under which Christians and Jews can converse. In the U.S. it once had a Protestant ring, more recently a Catholic emphasis. In, for example, Hong Kong, a place of great religious diversity, the Christian schools have several names for what they do, among which is "religious education." The Buddhist, Taoist, and Confucian schools do not use "religious education," although they do use "religious studies." Despite the possible Christian bias in the term, religious education is the best choice in English for a term to be an umbrella for Christian, Jewish, Buddhist, and other religions, as well as state-supported education.[11] "Religious studies" is also helpful, even more immediately helpful, although its restriction is on the educational rather than the religious side; that is, it is biased in the direction of education in the schools.

3. INTERGENERATIONAL

The third aspect of religious education, intergenerational, has always been desirable but has become more pressing in a world of religious pluralism. I pointed out at the end of chapter five that British writing on religious education is especially anomalous in almost always referring to the education of the *child*. If education is going to confront the religious complexity of today's world, then the student will need a lifetime to mature in understanding. All education needs to be lifelong, and religious education should appropriately lead the way.

Although the terms "intergenerational" and "lifelong" are not equivalent, I think one can help out the other. I usually shy away from either term because people often assume that one is talking about an exceptional case. Many people assume that there is real or normal education in which schoolteachers instruct children, and then there is a peculiar kind of educational exception in which adults learn. Adjectives such as adult, lifelong, and continuing still tend to be used as external additions to education. Of these terms, lifelong is the most helpful for my purpose, but all of them tend to connote individualistic ventures. As I noted in chapter three, the word "teach" is often avoided in the literature of adult, continuing, and lifelong education in favor of "self-directed learning."

Intergenerational provides a helpful reminder that we are being taught all the time by those who are younger than we are and those who are older. In a sense, of course, the teaching of children in school is intergenerational learning; and indeed that form of learning should not be excluded from intergenerational education. But it is only a small slice of the generations, usually young and middle-aged adults teaching pre-teen and teenage children. And even within that generational slice the learning may be scant in one of the two directions. Schools are not particularly well-designed for schoolteachers learning from schoolchildren.

The pairing of lifelong and intergenerational gives particular emphasis to the very young and the very old. The conversation of the generations begins for the individual at birth and ends at death. Religions have always given special attention to the moments of birth and death as well as to their interrelation. All religions resist the image of time as a series of points with the first called birth and the last called death. There is always a cyclical element in which we come back to the beginning or experience death as a rebirth. The conversation of the living generations is a reminder of a larger conversation with our ancestors, with nonhuman life and the voice of creation.

The most dramatic embodiment of intergenerational education is the conversation between the old a few years from death and the young a few years from birth. No relation is more powerful in its educational effects and yet it is totally absent from most treatises on education. Probably religious education has to remind the rest of education to include the relation of the very young and very old.

In this context, we might consider the twentieth century's recent interest in the elderly. One can applaud real advances here during the last two decades. In the United States, the old are generally better off economically than they were in the 1960s; ageism became one of those *isms* to be avoided. The image of the elderly has changed considerably. Within that progress and because of that progress some troubling issues have to be faced.

Daniel Callahan's *Setting Limits* drew strong reaction from experts on old age.[12] Callahan's specific policy recommendations are debatable (although he is surely correct in pointing out the long-term untenability of current economic policies). The more challenging thing he did was to question the premise of most writing on the elderly. The U.S. has not necessarily given up its obsession with youth as it uses every means to postpone death in old age, encourages older people to keep acting as if they were younger, and even tells older people to shed all their responsibilities for the pleasant life. A popular book of a few years ago was entitled *It Takes a Long Time to Become Young*.[13] Ostensibly a celebration of old age, the title betrays the fact that it is a glorification of youth.

One of the ways that Callahan challenges gerontology is by questioning the dismissal of "disengagement theory," which posited that people disengage themselves from prior interests as they get old. The theory emerged in the early 1960s and was quickly disputed.[14] Since then, one regularly sees reference to the "now discredited theory of disengagement." Callahan ventures to question whether the case is so clear-cut. It may be that people do or should disengage themselves from many youthful concerns so that their lives can take on new qualities in old age. Old age ought to have characteristics of its own that are valued in the culture. Callahan thinks that the elderly have a special responsibility to pass on what wisdom they have to the coming generations.

The Elder Hostel movement has had startling success in just ten years.[15] This movement, which had its start at the University of New Hampshire, has spread to hundreds of universities. College courses are offered to the elderly, usually during the summer; other social aspects accompany the academic program. This movement is all to the good provided it does not segregate the old into a new consumer market for universities. Such programs need to be related

to the twenty-year-olds in the university. Also, the education of the elderly should not be narrowed down to mean
only those who can attend universities.

The young—especially infants and teenagers—need the
presence of the old as partners in learning. I am always
happy to have elderly people mixed in with a class of
young people. I have met a number of remarkable old
people that way, perhaps the most extraordinary being an
eighty-year-old blind woman in a course on religious education. She said that she was taking the course to prepare
herself for helping old people. Her effect on the rest of the
students was transformative.

Religious education needs the presence of the elderly
and the elderly need the help of religious education. The
experts on old age and dying have generally been averse to
religion. Worse, the image of the old has been one of
constantly pushing forward and upward. If one were to
take the religious life of the elderly more seriously, the
image might be one of turning back to the very young, not
in the pretense of being young but in partnership with
those who are young. The old ought to have the physical,
social, and economic environment which allows them to
share their wisdom with the young. Who better than the
religious community should understand that the best examples of adulthood are the very old. Whether they are
preparing for reincarnation or resurrection, their lives are
not a waste product even though they may have infirmities.

The very old and the very young have a natural alliance
that can be realized if all of the other people in the middle
do not put up obstacles. The relation of grandparent to
grandchild often attains a mutuality not possible between
parent and child. Younger children and older adults may
have a profound religious sense, something that needs
preservation throughout the hurriedness of middle age. A
lifelong religious education is not necessarily a continuous
and straight line. There are moments of great intensity
and there may be years in which nothing seems to happen.
The individual does not have to get up each day and say: I
must educate myself today. Cradled in the embrace of generational conversation, an individual can be silent for long
periods knowing that he or she is never far from the start-

ing point which is also where the conversation leads in the end.

4. INTERINSTITUTIONAL

Despite much talk about lifelong learning, we seem unable to nudge the educational enterprise from its over-concentration on pre-teen/teenage children. I suspect we will never have lifelong education until we have *lifewide* education. And as lifelong education particularly correlates with religious education, so also does lifewide education. We cannot have effective education unless it engages the major institutions of society. As intergenerational education is a conversation across historical patterns of human life, interinstitutional education is a geographical interplay of human organizations.

The most obvious cooperation needed for religious education is between religious bodies (church, synagogue, mosque, temple) and a public education forum, most often represented by a state-supported school. An interinstitutional cooperation could take innumerable forms, but what the phrase excludes is total identity at one end and total opposition at the other. Before modern times what was thought to be the ideal by many religious groups was theocratic government. The religious leader was to preside over all of life, and a Christian, Jewish, or Muslim education was co-extensive with education.

One of the marks of the modern era is the emergence of the secular state. In countries where there is a single, unified religious group this development can lead to friction, hostility, or outright conflict. Sometimes education becomes not neutral to religion but aggressively secular. The religious group on its side may dream of the time when the old order will be reestablished and all of life will once again be under the direction of the Bible, Qur'an, or the like. Some groups try to maintain a subculture where this unified world can exist, as in fundamentalists' schools in the U.S. South. Occasionally, some group gets the chance to try it on a national scale, as did Iran in the 1980s. I do not think it would be intelligible to speak of religious education under the Ayatollah.

Leaving aside the cases of total identity or open warfare, the cooperation between religious body and secular state can range from very friendly and active engagement to a distant letting-live of the other. The cases vary according to whether there is a single religious group or whether there are several religious bodies fairly equal in size. Within the same nation there can be drastic differences; for example, Quebec with its historic relation to Roman Catholicism compared to British Columbia where Roman Catholicism is a minor part of the religious mixture. I do not think there is one ideal condition in which religious education flourishes, although some religious diversity is usually more conducive to it along with a tradition of academic freedom protected by the government or strong private associations.

The division of religious education into "teaching religion" and "teaching to be religious" roughly corresponds to the institutional cooperation described above. In many Western European countries the relation may seem the same, that is, the state school should teach the religion, the church liturgy should do the Christian formation. Even in those countries the division is not that neat. And other countries manifest the complexity of religious education which is not simply divided between state and religious institution. Actually, the more important institutional cooperation is indicated by my educational pattern, described in chapter two:

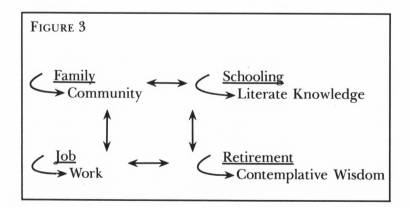

FIGURE 3

Family → Community ↔ Schooling → Literate Knowledge

Job → Work ↔ Retirement → Contemplative Wisdom

Notice that in this fourfold cooperation neither the state nor the church is a player. Each has an important part, but their efforts are more effective when indirect. The state has a duty to provide good conditions for family life, but the state ought not to dictate to parents how to raise their children. The state can see that jobs are provided and that workers are protected without the state necessarily being the employer. Likewise, the state has the duty to see that there are schools although the state need not administer all of them. And the state ought to see that retirement in old age is possible along with the existence of times and places of leisure throughout the rest of life.

The religious body has a similar relation to all four forms, with more attention to the bottom line in each case. Besides the economic and social conditions that are the state's primary concern, the religious body's vocation is to give examples of community, work, knowledge, and wisdom. Bringing families into relation with one another is an educational contribution the religious body can make to community. Liturgy and service programs can remind people of a deeper meaning of work. And the religious body ought to provide a refuge of contemplative quiet in an increasingly noisy world.

The most complex relation here is the religious body's relation to schooling. There can be a kind of religious schooling in which the religious group trains those who are members. Such training can be legitimate, especially for the interested adult and the potential leaders of the group. But school in the modern world and in relation to religious education has a wider function. It is a zone of intellectual freedom where all questions can be asked and where all loyalty oaths, except the quest for truth, are suspended. A religious body sponsoring a school should know what it is getting into. A child or adult who is exposed to critical church history or modern exegesis of the Bible is going to have potentially embarrassing questions for today's religious leaders.

Why, then, would any religious body in its right mind sponsor a school? Because hard questions are going to be raised anyway in the contemporary world. If the questions are raised with some intellectual discipline and within a community that cares about these issues, then the religious body in the long run is better off. Some religious leaders, of course, panic in the short run and wish to have a guarantee of where intellectual inquiry will lead. They seem not to trust the intellectual substance and integrity of their own religious traditions.

In my diagram, I have used the term "schooling" to refer to the double aspect of school. Schools are communities of socialization and transmission; they are also spaces of intellectual inquiry and academic freedom. These two sides of school can be in considerable conflict; their proper relation is one of healthy tension. A religiously affiliated school may have a greater tension if it is doing its job well of teaching religion. I do not think the tension has to be intolerable. Schoolteachers, school administrators and religious officials often have enough sense to realize that the tension is something to be lived with not something to be eliminated.

I am not claiming that the religiously affiliated school *alone* can teach religion. Rather, I have started from the other end of the argument in assuming that the public school is the most obvious environment for teaching religion to youngsters. The point I am making now is that the religiously affiliated school should not be *excluded* from the teaching of religion. The state school generally has the advantage of more easily establishing a zone of academic openness for the study of religion. Its disadvantage is that it may lack sufficient experiential data in the students' and teachers' lives and in the school environment. The religiously affiliated school almost reverses these two, that is, its advantage of environmental and personal data may overwhelm the open space needed for an intellectual inquiry into religion. If, for example, all the teachers are Christian, all the students are Christian, and everything in the syllabus (not to mention the art on the walls or the prayer before class) is Christian, it is possible but difficult to suspend Christian assumptions. The introduction of just a little variety in faculty, student body, or curriculum can make a course on religion be much more realistic.

I might add here a fifth *inter*: interdisciplinary. This

quality does not describe the whole of religious education, but it should typify the classroom part, the teaching of religion. Perhaps in elementary schools one could call the teaching multidisciplinary, a teaching of religion by addressing the issue within units of social studies, physical sciences, or literature. In secondary schools, where religion can be isolated as an academic topic on its own, the teacher of religion could still use the help of psychology, sociology, literature, history, and so forth. Even physical education, health, or home economics can provide insight into religion.

The religion teacher, instead of being looked at as an anomaly, might be a force for integration in the school, whether state or religiously affiliated school. That does not mean a push for Christian chemistry or Muslim mathematics but simply a recognition that religion has been important in people's lives, that instead of being an esoteric area where only a few experts can tread, religion is related to almost every sphere of personal interest and every academic discipline.

Interinstitutional religious education becomes actual as education is understood to include not only the form of schooling but the other three forms. The phrase "lifelong education" sounds to many people like an endless string of classrooms; not surprisingly, most adults are not thrilled by the idea. Middle-aged adults are more concerned with family and job issues; older adults are often withdrawing from the job into a time of more leisure. Schooling can be helpful for adults, but it needs to be integrated with the other three forms.

I suggested in chapter two that the collapsing of education into schooling for the young is an evasion of the religious issue in all education. To the extent that education does include all four of the forms in interplay, then religious questions will surface. Other forms of language besides discursive explanations will be recognized as educational: announcement, story, prophecy, parable, chant, poetry, dance, painting. Religious education will then be seen to emerge at the center of education not at the periphery. Religious education would be a place of both passion and tolerance, a place to stimulate the deepest intellectual search and invite a personal choice to follow the best way one has discovered through conversations with one's ancestors, with the generations of human travelers, and with the nonhuman lives that speak to us.

NOTES

1. Robert Browning, "A Sacramental Approach to Inclusion and Depth of Commitment," *Congregations: Their Power to Form and Transform*, ed. C. Ellis Nelson (Atlanta: John Knox, 1988), pp. 181-186.

2. John Westerhoff III, "The Liturgical Imperative of Religious Education," in *The Religious Education We Need*, ed. James Michael Lee (Birmingham, Ala.: Religious Education Press, 1977), pp. 75-94.

3. Graham Rossiter and Marisa Crawford, *Teaching Religion in Catholic Schools* (Winona, Minn.: St. Mary's Press, 1986).

4. Graham Rossiter, *The Practice of Religious Education in Government Schools* (Canberra: Curriculum Development Center, 1981); Donald Weeren, ed., *Educating Religiously in the Multi-faith School* (Calgary: Detselig Enterprises, 1986).

5. William Gilbert, "At the Crossroads: Public Education in Ontario," *Crosstalk* (January, 1986).

6. *Religious Information and Moral Development* (Ottawa: Ontario Department of Education, 1969).

7. Rossiter, *The Practice of Religious Education in Government Schools.*

8. Robert Crotty, "Teaching Religion in a Secular School: The South Australia Experience," *Religious Education* 81 (Spring, 1986), pp. 310-321.

9. Karl Ernst Nipkow, "Education's Responsibility for Morality and Faith in a Rapidly Changing World," *Religious Education* 80 (Spring, 1988), pp. 195-214.

10. Ulrich Hemel, "Religious Education, Catechesis, Evangelization: Some Terminological Difficulties at an International Level," *Irish Catechist* 9 (March, 1985), pp. 4-17.

11. Peter Ng, "The Challenge of Religious Pluralism and the Possibilities of Religious Education in Hong Kong." Paper delivered at the International Symposium on Religious Education and Values, New York, August, 1988.

12. Daniel Callahan, *Setting Limits: Medical Goals in an Aging Society* (New York: Simon and Schuster, 1987).

13. Garson Kanin, *It Takes a Long Time to Become Young* (Garden City, N.Y.: Doubleday, 1978).

14. Callahan, *Setting Limits*, pp. 34-36; E. Cumming and W. C. Henry, *Growing Old: The Process of Disengagement* (New York: Basic Books, 1961).

15. Huey Long, *Adult and Continuing Education* (New York: Teachers College Press, 1983), p. 128.

Index